The Changing Face of Chinese Management

The Changing Face of Chinese Management provides an invaluable portrait of Chinese business today. It is a portrait that reveals an intriguing mixture of the old and the new, for while certain features of management in China can be traced deep into the past, others have changed beyond recognition. New forms of enterprise and new ways of conducting business have emerged. Jie Tang and Anthony Ward present a far-reaching account of the continuities and changes in Chinese management today.

The book begins with an outline of the cultural background and its influence on a range of managerial behaviour, touching on topics such as attitudes to authority, communication, trust, negotiation and conflict resolution. The book then moves on to consider the changing role of the state in relation to enterprise management, before looking more closely at the work of management within the firm. Following this, the authors review management in the private sector, and the rich variety of other forms of enterprise that have emerged in recent years. A chapter is also devoted to the management of Sino-foreign joint ventures.

Alongside a discussion of the social and economic forces shaping management, Tang and Ward provide a wide variety of interview material and case studies, much drawn from their own extensive interviews with managers and from observations within Chinese enterprises. These offer a wealth of concrete examples of how managers deal on a daily basis with the opportunities and threats they face. *The Changing Face of Chinese Management* is a fresh insight into the mind of the Chinese manager.

Jie Tang is a native of Shanghai, and has worked in China and England. She is currently a researcher on Chinese management at the Judge Institute of Management Studies, Cambridge University.

Anthony Ward has worked in China for over 10 years, and currently divides his time between Cambridge and Shanghai, where he works for a leading Chinese publishing house. Before this, he lectured in sociology at Lancaster University. He is the author of *A Crane among the Chickens*, an evaluation of Sino-British training projects.

Working in Asia

General Editors:
Tim G. Andrews
Bristol Business School, University of the West of England
and **Keith Jackson**
School of Oriental and African Studies, University of London

This series focuses on contemporary management issues in the Asia-Pacific region. It draws on the latest research to highlight critical factors impacting on the conduct of business in this diverse and dynamic business environment.

Our primary intention is to provide management students and practitioners with fresh dimensions to their reading of standard texts. With each book in the *Working in Asia* series, we offer a combined insider's and outsider's perspective on how managers and their organizations in the Asia-Pacific region are adapting to contemporary currents of both macro- and micro-level change.

The core of data for the texts in this series has been generated by recent interviews and discussions with established senior executives as well as newly fledged entrepreneurs; with practising as well as aspiring middle managers; and with women as well as men. Our mission has been to give voice to how change is being perceived and experienced by a broad and relevant range of people who live and work in the region. We report on how they and their organizations are managing change as the globalization of their markets, together with their business technologies and traditions, unfolds.

Drawing together the combined insights of Asian and Western scholars, and practitioners of management, we present a uniquely revealing portrait of the future of working and doing business in Asia.

Titles in the series include:

The Changing Face of Multinationals in Southeast Asia
Tim G. Andrews, Nartnalin Chompusri and Bryan J. Baldwin OBE

The Changing Face of Chinese Management
Jie Tang and Anthony Ward

The Changing Face of Chinese Management

Jie Tang and Anthony Ward

Routledge
Taylor & Francis Group

LONDON AND NEW YORK

First published 2003 by Routledge
11 New Fetter Lane, London EC4P 4EE

Simultaneously published in the USA and Canada
by Routledge
29 West 35th Street, New York NY 10001

Routledge is an imprint of the Taylor & Francis Group

Reprinted 2004

© 2003 Jie Tang and Anthony Ward

Typeset in Times by Keystroke, Jacaranda Lodge, Wolverhampton
Printed and bound in Great Britain by MPG Books Ltd, Bodmin

British Library Cataloguing in Publication Data
A catalogue record for this book is available from the British Library

Library of Congress Cataloging in Publication Data
The changing face of Chinese management / Jie Tang and Anthony Ward.
    p. cm. – (Working in Asia)
   Includes bibliographical references and index.
      1. Industrial management–China. 2. Organizational change–China.
   3. Corporate culture–China. I. Ward, Anthony, 1947– II. Title.
   III. Series

HD70.C5 T344 2002
302.3'5'0951–dc21   20022072680

ISBN 0–415–25846–4 (hbk)
ISBN 0–415–25847–2 (pbk)

Contents

Illustrations

Boxes

Figures

Tables

Preface

This book grew out of a course on Chinese management given by one of the authors at the School of Oriental and African Studies of the University of London. It also builds upon many years of experience of working within China, supplemented by a further year spent in observing the operation of enterprises and interviewing managers in preparation for the writing of this book. We dedicate this book to all the managers in China who proved so willing to help with our research. We cannot, unfortunately, thank them by name, because of promises of confidentiality. To preserve this, details in our own case studies and interviews, such as names and locations, have at times been changed or left vague.

Others, however, cannot escape so lightly. Special thanks are due to John Child, Richard Mead, Peter Nolan and, in the case of one particularly long-standing intellectual debt, Salvador Giner.

Jie Tang
Anthony Ward

Introduction

> One day Deng Xiao Ping decided to take his grandson to visit Mao. 'Call me granduncle,' Mao offered warmly. 'Oh, I certainly couldn't do that, Chairman Mao,' the awestruck child replied. 'Why don't you give him an apple?' suggested Deng. No sooner had Mao done so than the boy happily chirped, 'Oh thank you, Granduncle.' 'You see,' said Deng, 'what incentives can achieve.'
>
> (*Time*, 30 April 1984: 62)

The story above may or may not be true, but if it is not, it is certainly a very happy invention. It captures nicely an important underlying strand to the economic reforms that have been going on in China for over 20 years now, leading away from reliance on ideological commitment and a totally planned economy towards material incentives and market forces. In the course of this transformation, those responsible for managing China's industry have had their world turned upside down. Old certainties have been eroded, new challenges have emerged. How these changes have been responded to is the subject of this book.

During the time this book was in preparation, one of the authors had the good fortune to spend a year observing, at first hand, management practices in a major joint venture project in China. The project was particularly interesting because it brought together managers and professionals from around the globe: Americans, Australians, Canadians, Germans and Chinese. Differences between the Chinese and their foreign partners abounded, not least in the way they sought to handle the running of the project. The author was naturally interested not only in recording these differences, but in going beyond to uncover what lay at their root. Most of the foreign managers, perhaps because of their broader experience of management in different countries, were quite happy to indulge the author's strange whim on this point and to put forward a number of interesting and often slanderous hypotheses as to why their hosts set about things differently. The Chinese managers were often ready to return the compliment, but were more likely to greet questions about why particular managerial practices differed with a degree of exasperation. As one replied in a fashion typical of his colleagues: 'What! Of course we are different from them. This is China and we are Chinese.' When pursued by further questions about why Chinese management must differ, the manager, following the customary Chinese pattern, turned to those who happened to be around us in the office for support: 'Listen to this, such ridiculous questions. How can I answer and where do I begin?'

Where, indeed? Setting out to paint a portrait of the Chinese manager is both exhilarating and frustrating. Immersing oneself in interviews and discussions with managers in China, one is struck by the variety one encounters. The range is broad, from those with traditional values to the most ardent individualism, from those clearly weary of yet another movement in the reform programme to those eager to search out new methods of running their businesses successfully. For every stereotype of a Chinese manager you entertain, you can be sure the next manager you run into will flatly refuse to fit in with it. We say this at the beginning because, when considering the general, it is easy to lose sight of the variety that it attempts to summarise, perhaps nowhere more so than in a country as vast and diverse as China.

Yet for all the differences within China, the contrast between the management of enterprises there and in advanced capitalist economies remains striking – the centre of gravity, the whole atmosphere, remains in many ways a world apart. In what follows, we try to provide some feel for what it is like to manage an enterprise in this world, set against the changes that have taken place and the course they are likely to follow.

To make a reasonable guess at the likely future path that management of Chinese enterprises will follow, we need some notion of the driving forces involved. This will also help to make sense of just why management in China differs from management in the West. Is management in China embedded deep in immemorial traditions that mark Chinese society off from the rest of the world? Or are its characteristics a legacy of more recent history, of communist economics and the planned economy? Are all such forces being overwhelmed by pressure towards worldwide convergence in business practices arising from the competitive pressures inherent in globalisation? Or are Chinese managers beating out their own unique path?

To make a start in answering such questions, we first set out the broad context within which business in China takes place. We begin, in Chapter 1, with Chinese culture. We look at a number of values widely shared within Chinese society that are of particular relevance to management and organisational behaviour. We start with attitudes towards individualism and the attention accorded to group ties. Individualism is not absent within China. It is, as we shall see, admired in certain contexts. Everything has the defects of its qualities, and there are few ways of life that do not breed some hankering after what they miss out on. Despite all this, it remains true that China is, in general, less individualistic in its view of the world than is the West. This colours the world of work as much as other spheres of life. Similar observations apply to the other values we look at, such as attitudes to authority. As we shall argue, patterns of deference formed in the Chinese home and school carry over into the workplace. We then move on to further aspects of Chinese culture that shape managerial conduct and the ethos of Chinese organisations. We look at communication and inscrutability, at preserving face and the boundaries of trust. We then move on to look at how disputes are settled or avoided, and at the way in which Chinese negotiations are conducted.

Much of this cultural tradition can be traced deep into China's past. Despite this, some have argued that the forces of modernisation are undermining traditional Chinese values to an unprecedented degree. We look at the issue of cultural change with specific reference to the values of managers. From this, it appears that modernisation need not entail the wholesale abandonment of one set of practices in favour of another. Some aspects of culture are superficial and may change rapidly. Paradoxically, these are often the most noticeable and attract the most comment. Others lie deeper and are often so taken for granted as to pass unobserved. Fashions come and go but, underneath, old sentiments linger, leaving the dragon free to don the three-piece suit while remaining much the same old dragon at heart.

The next two chapters concern themselves with the management of state-owned enterprises. Similarities between China and countries of the former Soviet bloc suggest that certain characteristics of Chinese management may well owe as much to the communist system as they do to the preservation of traditional virtues. With this in mind, Chapter 2 sets out to explore the institutional setting within which the management of state enterprises operates in China. We start with an overview of the state sector, tracing the continuity and the change in the relations between officials and state firms as the reforms unfolded. For all its similarities with other communist systems, China's transition towards a market economy has been unique in its gradualist approach. Understandably wary of great leaps, China has eschewed the 'big bang' approach to the transition to a market economy that threw other communist economies into chaos. Nevertheless, the gradualism was not without its costs. Supported by soft budgets, state enterprise managers were able to operate in a fashion quite unlike managers in a capitalist economy, expanding production in the absence of effective demand and accumulating debts they could never repay. Asset management companies have emerged in an attempt to relieve the state banks of some of the resulting bad debts. However, as we shall see, asset management companies in China, like so many other institutions, behave in quite a different manner from their counterparts elsewhere. This is true, for example, of the transformation of state enterprises into joint stock companies. The change in outward form conceals much continuity in how the organisation is governed by the state. Business and politics, as we illustrate, blend in a surprising variety of ways.

Chapter 3 takes us inside the state enterprise. We start with the Communist Party, tracing its changing role and looking at the relationship between the general secretary of the Party and the general manager within the enterprise. This leads on to an examination of managerial appointments and appraisal. We then focus on the way in which senior managers spend their time, and their preference for an informal style of management. Forces resisting and furthering delegation come next, leading to a consideration of the role of the workshop manager. Following that, we look at different forms of rationality. We see how formal rules adopted in a conscious attempt to get on track with international practice end up having distinctive Chinese characteristics.

Whether it is the similarities or the differences between China and the West that come most readily to mind depends on the topic under discussion and the level of generality at which one proceeds. Looking at the issue of strategic investment, for example, one is impressed by the similarities. Likewise, specific technological factors tend to favour certain forms of internal management structure wherever one may happen to be. These two topics are considered before turning to matters related to labour relations, including unemployment, trade unions and worker participation in management.

In Chapter 4, we consider the growth of the private sector and the manner in which it operates. We trace the route, at times devious, that private business has had to tread during the course of the reforms. Private business in China, as with business in overseas Chinese communities, remains very much a family affair. We look at how family connections shape their operation. Unwillingness on the part of owners to relinquish control has been blamed as one factor holding in check the growth of Chinese private businesses, but another barrier faced within China is the difficulty of securing outside funding. We review the accounting practices of private firms and how they are financed.

Private firms in China are frequently part of a broader conglomerate, their relationships mediated more by family ties than legal definition. Indeed, business relationships in general tend to be based on the development of relationships of trust in place of a reliance on legal mechanisms. This, as we shall see, is part of a broader cultural disposition.

The hand that is held out to private business by government officials is one that both helps and grasps. For both reasons, private entrepreneurs are attracted towards cultivating connections within the bureaucracy. The ways of influencing officials vary and we explore why one strategy is chosen in preference to another. Turning to a consideration of business associations, we find here also the hand of the state as it guides their development with a paternalistic solicitude.

The business world in today's China does not fall neatly into two distinct camps, private and public. An array of hybrid forms spans the divide between the two. Partly these forms have emerged from the surreptitious shifting of assets from the public purse into the private pocket – familiar to all transitional economies. The proliferation of business forms also takes place through more acceptable avenues. Of particular importance are the spin-offs from research institutes and universities that dominate China's high-tech sector. The professions are also being transformed. Some have effectively been privatised. Others are still vacillating as they attempt to find a way to transform their former status as state servants. All these developments are reviewed in Chapter 5, which concludes with a summary of the diverse forms of business organisation to be encountered within China today.

The growth in diversity is encapsulated in the history of township and village enterprises. These enterprises are the subjects of Chapter 6. Their growth, arising out of bottom-up local initiatives, came as a surprise to the Chinese leadership. It also came as a surprise to those who considered the involvement of officials in industry as a recipe for slow growth. Far from acting as a restraint on growth, the rural cadres provided dramatic increases in growth through their management of public enterprises. In this, local officials had the benefit over their counterparts at provincial and national level of being in more direct contact with the enterprises they led, making effective monitoring far easier. Success brought with it its own problems, however, as the increasing size and complexity of enterprises necessitated delegation to professional management and the accompanying need to align the interests of owners and managers. At the same time, while managers assumed responsibility for internal management, external management of the firm during the transition from plan to market necessitated the continued involvement of local officials for success. Increasing competition and the power of market forces led to yet further gains in independence for some of the enterprises. Even where the private sector has grown, however, local officials have continued to take an active role in steering the course of its development.

Joint ventures in China should flourish through combining complementary strengths. Bringing about such a happy result is, however, far from easy. One problem lies in differing aims. We look at these, and how they need to be addressed during the establishment of the joint venture, in Chapter 7, outlining the various trade-offs that can be made. Another difficulty encountered by foreign investors arises from the problem of deciding quite what is, and what is not, allowed, as laws and regulations are often vague, contradictory or silent on many points. Without firm knowledge in this area, cultivating the right connections to secure information and approvals becomes essential. It is work that calls for special talents, leading to the re-emergence of the comprador.

As they develop, joint venture partners learn to adjust to one another in a variety of ways. We look at the forces shaping modes of adaptation and at the differing expectations surrounding the role of the manager. National sentiments also inevitably enter into the equation. We look at how conflicts of interest may bar the flow of information and foil effective control of the enterprise. This leads to a consideration of the introduction of formalised approaches in an attempt to ease the transmission of information and to define the framework of managerial authority and responsibility. Next comes consideration of human resources management. This can be used for different purposes, from entrenching old practices at one extreme and to fostering a radical change in outlook at the other.

The chapter concludes with a look at ventures started in China by Chinese entrepreneurs from Taiwan and Hong Kong. The managers of these ventures have found themselves at an advantage in terms of language and many shared cultural traits. They nevertheless also encountered something of a culture shock in certain vital areas of business, areas that have proved quite unlike those with which they are familiar.

The conclusion expands upon the comparison of differences in outlook between the mainland and overseas Chinese before moving on to speculate about the impact of membership of the World Trade Organisation on China's enterprises. We end with one final case study that encapsulates many of the continuities and changes present in Chinese management today.

As will have become clear from this brief outline, we adopt a broad approach to what constitutes management. We do not confine ourselves to looking at managers as a professional group, but look at management as a function necessary to all businesses, whether undertaken by professional managers, private entrepreneurs, or government officials. Such an approach makes sense in the Chinese context, where, as we shall see, the management of internal operations and the external relations of firms may well be spread between different groups. Management here, then, is viewed very much in terms of getting things done through people and of steering the enterprise – tasks necessary to any business no matter who undertakes them. We paint a portrait of who undertakes these tasks and how they accomplish them in the Chinese context.

It is a portrait painted 'warts and all'. Our intention throughout has been to provide a rounded picture that encompasses more practices than those to be found, or at least found within the curriculum, in many management schools. Care needs to be taken when comparing Chinese management with management elsewhere. We need to compare like with like. Condemning Chinese practice as not living up to Western ideals is dubious at a time when fresh malpractices in the running of Western companies are never far from the headlines.

Continuity and change is a recurring theme throughout the book. Whether one is most struck by one or the other depends much on one's perspective and the issue being focused upon. From the perspective of China's past, many businesses have made enormous strides in the past two decades. Set against leading multinationals, however, all but a handful of these businesses remain, for the moment at least, fledglings.

Continuity and change within China can blend, with her leaders proving adept at using new approaches to the preservation of the established verities, as the anecdote with which we began illustrates. Even the leaders, however, have been surprised by the turn many of the forces they have unleashed have taken. More surprises doubtless lie ahead.

1 Of different minds

- Collectivism and individualism
- Power and authority
- Harmony and hierarchy
- Against being blunt
- Saving face
- Trust and suspicion
- Settling disputes
- Negotiation
- Decision making
- Tradition and modernity
- Diversity
- Ideals and reality: a sociology of hypocrisy
- Confucius or Marx?

> The abysmal ignorance of the foreigner about China and the Chinese cannot be more impressive that when he asks the question: do the Chinese have a sense of humour?
>
> Lin Yutang

The unfortunate fact that humour does not travel very well is just one more symptom of how radically ways of looking at the world can differ. It frequently results in accusations that one nation or another, never one's own, is devoid of all sense of humour. The inevitable huffy response is often illuminating. In Lin's case, it was to argue that the essence of the Chinese sense of humour resides in a well-developed – if rather grim – sense of farce:

> In spite of the serious style of their editorial and political writings, which are seldom relieved by humour, they often surprise foreigners by the extremely light manner in which they take important reform programmes and movements. . . . Political programmes and official statements are issued as matters of form, being drafted by clerks who specialize in a kind of specious, bombastic phraseology . . . and no intelligent Chinese ever takes them seriously.
>
> (Lin 1939: 65–66)

Many would find this rings as true today as it did when written over 60 years ago. This, at first sight, might seem a little odd, given the different political complexion of the regimes then and now. However, some habits evidently die hard. It is the depth and tenacity of such historical habits and how they impinge on management today that we shall be looking at in this chapter. In a word, albeit a very slippery word, we are looking at *culture*, at what has been termed 'the collective software of the mind' (Hofstede 1994).

Managers do not enter into their profession with minds that are blank slates. This sets limits on the ability of companies to impress on them whatever corporate culture they may choose. Which is perhaps just as well, for managers are likely to find themselves in a world of colleagues, clients and officials who were brought up to take for granted the same unspoken assumptions about how one ought to behave. Many of these assumptions have a direct influence on how business organisations operate. Much that is distinctive about Chinese management is seen by many to be rooted in attitudes and beliefs shared more broadly within Chinese society. To explore this notion, we start by looking at Chinese attitudes of particular relevance to the exercise of management and the operation of enterprises. These are attitudes towards authority and individualism. We then move on to look at further aspects of Chinese culture that have a direct bearing on management. These include Chinese preferences regarding communication, face, trust, dispute settlement and negotiations.

Collectivism and individualism

It is sometimes difficult for those living in individualist cultures to grasp that the values related to the individual, which they hold so dear, are far from being universal. Many more people in the world live in collectivist societies that take quite a different view of the nature of individual rights and duties. Misunderstanding can flow from failing to consider this difference when viewing Chinese practices from a Western perspective. This is because China, throughout its long history, has belonged well within the collectivist camp. Such societies tend to be characterised by participation in intense social interaction that affords little privacy, leading to a corresponding stress on the need to maintain harmony. Open confrontation is deemed rude and a flat refusal is replaced by delay or a 'yes' that everyone understands is not to be taken literally. Individualist cultures frown upon such behaviour rather than seeing it as good manners. Good character resides in telling the truth about how one feels in a straightforward manner. A child who reflects the opinions of others is regarded as a weak character. To the collectivist, in contrast, the child who continually disagrees with others is the one at fault. In such a world, much can be left unsaid, common knowledge and shared opinions can be relied upon to fill the gaps. In an individualist culture, diversity of thought and opinion flourishes and, consequently, spelling out explicitly what one has in mind is often necessary and a habit to be encouraged (Hall 1976). As we shall see when we come to consider the experience of Western firms seeking to establish themselves in China, training managers to challenge the opinions of others can run against the grain of conventional wisdom.

Trying to accommodate prevailing opinion is naturally likely to lead to less diversity of thought and smoother social relations than applauding those who strive to be different. Experiments comparing American and Chinese subjects in terms of conformity to peer group pressure lend support to this picture, with Chinese subjects moving more towards the majority position than Americans do (Bond and Hwang 1986: 256–57). Difficulties in comparing China with more individualist countries by means of attitude surveys reinforce this picture. They run up against a problem caused by the very values they are trying to unearth, as the Chinese are less prepared than Americans to express disagreement with any positively worded statement! They are also inclined to follow the traditional Chinese virtue of modesty in all things in their tendency to favour the middle range rather than extremes when asked to rank the strength of their approval or disapproval of a statement (Smith and Wang 1996: 326).

Central to the collectivist view of life is the distinction between those who belong to one's group and those who do not, between us and them, the former trusted, the latter ever suspect. This clearly has important implications for business. Enterprises are seen as ideally based on moral ties reminiscent of the family rather than cold contract. Favouring insiders over outsiders is expected rather than frowned upon. This contrasts with the universalism of individualistic cultures with their suspicion of nepotism and demand for the equal treatment for all. For the collectivist, entering into a serious business relationship with an outsider requires time spent first on establishing trust – the task has to wait upon the relationship. Only then can business be addressed, with the trust serving to obviate the need for contracts that cover every detail. All these cultural traits, as we shall see, have an affinity with characteristics of the Chinese business world.

Power and authority

The division between collectivist and individualist societies is related to another contrast that revolves around attitudes to power and authority. This concerns the extent to which the less powerful members of institutions and organisations expect and accept that power will be distributed unequally. In societies that place a high value on respect for authority, those wielding power can rely on deference from those below, with subordinates expecting to be told what to do rather than to be consulted. In such societies, authority figures can expect to be accorded respect and will not be amused if it is not forthcoming. Such societies have been dubbed high in *power distance* (Hofstede 1980).

Such attitudes towards authority are often thought of as being established very early in life. In large power distance societies, parents teach their children obedience and expect to be treated with respect. In small power distance societies, parents and children are more inclined to treat each other as equals. Similar differences prevail between teachers and students, while later in life the ideal boss for those valuing power distance is the benevolent autocrat, while for those of the opposite persuasion it is the resourceful democrat (Hofstede 1994: 37). In high power distance societies, people take with them into adulthood not merely the habit of outward respect for seniors but also comfort from depending upon them. There is the assumption that this is a quite natural desire. In low power distance societies, humans are seen in quite a contrary fashion, as impelled to struggle to break free of dependence.

Efforts to measure the values characteristic of the Chinese through attitude surveys have shown Hong Kong, Singapore and Taiwan sharing with mainland China scores high on power distance and low on individualism (Hofstede 1980, Bond and Hwang 1986). This particular configuration of values is not unique to Chinese societies, however, as it is shared by others such as Greece, Iran, Turkey, Pakistan, Thailand, India and the Philippines. It is a pattern that does, however, stand these Chinese societies in marked contrast to many societies in the West. These include the United States and Britain, both of which score high in terms of individualism and low on power distance.

Management development programmes devised in one cultural setting can run up against difficulties in another because of these cultural differences. Management by objectives (MBO) is an example. First established in America, this technique relies on the negotiation of a performance contract between subordinate and boss, followed by periodic meetings to assess progress. This requires a willingness on the part of superiors to delegate and to refrain from cutting across intermediate hierarchical levels. It also requires subordinates to be sufficiently independent to be able to negotiate meaningfully with the boss and a willingness on both sides to take risks. These conditions are simply not present in Chinese organisations to the extent necessary for MBO to be introduced effectively.

Harmony and hierarchy

Collectivism and deference to authority have, for many centuries, been so central to life in China that the value placed upon 'harmony-in-hierarchy' has been suggested as the key to understanding Chinese social behaviour (Bond and Hwang 1986: 213–14). It is a value that can be traced deep into Chinese antiquity, to the philosophy of Confucius and his fundamental concern with achieving social harmony.

This philosophy has no truck with the Western tendency to make the isolated individual its starting point. From the Confucian perspective, the idea of the isolated individual appears as an unnatural and absurd abstraction. Instead, we are viewed as inseparable from our relationships with others. Fulfilment is to be found in the performance of one's social roles and obligations rather than in breaking free of them. Foremost among these roles are the *wu lun*, the Five Cardinal Relationships that bind emperor and subject, father and son, husband and wife, older brother and younger brother, and friend and friend. These, even the last, are seen in hierarchical terms, with the senior permitted authority over the junior. Such rights are, however, balanced by rules of correct behaviour (*li*). The senior is expected to display benevolence and justice.

Filial piety lies at the heart of this system. This has, for centuries, governed relations between generations, requiring children to obey parents, and provide for their welfare in this world when old and in the next world through sacrifice. It even exhorts children to avoid all harm to their bodies in case they should be unable to fulfil their filial duties. Blind obedience in the face of unrighteous conduct by parents is not expected, but patient remonstration rather than outright defiance is the only permitted remedy (Ho 1996).

The Confucian tradition, then, stresses that man exists through his relationships to others; that these relationships are hierarchical in nature; and that social harmony rests upon honouring the obligations they entail. Some have seen it as a philosophy born of strife, as Confucius' attempt to remedy the ills of an age torn by political intrigue through the restoration of traditional virtues. Its continuing influence down the ages may be attributable to a similar wish to ease the threats posed by a history marked by recurring economic hardship, natural disasters, and frailty on the part of the traditional Chinese state (Gabrenya and Hwang 1996: 310).

Modern China carries forward these traditions. Child-rearing practices aim at training for obedience, impulse control and the acceptance of social obligations, in contrast to the emphasis on independence, assertiveness and creativity encouraged in more individualistic societies. The authority exercised by parents is put to the service of developing moral character in the child rather than responding to the child's internal needs and feelings. Children are looked after, they are not expected to experiment for themselves or encouraged to take control of their own affairs at the earliest opportunity, as in less authoritarian societies (Ho 1986).

The attitudes towards authority established in the family are reproduced in the school, the pupil–teacher relationship mimics that of the parent–child, gratifying needs for dependence already established. From as early as kindergarten there is an emphasis on discipline and learning rather than free play. Teachers are treated with respect and learning is teacher-centred. Students are generally expected to speak when spoken to and not otherwise. In the case of misbehaviour, the child's family will be contacted and expected to support the teacher's authority and bring the child into line.

The attitudes towards authority thus formed stand ready to be carried forward into the workplace where they sit at ease with the hierarchical, top-down structure of the command economy and the care that needs to be taken with officials. However, they have less affinity with attempts to delegate responsibility down under the reforms.

Box 1.1 On the difficulty of dealing with officials

Gangs of thieves getting on to the site at night troubled the construction site for a new plant. One local government official involved in overseeing the project suggested to the managers that they should have a guard dog. The managers replied that they would organise a security team to tour around at night.

Thefts continued, the security patrols being intimidated by the gangs. The official repeated the necessity of having a dog. The managers replied that they would find a way to resolve the problem and that the leader could put his mind at rest.

However, a few weeks later there were more thefts. This time the government official was adamant that a dog was needed and he criticised the managers for inaction and neglect of duty.

One of the management team later explained to us the dilemma they faced. Now that the leader insisted upon a dog, they would have to have one, otherwise the leader would bridle at not being given proper respect. But the notion of a having a dog was regarded with grave misgivings. Large dogs are rare in that part of China and, apart from their occasional appearances at the dinner table, tend to inspire fear. They are generally viewed as dangerous and unreliable beasts liable to take a chunk out of anyone unlucky enough to get within biting distance. Thus, while it was granted that it might well frighten thieves, it was viewed as equally likely to savage any innocent worker out roaming the site at night to relieve himself.

When asked why he did not point this out to the official himself, the manager explained:

> It is quite natural and easy to realize that a dog might solve one problem only to cause another. Besides, the leader knows that we have many workers on the site at night. He should have thought about the possibility of the dog biting the workers. However, it is precisely because it is such a simple fact that makes it difficult to point out to him. It might make others assume that one is poking fun at the leader and showing disrespect. It is very difficult to deal with officials, you have to think a lot before you open your mouth, otherwise you will offend them and bring down trouble on yourself.

Fieldwork notes, 2001

Against being blunt

Despite the stress on harmony in Chinese society, tensions inevitably arise. Where they do, Chinese strategies for resolving them remain shaped by the desire to avoid open conflict. This has a wide-ranging impact on how Chinese communicate with each other (Gao *et al.* 1996). Open debate requiring direct confrontation is avoided. In discussions, the Chinese are likely to preface their own opinion with a review of the

Box 1.2 Avoiding trouble

'There are a lot of things missing, steel plates here, nuts and bolts there,' the manager commented, pointing at the places where the missing parts should be. 'The contractor deliberately omits quite a number of details from the design drawings by the architects. But no one wants to stir up trouble by bringing this out into the open.'

'But what happens if it falls down?'

'If one brings these problems up for discussion, then they have to be solved, and the persons to be held responsible have to be found. This will be very painful. So it is much better not to bring the problems out into the open now. After the building is completed, everybody will have left the site, and the problems are discovered, then it will be much more difficult to find out whose fault it is. Usually everybody will be blamed. And if everybody is blamed, then nobody will suffer much. So it is much better that way.'

From an interview with one of the managers of a construction project in northern China during a tour of the site, 2001

common problems and constraints facing all parties. While Westerners may find this unnecessarily vague and diffident, it does serve to reduce the possibility of a polarisation of opinion within the group (Young 1982).

Chinese communication stands in direct contrast with the American aversion to ambiguity and preference for blunt and direct speaking (Mead 1990: 132ff.). The Chinese favour the reserved, the implicit, and the indirect (*hanxu*). Consequently, the Chinese are constantly on the alert to 'read between the lines' of any message. Things stated baldly leave too little room for manoeuvre, for tactical retreat to preserve harmony. *Hanxu* also inhibits the forthright expression of emotion, particularly negative emotion. This is inculcated from an early age, with children discouraged from displaying anger or disappointment. This cultural emphasis on restraint has deep roots. As Chen Dexiu (1178–1235) recommended in his rules for educating sons so that they might develop into the ideal Confucian gentleman: 'The little ones are exhorted always to walk slowly with arms held within the sleeves, with no waving of the arms or jumping' (Dardes 1991: 79). Children were expected to learn to control their facial expressions, posture and speech. This is training in inscrutability, in never revealing one's thoughts or feelings (*bugou yanxiao*), leaving the surface of public tranquillity undisturbed.

In many situations, silence is often considered the safest course in a culture that sees the mouth as the fount of misfortune (*huo cong kou shu*). Children are expected to be seen but not heard in family gatherings at which the senior adults hold the floor. The good child is one who heeds what he or she is told (*ting hua* – 'listens talk') and does not interrupt or talk back. This pattern of the superior having the prerogative of speaking with the inferior relegated to listening reverently is repeated at school and at work, with acceptance rather than argument expected of students and employees. One consequence is that Chinese managers tend to rate oral fluency as of little importance in their staff (Hildebrandt 1988).

Box 1.3 Having the last word

Business meetings tend to be long, especially when senior managers or officials are participating. The chairman is obliged to invite all of such managers to give their guidance on all the various matters under discussion. The course of the meeting then takes the form of a series of lengthy speeches rather than any open discussion. These are made in order of rank, from low to high.

When managers and officials of the lower rank begin their speeches, they usually have to show proper deference to their seniors. Most of them start with something like this: 'Dear leaders, dear gentlemen, I will say a few words, anything wrong should be pointed out by you and anything more important will doubtlessly be addressed by our leaders.'

During their speech, the lower ranks also have constantly to defer to the senior leaders to make sure the latter condone what they are saying. It is an art to strike a balance between addressing the problems properly to show one is competent while at the same time leaving the important and final words for one's seniors.

At one such meeting, one middle manager was observed embarking on a long speech that laid out a number of definite conclusions concerning the problems under discussion. To make matters worse, he appeared to became so lost in reading from his script that he forgot the normal code of behaviour concerning due displays of deference. This made the rest of the people at the meeting bored and upset. As his colleague commented to one of the authors: 'He is a very silly person. He said all these things that should be left for the leaders to say. Now what have the leaders left to tell us? He bores us and the leaders won't like him either.'

Heated discussion showing emotions in the presence of the senior officials is regarded as disrespect towards authority, an unseemly contempt for their presence. At one meeting, one junior manager disagreed with a colleague's speech by pounding on the table. The government official at the meeting indicated later that he thought he should be dismissed. While he managed to retain his post, he was subsequently barred from attending such meetings.

Fieldwork notes, 2001

The flow of information in Chinese society is also influenced by the intense loyalty commanded by small face-to-face groups, most notably the family. What people are told and how they are treated will depend upon whether they belong to the same group or not, whether they are insiders (*zijiren*) or outsiders (*wairen*). 'Dirty linen' will not be aired in public so that, in the event of disputes, a close friend of both parties is often chosen, for 'a *wairen* would not know what has happened. The two in conflict won't talk about their conflict to a *wairen*' (Ma 1992: 274). Similarly, workers viewed by management as causing problems may be advised by the latter to discuss the matter with their co-workers, friends and family. The hope is that these will bring their influence to bear on the employee to mend his or her ways (Krone *et al.* 1992).

Saving face

Chinese people are the first to acknowledge the influence of 'face' in their lives, and yet even they have difficulty in setting out precisely how it works. Lu Xun, the famous Chinese writer, said of it: 'It is all very well if you do not stop to think, but the more you think, the more confused you grow. There seems to be many kinds: each class in society has a different face' (Worm 1997: 148). In many ways, the concern with social standing and self-esteem to which it relates is universal. Yet, it is arguably felt more keenly in collectivist societies such as China than elsewhere. Here, face serves as the lubricant necessary to sustain harmony amongst those living in situations where moving away is not an option. As Bond and Lee (1981) have argued in discussing face-saving in Hong Kong, face assumes particular importance where the same people meet repeatedly; where identity derives from group rather than individual activities; and where criticism of superiors is suppressed in favour of knowing one's place.

In such circumstances, attention must be paid to avoiding giving offence. Care is needed to preserve the face of others, particularly the face of superiors. Criticism of others is often phrased in vague or moderate language to avoid loss of face. Similarly saying 'no' to a request may be interpreted as not giving face. In this case, a rejection may be concealed in an undertaking to consider the matter, or accompanied by excuses to 'pad the face' of the one disappointed. The matter of face is further complicated by the relative nature of prestige. To give face to one may throw the face of another into the shadows (see Box 1.4).

Box 1.4 Face

Redding and Ng (1983) illustrate how giving face can be a delicate matter with the case of a Hong Kong businessman who, when inviting clients to regular seminars, would telephone his less important clients, but would deliver invitations to the more important clients in person. He also gave representatives of the more important firms the front seats. This worked well for a while, but then the smaller companies began to take offence, thinking he was not giving them sufficient face. This led them to stop attending, putting at risk the organiser's face as the more important companies looked askance at being invited to a poorly attended seminar. As the manager remarked of the smaller companies:

> Some of the more face-conscious ones began to complain and even challenged me. 'We are a small company, so our attendance is not so important as that of the big companies!' Usually such shipping companies in Hong Kong are run by Shanghainese people, who are known as the most face-conscious among Chinese people.

Source: Redding and Ng (1983: 109–10)

The circumspection required in preserving the face of others in public has its negative side. It fuels a lively inclination among the Chinese to vent less polite thoughts and feelings about others behind their backs. Gossip enjoys universal popularity, of course, but in close communities it becomes particularly powerful. Among the Chinese, concern for face mixes with fear of gossip (*yulun*) to strengthen even further pressures to conform. It also influences attitudes towards self-disclosure. Often used as a tactic for initiating personal relationships by Americans, self-disclosure is treated with more caution by Chinese. This is partly through fear of providing ammunition that may be turned against them. As a result, the Chinese sometimes end up knowing more about the personal lives of American acquaintances than they do of Chinese friends. Attacks can also be made indirectly through poison pen letters and there is some evidence to suggest that these may be more common among the Chinese than among other East Asians (Worm 1997: 175). In China, the authorities encourage it. It is not unusual to come across special report boxes (*jian ju xiang*) specifically for people to deposit denunciations anonymously.[1]

Trust and suspicion

In speaking of societies in which harmony and forbearance are much in evidence, Colson observes that 'some people live in what appears to be a Rousseauian paradise because they take a Hobbesian view of their situation: they walk softly because they believe it necessary not to offend others whom they regard as dangerous' (Colson 1975: 37). Her remarks could well be applied to China. Traditionally, as Weber remarked: 'The Confucian gentleman, striving simply for dignified bearing, distrusted others as generally as he believed others distrusted him' (Weber 1951: 244). This lack of trust in the wider world beyond one's immediate family has been made much of by Redding in analysing what he sees as the limits on growth of Chinese private enterprises. Among the Chinese, he argues, 'you trust your family absolutely, your friends and acquaintances to the degree that mutual dependence has been established and face invested in them. With everybody else you will make no assumptions about their goodwill' (Redding 1993: 66). Networking beyond the family (*guanxi*) relies upon establishing trust, but this trust is specific, limited to partners bound by personal obligations and not by any community of faith. Universalistic moral rules concerning protecting the welfare of all people are not as strong as those urging benevolence towards the circle of those with whom you are in frequent contact (Schwartz 1992: 39). Giving the same consideration to those beyond one's primary groups – the small intimate face-to-face groups of family, friends and workplace – can be frowned upon as devaluing the worth of these primary groups. The result is a culture in which nepotism and favouritism is, if not condoned, at least regarded as, in many ways, understandable and natural.

Settling disputes

Despite the best endeavours, conflict can still break through the surface of tranquillity that the Chinese long to maintain. Wherever in the world this happens a number of choices concerning how to settle the matter lie open to the disputants. Thomas (1976) has delineated these in terms of two dimensions, as illustrated in Figure 1.1.

The first dimension, shown on the vertical axis, measures the desire to satisfy one's own concerns, varying in strength from unassertive to assertive. The second, shown on the horizontal axis, measures one's desire to satisfy the concerns of another, varying from the uncooperative

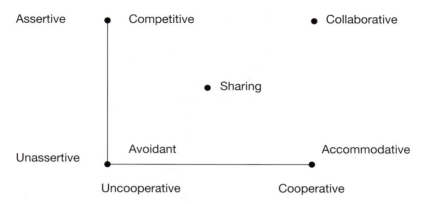

Figure 1.1 *Approaches to dispute resolution (adapted from Thomas 1976: 900)*

to cooperative. Taking the two dimensions together, we can identify five ways of handling conflict. The competitive reflects a desire to have one's own way regardless of anyone else, yielding no quarter. In contrast, the accommodative approach is one of appeasement, of generous self-sacrifice for the sake of the relationship. Intermediate between these two approaches we find sharing, a taste for 'splitting the difference' in which both parties compromise to gain moderate if incomplete satisfaction. The collaborative orientation seeks to integrate the concerns of both parties by fully satisfying both through devising a mutually beneficial solution. Avoidance is the path of benign neglect.

Which of the five approaches is favoured appears to depend, in part, on the cultural background of those involved in the conflict, as can be seen from the comparison of Chinese and British attitudes undertaken by Tang and Kirkbride (1986). Using a questionnaire designed to measure which of the five solutions identified by Thomas were most preferred, they compared two groups of British and Chinese Hong Kong government officials with similar rank and background. A third group of Chinese managers from the private sector was also included. The Chinese managers, both public and private, favoured the less assertive 'compromising' and 'avoiding' solutions, in contrast with the British officials who preferred the more assertive 'collaborating' and 'competing' styles. A similar Chinese preference for compromise can be seen in the study by Leung (1987), which found that Chinese subjects from Hong Kong preferred mediation over adjudication as a way of resolving disputes, whereas American subjects had no preference for one over the other.

Negotiation

Negotiation is a peculiar mixture of conflict and cooperation. It takes place between parties with interests that conflict. The parties share, at the same time, a common need to agree because of the expected gain from such agreement. Chinese managers bring to the table the distinctive values we have touched upon earlier and this influences how they blend these two elements. Concern with harmony and hierarchy shape the style of communication. Ideals of Confucian gentility promote respect for those who maintain self-control, who embody 'perfect calm' (*xinping qihe*). Emotional outbursts, on the other hand, arouse strong distrust and antipathy. In the context of cross-cultural negotiations, Chinese preference for restrained, moderate behaviour means that the 'American task-oriented approach, which allows for the admission of differences in the positions of the parties to a negotiation so as to promote "honest confrontation" is viewed by the Chinese as aggressive, and therefore as an unacceptable mode of behaviour' (Shenkar and Ronen 1987: 268).

Areas of disagreement are not merely skirted through vague and non-committal responses resulting from a desire to keep up appearances. Forces that are more self-interested may also be at work in a desire to avoid indebtedness. Chinese society makes great use of gifts to establish relationships of trust and dependence. Refusal is difficult without causing loss of face, and yet once accepted a debt is incurred, and a strong duty to reciprocate is formed. This duty means that receiving favours creates anxiety that one will incur obligations requiring real, yet unspecified future repayment. This possibility may well come to mind in discussions that threaten to stray into areas of known disagreement. Any concessions that result will create a 'debt' that has to be repaid. In such circumstances, the contentious issues may well be brushed under the carpet in the hope that they will fade with time.

It is interesting in this context to see that the Japanese, who take a similar attitude towards indebtedness (Black 1993), tend to resist Chinese overtures to establish ties of friendship by seeking to be more businesslike and impersonal than are Americans (Pye 1982: 90–91). In this, they are probably wise. Westerners who have heard about the importance of such relationships in China may welcome the opportunity to be included in the networks of mutual obligation and friendship that are so important in everyday Chinese life, but in reality Chinese officials are unlikely seriously to consider foreigners suitable candidates for such a role. They are too much outsiders and lack any pull within Chinese society to reciprocate with favours through friends of friends. Not embedded within the system, foreigners lack face to lose and, as such, cannot be relied on to meet obligations. As such, appeals to friendship by the Chinese side are often, in reality, little more than a matter of habit and an attempt to shame foreigners into giving special consideration. Different understandings of the nature of friendship compound the problem. Close relationships in the Chinese mind are associated not so much with effusiveness, as they are in the minds of Americans, but with reliability and permanence. As Pye remarks: 'Although the Chinese may be quick to say that someone is an "old friend" and although Americans enjoy calling Chinese "old friends," the Chinese notion of true old friends is one based on a blend of dignity and pleasure' (Pye 1982: 93).

Pye further suggests that the heart of the problem faced by Americans negotiating with Chinese authorities is a different attitude to power and authority. The Anglo-American attitude is to assume power and responsibility go hand in hand. Those with the power are accountable for its exercise, the buck stops at the desk of the person in charge. However, in Chinese bureaucracy and politics, the critical art is to avoid responsibility. Proof of importance lies precisely in protection from accountability. Those in command act as if they have complete authority, taking care to avoid situations where their powers are visibly circumscribed. This accounts for the absence of the most important players from the negotiating table, with the inevitable lengthening of negotiations that this entails. Staying behind the scenes allows important figures to change their position without loss of face.

Decision making

Let us pause for a moment to consider the humble potato. We know this may seem to be wandering from our subject, but bear with us for a moment. Let us take a general-knowledge question about this modest vegetable and see what answer you come up with, what decision you make. The question is this: does the potato grow better in a warm climate or in a cool climate? Having chosen your answer, now estimate the probability that your answer is correct on a scale from 50 per cent to 100 per cent where 100 per cent is absolute certainty. If this is your answer, you clearly regard yourself as an authority. Fifty per cent, on the other hand, is pure chance.

Now the point of all this is to give you some feel of how social psychologists have set about studying the issue of cross-cultural differences in decision-making (Yates and Lee 1996). Subjects are asked not one but many such general-knowledge questions. Their estimates of their confidence in their own judgements are then calculated and compared. This has been done, for example, with Chinese and American subjects. Both tend towards overconfidence, thinking their answers correct more often than is the case. However, when their scores are compared, one group shows itself more overconfident than the other. Before reading on, can you guess which?

The experiments showed that the Chinese subjects were more liable to be overconfident than the Americans. In some ways, this is surprising, as overconfidence might suggest an inflated opinion of oneself, a lack of modesty. Chinese culture strongly discourages such feelings. The explanation for Chinese overconfidence must lie elsewhere, possibly in differences in attitudes to learning, between America and China. America is very contentious, with roughly one new lawsuit for every ten adults filed each year. Arguments are settled in adversarial combat, each side putting forward its case, and the evidence being weighed by the jury. Parallel approaches to learning take place in the classroom with a high value being put on critical thinking. China, by contrast, the oldest continuous civilisation in the world, places far greater emphasis on its past. Even Confucius claimed simply to be transmitting the wisdom of the ancients. To learn is to imitate rather than debate. Overconfidence may well rest, in part, on less value being placed on promoting a questioning attitude.

The hierarchical nature of Chinese society also militates against making decisions and submitting them to public scrutiny. Many Chinese consequently avoid making individual choices when confronting new problems. This can make it particularly difficult to introduce Western management techniques, such as normative decision analysis, into a Chinese setting (Pollock 1986). Research comparing decision making among Taiwanese and Western subjects has found the former more ready than the latter to panicking under the pressure of time, passing off responsibility, procrastinating, and rationalising away problems (Bond 1991: 85). The difference owes much to a tradition of training from childhood to rely on superiors and the group for guidance in dealing with the unexpected.

Tradition and modernity

However, can traditional Chinese values such as collectivism and its stress on harmony, survive in the face of the forces of modernisation? There are broadly two schools of thought on this question. One sees core Chinese cultural values as deeply embedded in traditions that have survived thousands of years. As such, they are unlikely to be casually cast aside. Others have argued that China's traditional culture was the product of an agricultural society and that as Chinese communities become more industrialised they will abandon outdated values. An example of this approach can be found in the early work of Yang (1986). Surveying findings from numerous psychological studies that mainly centred on comparisons between Chinese and Americans, he concluded that the former were indeed more likely to display social harmoniousness, group-mindedness and mutual dependency. However, he also noted that evidence from Taiwan suggests that its inhabitants are moving away from such a 'social' orientation towards a more 'individualistic' one. This he attributed to the rapid industrialisation of Taiwan favouring such characteristics. The implications are clear. Given industrialisation, Chinese people will become much like other members of advanced industrial societies.

Recently, however, under the influence of critics of modernisation theory, Yang has chosen to follow the Confucian rule and adopt a middle way. His argument now is that modernisation theory is an oversimplification. It assumes that modern values are all the polar opposites of traditional values so that if you have more of one you inevitably get less of the other. This stems from the idea that values are all tied to each other and move in unison. Such assumptions are questionable. Many traditional values can continue alongside modern ones (see Box 1.5). Reviewing the evidence from recent Chinese studies Yang now concludes that 'some collectivist and individualistic characteristics may coexist in persons in a modern society, and the former need not be eventually replaced by the latter through the process of societal modernization' (Yang 1996: 492).[2]

It is interesting, with respect to this problem, to look at Hong Kong in comparison with mainland China and the United States, as Hong Kong residents are betwixt and between in exposure to both Western and Eastern influences. When asked, 79 per cent of respondents in Hong Kong reported themselves Westernised in some respects, while at the same time 71 per cent considered themselves as being Chinese with regard to other aspects of their character (Bond and King 1985). Looking

Box 1.5 Managing luck

At lunch, staff at a construction project were talking about accidents that had occurred during the construction of the Jinmao Building, China's tallest. The general manager commented:

> The Jinmao is bad, even a foreigner was killed by a piece of falling curtain wall crashing into the meeting room he happened to be in. This is because the Fengshui master they used was not very good. I asked the best one in this city, Fengshui Ma, we use him for all our projects, he said that building is too aggressive and too high. It disturbs the dragons in the clouds.

> I know one of the people in charge of building the Jinmao, he always seems to have bad luck. The China Trade Tower he built in Beijing had several deaths, and, later on, the Jinmao had more deaths. After the completion of the Jinmao, he was hospitalised immediately because of liver cancer. That is why before I came to do this job, my friends dragged me to the temples on Jiuhua Mountain, because it is the only place with any real monks left. They forced me to be a vegetarian for three days! Only then was I allowed to come back to take up this post.

He assured the staff that this project would not have such bad luck as the Jinmao:

> The Fengshui master said that our plot is a good one, full of energy. But he warned us that with so much energy, there is the danger of fire. So everybody should be careful.

Fieldwork notes, 2001

specifically at the values held by managers in the three locations, Ralston and his colleagues confirmed this picture of Hong Kong as something of a melting pot. It was found to mix influences from both China and the West, occupying a point midway between the two with regard to some values, such as thrift and perseverance, while holding firm to the Chinese pattern with regard to others, such as placing a greater emphasis on trust and personal relations over contracts (Ralston *et al.* 1993).

Diversity

So far our portraits have been drawn in deliberately bold lines, but we need to bear in mind that the distinction between collectivist and individualist societies is not so much categorical as a matter of degree.

Moreover, within societies, the extent of collectivist sentiments will vary. Although the centre of gravity of the Chinese cultural ethos lies well within the collectivist sphere, individualism is not completely absent and in certain realms is much admired. Such is the case, for example, among investors on the Shanghai stock exchange, where the unbridled individualism of the wealthy players attracts widespread admiration. This is in large measure precisely because of their being self-made rather than reliant on family and connections for their achievements (Hertz 1998). Finding the rugged individualist as hero is not quite what one would expect from notions of the Chinese as governed by traditional Confucian values. In truth, individuals in all societies seldom escape ambivalence towards forbidden fruit.

Turning to the values of managers in today's China, we need to take the diversity within their ranks into account. First, it should be borne in mind that many of China's provinces are larger in both area and population than many countries in Europe. Geographical barriers that have resulted in a large number of mutually incomprehensible dialects separate them. Movement between them has been restricted for much of the communist era by a system of residence permits that has only recently begun to loosen its grip. The provinces are also different in terms of history and economic resources and development. These all find a reflection in differences in business ethos between the localities. Managers in the thriving coastal cities of Shanghai and Guangzhou, for example, are far more individualistic in their openness to change and unabashed pursuit of individual self-interest than are those in the more remote and less developed inland cities of Chengdu and Lanzhou (Ralston *et al.* 1996).

Consideration also needs to be given to a growing generation gap. As one might expect, the new generation of managers, those in their 20s and 30s who have spent a greater proportion of their upbringing and professional lives in the era of reform, are more individualistic than their elders. Living in a world that has altered so dramatically, from one of planning and the mentality of the iron rice bowl, to one of market forces and the glorification of getting rich, has naturally had an impact.

Even the younger generation of managers are still, however, far more collectivist in approach than their American counterparts (Ralston *et al.* 1993, 1999). To the extent that attitudes towards authority are rooted in patterns of upbringing within the family it would be foolish to expect such differences to fade into insignificance, because traditional patterns of child rearing by Chinese parents are resilient to change. Even among

Box 1.6 Trust, contract and age

A team of managers from a steel manufacturing company came to sign a manufacturing contract with a company in Shanghai that one of the authors was observing. Before their arrival, the author had proof-read the contract at the request of the purchaser. The steel company team was presented with the revised version.

The older managers asked whether there had been any changes from the draft sent to them a few days earlier. On being informed that there were only a few minor spelling corrections they said that they were happy with the terms and were ready to sign. However, the younger managers objected. They dragged their older colleagues aside, warning them against the possibility of the purchaser having changed the terms of the contract.

While other old managers ignored this and prepared to sign, one older manager assured the younger ones: 'Don't worry, if they put some extra work in, we simply won't do it.'

The younger ones insisted: 'But if we don't do it, they can take us to the court and sue us for a lot of money.'

The older managers laughed. One said: 'But we are all from the same locality, we all know each other. After all, business is based on trust.'

Very surprisingly, the younger ones still insisted and the older managers decided to compromise. They asked the author to point out the pages that had been revised for their young colleagues to check for any changes of significance. The younger managers then went over the pages very carefully while their older colleagues sat back smoking and chatting to the author.

Fieldwork notes, 2001

the third generation of Chinese immigrants to America, such patterns remain distinctly different from the rest of the population in their adherence to traditional Chinese virtues (Wu 1996: 154).

The issue of diversity also occurs with values themselves. Some virtues often considered typically Chinese, such as respect for tradition, concern to protect face and the meticulous reciprocation of greetings, favours and gifts can come into conflict with other equally traditional values, such as perseverance and thrift. The former are more oriented to the past or present, the latter to the future. And it is the dynamism of the latter group that has been credited with fuelling Chinese economic success. The Chinese may indeed value tradition and face, but when these conflict with what can be gained by hard work and deferred gratification, they are likely to be sacrificed (Hofstede and Bond 1988).

In a similar vein, in assessing the sway over conduct that values are likely to exercise, we also need to take into account the all too familiar clash between the dictates of morality and the temptations of self-interest. The simulation exercises referred to earlier, in which the Chinese revealed a preference for a more accommodating style of dispute settlement, doubtless do reflect a Chinese preference under circumstances where little is at stake. However, experience of Chinese business practice leaves one in no doubt that such preferences are forced to take second place to a more aggressive stance when substantial matters of self-interest are at issue.

Ideals and reality: a sociology of hypocrisy

While the clash between ideal and reality is universal, the high ideals and self-sacrifice demanded by Confucianism and communism render admission of the pursuit of self-interest less acceptable than under the private vices–public virtues philosophy of capitalism. The resulting gulf between public rhetoric and reality has been so long established and characteristic of Chinese thought that it is taken for granted. This can be seen as far back as in classic works on Chinese imperial military strategy dating from the time of Sun Tzu's *The Art of War* over 2000 years ago. All felt the need to utter pious Confucian platitudes about the efficacy of relying on setting a virtuous example as sufficient to win over neighbouring states before moving on to devote the greater part of their advice to using force and guile to undermine these other states at every opportunity. The inconsistency was handled adroitly by simply ignoring it.

Much the same might be said of contemporary business strategy. In interviews with Chinese managers, we found ourselves frequently hearing descriptions of their business life familiar from official pronouncements. As the interviews progressed, however, respondents reaching into their own experience to illustrate their situation just as frequently contradicted these descriptions without turning a hair. The high standards set combined with experience of fluctuating fashions in political campaigns add to a readiness to accept that what is said on the surface of things is unlikely to be the final word. This promotes a certain tolerance of undertakings, serving more as statements of good intent than as deliverable in every detail. It breeds the amused disbelief of Lin Yutang's humorist to yet another new campaign.

Confucius or Marx?

Much of the present chapter has been concerned with what is distinctive about Chinese values and how they may impinge upon management practices. There can be no doubt that values do play a part here, but they are not the only factor in the equation. If management practices in China are compared with those in Hungary under communist rule, for example, a number of striking similarities emerge in areas such as decision making, communication and personnel practices. Compared with their counterparts in advanced capitalist countries, managers in both China and Hungary exhibit a reluctance to make decisions and an inclination to shift responsibility and blame on to others. As for communication, they are unwilling to share information, failing to pass this on to their subordinates or other departments. A great deal of paperwork such as reports and signed authorisations are generated, usually more for protecting managers from blame than furthering the effective operation of the enterprise. In the personnel area they stand in contrast with advanced capitalist countries in their lack of effective systems for hiring, firing, and rewarding staff (Child and Markóczy 1993).

Obviously, these similarities are not attributable to any shared familiarity with the Confucian classics. What they do appear to have in common is a shared system of state ownership and control of industry. This system produces the defensive behaviour outlined above through the dependence of managers on cultivating good relations with officials outside the enterprise and political organs within it. It is therefore to the workings of the system of industrial governance in China that we turn our attention in the next chapter.

Box 1.7 Through different eyes

We conclude this chapter with two character sketches of private businessmen.

Zhang Wenguang and Lu Xin form a vivid contrast in attitudes on how to run a business. Both manage their own enterprises, situated on the outskirts of Shanghai. Zhang is 75 years old and owns four shoe factories and two shoe shops in his hometown, employing about 100 people. Lu is in his mid-30s and owns eight fashion shops in five different locations employing 35 people.

The two private entrepreneurs come from different backgrounds. Zhang used to be a technician in a state-owned shoe factory in the city. During the 1980s, Zhang's factory formed an alliance with a village enterprise. Zhang was sent down to the village to help the enterprise in technical matters. Upon retirement, the enterprise persuaded him to stay and manage the enterprise. In the mid-1990s, the village leadership leased the enterprise to Mr Zhang. At the end of 1990s, Mr Zhang bought the enterprise.

Mr Lu followed a different path. He was a peasant and planted rice for eight years after school. In the early 1980s, the urbanisation of Shanghai's suburbs took away the land allocated to his family. With the compensation for the land, Lu opened a cafe but it was knocked down by another property development project. Lu then rented a stall in the local market selling fruit. At the beginning of the 1990s, with the proceeds from the fruit stall and money borrowed from friends, Lu opened his first fashion shop in the county seat.

Zhang received us in the sitting room of his home. The room was bare apart from one old dining table and four hard benches. The rest of the house was equally spartan. Zhang said he did not have an office and received all his guests and business contacts at home. 'I never took anybody to a restaurant. It is a waste of money. My wife cooks well. Her food is good enough for the guests. Besides, when you receive business contacts at home, they feel you are treating them like part of your family.'

Zhang said that he did not spend the money he owned, 'I have made a lot of money, but I do not use it much. See, I do not have anything expensive in my house or on myself. My wife does not wear lots of gold. I do not give my money to my children either. That will only spoil them. Besides, they all have good jobs in government-owned companies . . . I work hard because I like it. It is a great pleasure to see the business grow to dominate the local market . . . I saved all the money so I can expand the business without borrowing money from others.'

While sparing with himself, Zhang is very generous with his money to others. He donates to local schools and hospitals. He also helps his employees when they need money to build a house or when they have sick family members. 'I don't have much use for the money myself. Besides, if you are not generous with them, people will be very jealous and do nasty things against you. You've got to scatter some money to avoid trouble.'

Zhang's workshops and stores are a few hundred yards away from his house. He spends all his days touring around them. Zhang said: 'I do not like to leave matters in other people's hands. I want to know about them and solve them by myself, so that I know everything that is going on in my company. Everybody says in the company, Old Zhang still has a good brain, you can't cheat him.'

As to the shoes produced by the company, Zhang said: 'I don't worry much about the styles as long as they are not too old. The most important thing for shoes is quality. We have lots of migrant workers here. They want to buy cheap but tough shoes. The market for them is big enough for me. But I want to attract more town people. Now I am offering a deal at the stores. If they bring their old shoes to the stores, they can have a 20 per cent price cut on the new pair they buy. My ambition is to have everybody in the town buy two pairs of shoes from me every year.'

When asked whether he participated in any political or social activities organised by the local government, Zhang said: 'Well, if they come to ask me to do things, I always do according to their wishes. But I do not volunteer for anything. I have learned from experience in the Cultural Revolution that you can get into big trouble if you are too active in politics. I do not hobnob with the local officials. But I pay all the taxes. The most important thing for business is hard work.'

When we were leaving, Mr Zhang gave us the following advice: 'You know it is much better to be your own boss. You don't earn much working for other people, even as a university lecturer. There are plenty of opportunities here. The shop near the bus station has just closed down. I figure if somebody turns it into a cafe, it will be a success, because there is not a clean and cheap cafe in the town. People like you can invest in it. You must have saved some money. It is very easy. The only trick is hard work.'

Lu's office is a sharp contrast to that of Zhang's. The office is above his biggest shop in the centre of the county seat, it is spacious and grand with wood panelled walls, a huge round conference table and leather sofas. Lu dresses in brand-name suits with his hair immaculately styled in the latest fashion. He said he needs a big office because he also uses it for staff meetings and staff training. He proudly told us that he learned the importance of staff development from the courses organised by the local government-run small business association and from management books. However, he acknowledged that, in spite of his efforts, the employees did not take the trainings seriously. 'They giggle when I introduce to them new sales techniques from the books,' Lu sighed.

Lu is an active member of the small business association and has just been elected vice-chairman of the local town branch. He told us that recently he organised members of the branch to sweep the streets in the town.

'The town people were amused by us. . . . The position is very useful to me. In addition to helping fellow private traders, I get the chance to know many township and county officials. The association also organises tours to other provinces and even abroad. Last year my wife and I went to see Thailand, Singapore and Hong Kong.' Lu donates money, like Mr Zhang, but mostly to campaigns championed by government organisations. For these donations, Lu has been awarded titles such as 'Patriotic Private Businessman'. Lu hangs these awards in his office.

Although Lu sells anything in fashion, he has an ambition to run a chain of stores selling fashions carrying a brand name of his own. Recently, Lu has been developing connections with brand name manufacturers and they appear willing to take Lu on as a retail outlet if he expands. Unfortunately, Lu cannot expand since he has invested all his money in shares in another private business. Lu told us the reason behind this investment: 'In China now everybody is talking about how to make money not by sweating yourself, but through buying shares in other companies. So other people work hard to make money for you.'

Unfortunately for Lu, the businesses he has shares in, which produces car parts, is not making any money. Consequently, he has had to try borrowing money from friends. He is also thinking of pulling strings with government officials to see whether they could help him to get a bank loan. 'Connections are the most important thing for business. If you work on your own, no matter how hard you work, you cannot make it big. You know, most of the big businesses in the south have big fish supporting them. I am sure Bill Gates has hard backing too.'

Fieldwork notes, 2001

2 Mandarins and managers

- The state sector
- The command economy
- Reform
- Nobody's business
- Principals and agents
- The institutional framework
- The state banks
- Asset-management companies
- 'Too many mothers-in-law'
- 'Do not falsify accounts'
- Corporate governance
- Blending business with politics
- Bureaucratic entrepreneurs
- Paths to growth
- Transforming the bureau

A Western manager let into the office of his Chinese counterpart at the height of the command economy would have had no hesitation in admitting to being lost in a totally alien world, one dominated by the plan and which was totally innocent of market forces. Today, he or she returning to the same state-owned enterprise would find a more familiar scene, with managers cut loose from the plan and given the task of having to purchase their own supplies and to sell their products at prices set by the market. The conversation would sound more familiar, peppered with references to profit in place of output quotas. The firm itself may well now have a familiar corporate structure, with shareholders and board. It would seem, to all intents and purposes, that the enterprise management were now firmly in the driving seat. The driving could be expected to be a little erratic, but nothing that a little experience and some sound management training, perhaps the odd MBA, could not set to rights.

Appearances, as ever, can be deceptive. Closer familiarity would reveal the managers behaving in ways decidedly odd from a Western perspective. The approach to pay and benefits provides an example. For 20 years before the reforms began in the late 1970s, incomes had remained more or less unchanged. The reforms eased the brakes, granting greater freedom to enterprise managers in setting wage levels, most notably through the power to award bonuses. The consequence over the ensuing 20 years has been a surge upwards in remuneration, often regardless of performance. Why this generosity? Certainly not pressure from trade unions. Neither was shortage of labour a problem. Quite the reverse. And yet the government has repeatedly felt the need to rein in the generous impulses of managers of state enterprises by regulations limiting the size of annual increases, a move that would be superfluous in a system with functioning labour markets and mechanisms to ensure managers acted in the interest of owners. Despite such prohibitions, the liberality of many state enterprises found ways to flow round them through the provision of a variety of additional benefits.

Traditionally, state-owned enterprises have provided a broad range of social benefits to their employees. Throughout the reform period of the last 20 years, until very recently, these continued, covering the provision of housing, medical expenses and pensions. Moves are underway for the enterprises to shed direct responsibility for these tasks, but progress is uneven. In 1998, for example, new regulations were introduced in Shanghai stating that henceforth housing was no longer to be provided as a benefit by state units, but purchased as a commodity. Many local state enterprises and institutions, far from seizing with relief the opportunity to divest themselves of a costly burden, went on a last minute spending spree, buying up blocks of housing still on the drawing board for distribution to their workers at subsidised prices (Brahm and Lu 1999: 190).

State enterprise staff can enjoy a variety of other fringe benefits, partly favoured as a means of avoiding income tax on direct payments and ceilings on the total wage bill. Much of the revenue of larger restaurants throughout the land relies on lavish banquets funded by public units. The same source provides for the majority of domestic tour groups (Gore 1998: 45–46). Consumer goods are provided free of charge or heavily subsidised, either directly or through coupon schemes (see Box 2.1). One loophole is plugged by government edict only for enterprises to find another through which to divert resources to their members.

The new enthusiasm for profit is perfectly genuine. It is just that what would seem to a Western manager some rather obvious ways of achieving

Box 2.1 Fringe benefits

In the early 1980s, when commodities were in short supply, companies spent a considerable amount of time and effort to get them for free distribution to their employees. Such distribution was crucial for the popularity of the managers, especially with the approach of a major national holiday. The procurement and distribution was usually organised by the trade union. Companies in Shanghai, for example, would send trucks to Shandong province to buy apples in autumn and to Anhui province in winter for cabbages.

Between the late 1980s and early 1990s, with a growing availability of basic commodities, apples and cabbages were no longer appreciated. More exotic and expensive goods were sought instead. There was a shift towards distributing foreign brand name goods produced by Sino-foreign joint ventures, or Chinese delicacies such as Jinhua ham or shark fins.

By the late 1990s, both managers and staff were complaining about the tiresomeness of this practice. Either the goods were not to one's taste or family members brought the same goods home. This led to the adoption of coupons. Producers and service providers, including major stores, issued these. They proved popular with companies for a variety of reasons. Those responsible for the purchase frequently benefited from kickbacks. Their purchase could be concealed as the purchase of office supplies through vaguely worded receipts, thus circumventing tax and state-imposed wage ceilings. Staff could accumulate store coupons to purchase expensive goods or swap them for cash with one another or on the black market. Another reason the coupons proved popular was that they could replace money as gifts to business contacts and government officials. Not being cash they smacked less of outright bribery.

Losing a large amount of tax revenue and faced with the need to stimulate consumption to combat deflation, the government decided to act. In late 2000, it announced that the use of the coupons in shops would cease at the end of the year. Overnight, the extent of their use became visible in long queues, as a shopping spree got underway.

Fieldwork notes, 2001

it are neglected. Labour costs, as mentioned, are not held in check. Overstaffing is common. Periods of recession are not met with cutbacks in output, but with desperate attempts to continue expansion. Evidently, the management of state enterprises have other matters weighing on their minds than maximising profits alone.

Other contrasts abound. Faced with financial difficulties in meeting their debts we find senior managers of state enterprises eagerly seeking the embrace of asset management companies, a move likely to be contemplated more with dread than enthusiasm by managers of troubled corporations in the West. Clearly, things that mean one thing in one business world can mean something quite different in another. Quite different constraints and opportunities face the Chinese manager from those confronting their counterparts in more fully developed market economies. Chinese managers not only come from a different world in terms of the cultural heritage they bring with them to the job. They also find themselves inhabiting a different world in terms of the business system in which they find themselves operating. It is a world full of strange paradoxes, one in which, as we shall see, well-intended reforms can lead to results quite contrary to those intended.

The state sector

The public sector continues to dominate much of the economy. This remains true despite the decline in its overall share of gross domestic product since the beginning of the economic reforms in the late 1970s. Arriving at a clear figure is complicated by a number of factors. One is the shifting of firms out of the state-owned enterprise category in official statistics when they adopt a corporate form. This can create the illusion that the state sector has shrunk more than it actually has, for the state almost invariably continues to dominate the enterprise through a majority shareholding under the reformed structure. Another factor is the presence of collectives and how to treat them. At one end of the spectrum there are collectives that differ little from officially designated state-owned enterprises in terms of being clearly under government control, while at the other end there are collectives that are just as clearly private enterprises in all but name. Placing the former group of collectives together with state-owned enterprises, we can say that they jointly account for around one half of gross domestic product (International Finance Corporation 2000: 18).

The situation varies between different industries and services. Competition has eaten into the position of state enterprises in areas such as textiles, clothing, computers and electronics, but elsewhere state enterprises face little, if any, competition. They continue to enjoy a position with little or no non-state competition in areas such as electric power, coal, petroleum, steel, chemicals, rail and operating telecommunications. State-owned enterprises continue to be the largest provider of urban employment. They also provide the bulk of the tax revenue for the government, partly because an over-stretched tax service finds it easier to target collections on a few large firms than on a multitude of small ones.

The command economy

To understand the current operation of state enterprises it is necessary to look at how they functioned in the command economy of the pre-reform period. Only then is it possible to appreciate the extent of the changes that have taken place and to understand the path these changes have taken.

Under the command economy, workers, along with all other inputs, were allocated to the firm by the state. They then became the responsibility of the enterprise. At the height of the planned economy, the work unit, the *danwei*, was, for its employees, a small self-contained society, one catering to all their needs. Remuneration may have been modest and slow to rise, but security of employment was guaranteed. Workers were allocated to a unit that they could expect to provide them with lifetime employment and the provision of a pension upon retirement. Mobility of labour was minimal: you were stuck with your unit and your unit was stuck with you. Housing was provided free or at minimal cost by the unit, control over its allocation proving both a drain on managers' time, but also a buttress to their authority. Other social welfare responsibilities included medical care and could extend to the provision of schools for employees' children, often with the expectation that the *danwei* would also provide for their future employment. With the arrival of the one-child policy, the task of promoting and policing family planning fell naturally to the all-inclusive work unit, remaining with them to this day.

Work units found themselves under dual control at the local level. The enterprise was subject to a vertical chain of authority stretching down from the national department that held special responsibility for its operation to the department's local bureau. At the same time, the local authority in which the unit was located also took a hand in directing its affairs. This criss-crossing of authority was made still more of a maze by the operation of planning to dictate what was to be produced and how it was to be disposed of. This left the firm reporting to, and dependent upon, a whole range of ministries charged with allocating workers, materials, machinery and finance. Direct dealings between units were rare: information flowed up and down the chain of command and careers followed the same path.

The command economy gave managers the incentive to behave in certain characteristic ways. There was, for example, the tendency to deflate estimates of output in the hope of lowering the targets set by government officials. The bureaucrats, in their turn, regularly discounted such estimates on the understanding that this would occur. Here, it is as well to bear in mind that mandarins and managers are not alien species. Government bureaux will have built up a fund of knowledge about the industry for which they are responsible. Added to this was the direct experience of managers promoted up into the bureau. They had direct knowledge of how enterprises would manipulate information disparities to their advantage. Once the reforms arrived, this insight would be seen in the ingenuity put into devising a range of different contracts for enterprises, tailored to make managers reveal rather than conceal their true economic position.

Given that output targets were, in the end, set by those outside the unit, there was a tendency for managers to hoard capital and labour. Not operating on profit principles, such conduct did not impinge on the main economic criterion by which they were judged – meeting output targets. As such targets were likely to move, often being ratcheted up in response to earlier achievements, it made sense to hold on to as many resources as one had managed to acquire.

Reform

The difficulties faced by the planning apparatus in monitoring enterprises and encouraging efficiency led, with the death of Mao and the eventual ascendancy of Deng, to a series of reforms intended to breathe new life into state enterprises. These can loosely be divided into three stages. The first, starting from the end of the 1970s, handed increased autonomy to enterprise managers, principally over the retention and allocation of a proportion of profits. This could be used for investment and, for the first time, the payment of bonuses. At the same time, however, price controls remained in place.

From the mid-1980s, the reforms entered a new phase with long-term contracts being struck between the enterprise and the state, stipulating financial targets in terms of profit and tax delivery. This broke with the reliance on output targets as the principal guide and judge of performance. Long-term contracts were intended to provide some assurance for firms that increasing profits would not be met with moves to ratchet-up the amount of profit extracted from the firm. At the same time, a dual track system mixing plan and market was introduced, with any excess output above that stipulated in the plan allowed to be sold at unregulated prices. This move towards the market was typical of the gradualist approach of the Chinese path to reform. The unhappy experience with the disastrous Great Leap of an earlier era doubtless played a part. The reforms were to move more cautiously, 'crossing the river by groping for stones'. The dual track system was also typical in generating unanticipated consequences that were quite contrary to the hopes of the innovators. It produced enormous incentives for the illegal transfer of goods from within the plan to outside it, a move that, at a stroke, could double the price of some commodities. Another shortcoming was that, with the retention of price controls, the losses or profitability of some firms were largely set by fiat. Those enjoying inputs with prices set low and outputs high were naturally profitable. Those with input prices set high and output prices held in check equally inevitably ran into losses. This made it impossible to impose strict budgetary controls on loss makers, rendering the introduction of the Bankruptcy Law of 1986 more symbolic than real. This situation also required the negotiation of enterprise contracts on a one-by-one basis, precluding the introduction of a uniform system and some semblance of an even playing field.

The third period can be dated to the policies set by the Fourteenth Chinese Communist Party Congress in 1993. This allowed for the diversification of forms of ownership and the introduction of systems of corporate governance based on those in fully developed market economies. The result has been for most small, state-owned enterprises to have been shifted out of state and collective ownership, often through the device of stock cooperative companies. With large and medium state-owned enterprises, many are reshaping themselves into joint stock companies complete with the panoply of boards and shareholders while remaining under public ownership.

Overall, the reforms have led to the current situation in which managers find themselves responsible for obtaining inputs and selling output. Prices are free, with one or two exceptions, such as fertilisers and some food products. Managers extol the pursuit of profit. Yet, in their conduct many state enterprises retain more than a vestige of their former selves. This is not simply a matter of finding it hard to break with old habits. Under the reforms, state enterprises found themselves operating within a system that, in certain respects, made continuing with the old ways of doing business more congenial than abandoning them.

The appetite for hoarding, for example, continued, fuelled by lax budgetary constraints. The reforms shifted investment funding from direct state subsidies to loans from the state banks, but loans provided at artificially low rates of interest and without strict enforcement of debt repayment. This placed little pressure on state enterprises to optimise the use of their current holdings.

Nor did the reforms eliminate compartmentalisation along departmental and regional lines. A variety of uncoordinated government agencies continue to enter into the running of state-owned enterprises and to extract resources from them. Lines of command continue to be muddied by the fusion of the Party-state and the enterprise, with the confusion in the system of government between the role of state and Party stretching down into the state-owned enterprises.

The system continues to produce bottlenecks in some areas and over-capacity in others. This has partly been the result of price distortions upstream, with the price of raw materials, energy and transportation held back. At the same time, localities have preferred to put their resources into light consumer and processing industries, where investment requirements are less and returns faster. This has fed over-capacity on one hand and put pressure on a neglected infrastructure on the other. The provinces, repeating at a local level the national policy of choosing and promoting key industries, have further increased excess capacity. Unfortunately, more or less the same list of what industries are key occurs to each province. Each feels it must have a production capacity that embraces automobiles, electronics, chemicals and machinery manufacture, with the inevitable duplicate construction across the nation (Gore 1998: 208–18).

The problems of state enterprises in China resemble those observed in other communist states (Kornai 1992). Under such systems, state enterprises may operate as net destroyers rather than creators of wealth, consuming more than they produce over extended periods. This has been true of many state enterprises in China, and is tied to low productivity, declining profits, and a lagging export performance in comparison with non-state firms and joint ventures. A major problem is over-staffing, with redundancies sufficient to resolve the problem long delayed by concerns over the threat posed to social stability. Estimates on the overall size of the workforce that is technically redundant vary, but one puts the figure at between 20 and 30 per cent (Tam 1999: 45).

Another source of the problems facing state enterprises has been the slow pace at which they can divest themselves of the social welfare burdens inherited from when the *danwei* was expected to provide a miniature society caring for the needs of workers and their families from cradle to grave. These burdens continue to distract managers and drain resources. The number of retired workers that an enterprise has to provide for, for example, can vary from between 20 and 100 per cent of the current workforce (Tam 1999: 46).

Yet, far more of the difficult situation in which state enterprises now find themselves was not inherited from the command economy, but arose during the period of reform itself. It was during this time that many amassed large and increasing liabilities in the form of bank loans and credit from other enterprises. Concurrently, the quality of their assets declined as these assets became increasingly composed of unmarketable inventories and non-performing loans. The result has been endemic liquidity crises. Enterprises are forced to rely on short-term loans to meet their wage bill, as their liquid assets tend to be comprised almost entirely of inventories and receivables that are stubbornly resistant to being realised as cash. Such conditions mean that attempts by the government to tighten credit quickly run up against increasing unrest as wages remain unpaid.

The situation has promoted a web of inter-enterprise debt. Managers frequently complain about the difficulty of getting customers to pay for goods and services. Yet their own enterprises very often contribute to the problem. This is not simply a matter of they themselves delaying or defaulting on payments due to their own suppliers. In addition, in their eagerness to dispose of goods for which there is no real effective demand, they often resort to inducing demand through the extension of credit with little attention to ability to pay. The result is the build-up of a network of debt throughout the system that everyone bewails and everyone contributes to. Even the government is not guiltless in this, and frequently initiates the chain through withholding payment.

Nobody's business

Another unwelcome consequence of the reforms has been the opening up of new avenues for the depredation of state assets. Where no individual has a secure claim on the revenues generated by public assets, few are ready to stand out in their defence. In the absence of such vigilance, resources frequently find themselves diverted into the pockets of managers and employees. Assets, for example, may be funnelled into

Box 2.2 Nobody's business

The following comes from an interview with the chief accountant of a joint venture in Beijing.

> The Chinese managers do not worry about money because it is not their money. At this joint venture, the foreign partners are always talking about money, how we should get everything going because we borrowed money from the banks and we have to make money quickly in order to be able to return it. However, I have never heard anybody from the Chinese side worry about paying the interest or returning the money. It is not their money so they throw it away like water without batting an eyelid.

> I used to work at a state-owned company. It was the same there. The bosses used the state's money to make loans to friends who wanted to open companies. They also provided financial guarantees to friends involved in business. Yet things are gradually getting better, because all the accountancies are now independent from the state and there is an accountancy law. In the past, the general manager responsibility system made him so powerful he could make almost all the decisions on his own. However, with companies having shareholders and boards of directors now, it is less easy to steal money, because at least decisions have to be approved collectively.

Officials from the headquarters of two state banks were subsequently questioned about the practice reported of state enterprise loans being passed on to others. This came as no surprise to them. It was, as one remarked, 'an everyday occurrence'.

Interviews, 2001

non-state firms with little regard for market value, either directly or through establishing real or fictitious joint ventures.

The siphoning of state assets can also take place through leasing out or contracting their use to employees. This can take place under terms that cannot hope to cover repayments on the loans from state banks taken out to cover the original purchase. The income generated by the offshoots is then turned to the benefit of the staff of the founding unit. Supervisory authorities may decide to wink at the arrangement. As Tam (1999: 46) remarks of such practices: 'Given the continuing strong influence of supervisory departments over [state-owned enterprise] operations (particularly decisions on major investments and managerial appointments), some form of collusion cannot reasonably be ruled out.'

Principals and agents

The sad possibility that managers may give way to the temptation to feather their own nests or indulge in unwarranted empire building is not unique to China. The problem of how to coax, coerce or cajole agents into serving the interests of their masters is universal. It is the problem made familiar by the separation of ownership from control, which is characteristic of large corporations under capitalism. How can the principals of a corporation – its shareholders – ensure that their agents – the managers – maximise returns on their investment? The answer has been to establish a range of institutions that monitor managers and seek to align their interests with those of the owners.

The resulting controls are both internal and external to the firm. Internally, the board acts to protect the interests of owners through monitoring performance and exercising a veto over strategic decisions. In addition, directors will use their power over setting pay packages to align the financial interests of managers and owners, such as linking rewards to performance through stock options. External monitoring is facilitated by the enforcement of strict accounting standards and rules of financial disclosure. Capital and equity markets measure performance and guide funds towards the more profitable firms and away from the less successful. Managers of unprofitable firms face the prospect of losing control over the firm through bankruptcy or takeover.

Viewing state enterprises in China as presenting a principal–agent problem yields some interesting results. Principals seem, at times, difficult to locate, at others all too numerous. Their agents, the managers, are not maximising profits. Part of the reason is that they do indeed at times favour their own interests over those of their principals. Yet another part of the reason is that they are doing the best they can as agents given the variety of economic, political and social tasks entrusted to their care. All this results from the institutional framework within which state enterprises operate.

The institutional framework

Much of the reform effort directed at state enterprises has been aimed at managerial aspects of the enterprise itself. Despite the best intentions, these efforts have not achieved all that was hoped for. State enterprises cannot simply be reformed one by one because much of what goes on inside their walls reflects the peculiarities of the institutional framework within which they operate. It is only through appreciating these peculiarities that one can avoid the temptation to prescribe remedies drawn from circumstances quite remote. It makes little sense, for example, to talk in terms of the importance of clarifying or transferring property rights where the institutions necessary for property rights to exist are absent or fail to function in any effective manner. The necessary legal, financial and regulatory institutions have only begun to make an appearance. They have a long way to go before they attain sufficient strength and independence. For the moment, they remain fledglings.

Under such circumstances, devolving authority to enterprises has certainly resulted in changes to their management, but not quite those anticipated. Granting managers greater control over enterprise funds within this setting is as much likely to lead to unfettered expansion and the diversion of working capital into non-productive avenues as it is to result in commercially viable business conduct. The institutions required to enforce the necessary element of discipline simply do not operate as in fully developed free market economies.

The market itself has not been given free play as a means of selection. From the start of the reforms, managers and policy makers have leaned towards a benign view of markets. They have been seen as of positive benefit to all enterprises, a source of incentives that will raise the standards of all. Allowing the market not only to funnel funds towards the successful but also to weed out the unsuccessful is still in many ways a novel idea. This finds reflection in many ways, including the need felt by the chief economist of the World Bank to promote the idea of 'creative destruction' to a Beijing audience, attempting to stiffen resolve by alluding to the third of US manufacturing firms that are wiped out to be replaced by others over a five-year period (Stern 2001).

The state banks

The state-owned banks have hardly proved themselves red in tooth and claw as instruments of 'creative destruction'. Quite the reverse. Since 1984, they have been almost the sole source of investment funds for the state enterprises. The intention was to force enterprises to bear a cost for capital in place of the former direct government subsidies, thus encouraging its more effective use. However, this good intention was undermined by the provision of loans at low or even negative rates of real

Box 2.3 Loans

A chief accountant of a state-owned food trading company mentioned that it was very easy to get loans from the local branch of one of the large commercial state banks. An official in the headquarters of the bank interviewed subsequently made the following comment on this:

> Yes, they are a major state-owned company, they have a big name. The bank will be very eager to give loans. In fact, it is not they who come to ask for loans, it is we who chase them to give loans. Being so large and backed by the state there is no danger of them failing. In addition, they are trading in foodstuffs, which is not strategically important, so the bank automatically gives them loans without questions asked. Where we are cautious with state companies might be with a state mechanical trading company wishing to trade overseas in strategically sensitive materials. Funding this without making sure of official support could get us into trouble.

Fieldwork notes, 2001

interest. In addition, the banks have operated without careful commercial selection and monitoring of loans. The result has been a huge build-up of liabilities by many state enterprises.

With interest rates held low, excess demand requires administrative allocation, giving free play to the political directives and pressure that, throughout the period of reform, have shaped the provision of loans. In addition to the policy loans backed by the central government, local Party and government officials have frequently requested Chinese banks to make specific loans to enterprises under their aegis. As Lardy remarks: 'The structure of authority in the Chinese banking system would have made it difficult to limit political intervention in loan allocation, even in the absence of excess demand. But chronic excess demand for loans reinforced the tendency for lending to be based on local political considerations and corruption' (Lardy 1998: 126). Such practices leave many enterprises that would be better able to support loans unsupplied, leading to unofficial banks repeatedly springing up, often with the involvement of local officials, offering loans at rates well above those set by the state banks.

A legacy of poor lending decisions, added to the high operating costs resulting from the over-staffing characteristic of the state sector in general, has left the state banks in much the same financial straits as many of their clients. Banks are constrained from calling in bad loans from state enterprises on any scale when to do so would lay bare the underlying insolvency of both. For, like many countries in the region, a rapid growth in bank lending in China has gone hand-in-hand with political considerations and connections at times taking precedence over sound commercial judgement. The Asia crisis has focused attention on this unfortunate similarity, and attempts have been made to address the problem through restructuring and greater commercialisation, but financial and political considerations continue to weaken the impact of such moves.

Efforts to get the commercial banks to behave in a truly commercial manner have taken a number of routes. New policy banks were created with the intention of relieving the commercial banks of the burden of subsidising state industries and allowing them to concentrate more on allocating loans according to commercial principles. Yet, the burden was not entirely escaped as the new policy banks are financed by the commercial banks through the enforced purchase of bonds at low rates of interest (Lardy 1998: 179).

The banks have also been reorganised with new regional offices spanning several provinces. These were specifically introduced in an effort to end the common practice of provincial governors influencing the direction of loans. Yet in a situation where the central bank has publicly commented on the increase in banks lending funds without recording them on their books and inventing funds to cover up for losses, the market is clearly not the only hidden hand at work (Lardy 1998: 206). Forcing the banks to operate along purely commercial lines meets resistance from state and Party officials reluctant to give up their last powerful instrument for controlling resource allocation. It is a struggle made still more difficult to resolve because officials themselves often express views on the matter that reveal a deep ambivalence, directing banks one moment, telling them to be guided by the market the next.

Asset-management companies

It was against the background of a massive build-up of bad loans owed to the banks by state enterprises that asset-management companies were introduced in 1999. Each of four major state banks, the Bank of China, the Industrial and Commercial Bank of China, the Agricultural Bank, and the Construction Bank, have been paired with a newly established asset-management company. These purchase the bad debts of selected enterprises from the banks and, in exchange, receive shares in the firms responsible for the debts. From similar operations elsewhere in the world, one might expect the banks to welcome such asset-management companies as offering the opportunity to rid themselves of non-performing loans. The management of target firms, on the other hand, could be expected to view the prospect with alarm, the writing was on the wall as far as their futures were concerned. Yet curiously in China, quite the reverse occurs. Banks are at times reluctant. This springs from a variety of reasons. The bonds offered to the banks in exchange by the state asset management companies come at a low rate of interest and with doubts as to whether even this will be paid. At the same time, the banks tend to be losing their 'best' bad loans rather than the worst, either in the sense that they still yield interest or come from asset rich companies.

Box 2.4 Debt for equity

An illustration of the restructuring resulting from the operation of asset-management companies can be seen in the debt–equity swap plans for the Zhengzhou Coal Industry Group reported by Gilley (2000b).

Zhengzhou Coal, situated in Henan, has 43 000 workers in seven mines and 30 subsidiaries. In recent years, protests from workers at unpaid wages have grown more common as the financial situation of the company deteriorated and its debts mounted. Under the rescue plan, Zhengzhou Coal had 970 million yuan (117 million dollars) in debt transferred to Cinda, one of the four asset-management companies, in exchange for a 51 per cent shareholding of a new company, Zhengxin Energy, to be formed out of the best parts of the old. The new company is also to be relieved of all its 'little society' functions, with provision for retired workers, schools, hospitals and other social services being taken over by the provincial government. Zhengxin Energy takes with it half the net assets and revenue, but only a third of the workforce.

The plans met with resistance from creditor banks, however. It is not they but the State Economic and Trade Commission that is responsible for choosing enterprises to be included in the debt of equity scheme. The Commission had originally hoped to transfer debts totalling 1.2 billion yuan to Cinda. The banks, however, have a fixed quota on the amount of bad debt that can be offloaded in such swaps, and Zhengzhou Coal was far from being the worst of their customers. It was asset rich and still paying some interest on long term loans at 8 per cent, in contrast to the asset-management company's 2.25 per cent bonds.

Based on Gilley (2000b)

State enterprises and their local authority sponsors, on the other hand, vied with one another to be among the 600 chosen to participate. This choice lay not with the banks nor the asset management companies but with the State Economic and Trade Commission. Selection was fought over as an easy way of wiping the slate clean of accumulated debt. In the resulting competition, it was the large and politically connected state enterprises that were best placed to succeed and, for the same reasons, to survive the aftermath. Leaders of the asset management companies are clearly aware of the political parameters within which they must operate. As the head of one remarked, 'We must avoid a lot of bankruptcies that would affect social stability' (Gilley 2000a: 60). Even in economic terms, resorting to winding up firms holds little appeal in circumstances where the bankruptcy laws assign priority to pension and welfare obligations, leaving little over from any forced liquidation. Politically, the debt–equity swaps also came at a convenient moment for meeting the 2001 deadline set by Premier Zhu Rongji for 'resolving the difficulties' (*jie kun*) of state enterprises. By removing interest payment, profitability is instantaneously improved. Whether the underlying problem of low returns on investment that led to the build-up of debt in the first place will be resolved remains another matter (Steinfeld 2000).

While the asset-management companies labour under restraints, they have not been inactive. They have a motive to recover funds, with staff joining from banks taking a cut in salary on the promise of bonuses on amounts regained. Their sweep is wide, with the 580 firms remaining in the programme estimated to account for around 40 per cent of the state enterprise sector in terms of assets, sales and profits. In the first half of 2001, the four asset-management companies were reported to have recovered 8.72 billion yuan in cash (World Bank 2001b). This, however, needs to be set against the 1.4 trillion yuan of bad debt transferred to the asset-management companies (equivalent to 17 per cent of gross domestic product) and reports that they have failed to meet interest payments on their bonds. As for the banks, even after this transfer, one central bank estimate suggests that the banking system would need a further 2.5 trillion yuan (equivalent to 25 per cent of gross domestic product) to absorb the rest of the non-performing loans remaining on their books (World Bank 2001a).

'Too many mothers-in-law'

'*Gong-gong shao le, po-po hai hen duo* – fewer fathers-in-law, still too many mothers-in-law', sighed one of our interviewees. Similar sentiments trip readily off the tongue of state enterprise managers asked to sum up their relationship to government agencies. The familial metaphor is quintessentially Chinese. In it, the state enterprises figure as the daughter-in-law, traditionally seen as bossed around by her in-laws and made to do all the work while they sit back doing nothing. The line ministry and its local bureau feature as the father-in-law, the *gong-gong*, whose hold has loosened as more decisions have devolved downwards to the enterprise. However, there remains a wealth of *po-po*, mothers-in-law, in the form of a variety of regulatory agencies to make life difficult.

Box 2.5 The *po-po*

The strength of the regulatory agencies, the *po-po*, varies with the industry. Paradoxically the *po-po*'s grip is lightest where arguably it should be tightest, as the following interview with a manager from a state-owned telecommunications company illustrates.

For the telecom business, the *po-po* are still there, the number of them is not much less than before the reform, but they have less power over our industry. This is because our business is still much of a monopoly; the regulatory agencies have never been very powerful over monopoly industries such as telecom, power, gas, and water. Another reason we do not get bossed around by them is that the telecom industry is a new one with higher technology, the *po-po* do not know much about the business, so this stops them interfering too much.

However, the local provincial government has an office called the Information Industry Office. The Office is there supposedly to coordinate all telecom or related industries, such as broadcasting and TV. However, the Office does not simply coordinate. Instead, it sets up companies such as an Internet server to compete with us. The Information Industry Office set up this server together with the Party Secretariat of the provincial Party with money from the service industries that the provincial bureaux run as a sideline. The Office gives preferential treatment to its own companies and this creates unfair competition. The Information Office will also order us to do things that are good for the province, but which conflict with the orders we get from our parent company. Of course, in the end we will obey our parent company, but we cannot afford to rub the Information Industry Office up the wrong way too often. These conflicts are difficult to solve.

Interview, 2001

A state enterprise contemplating setting up a new factory would first need to secure the approval of its governing bureau. The bureau may well, indeed, have initiated the project. Either way, the position of the bureau remains bolstered by banks being unlikely to grant loans without evidence of the bureau's agreement. The enterprise then has to embark on negotiating its way through a maze of *po-po* in an effort to secure from each the ubiquitous red stamp of approval. Each operates independently, with little coordination between them. Each can demand certain conditions are met and many can effectively veto completion of the project.

First, the plans are reviewed by the local planning bureau and the economic committee, while the permission of the financial bureau is sought to raise finance. If there is any foreign investment or trade involved, permission has to be obtained from the foreign economic and trade committee and the foreign exchange control bureau. Next comes the industry and commerce bureau to obtain a licence to operate. This is followed by registration and approval by the tax bureau, the public security bureau, and the labour bureau. For building to commence the construction committee will need to review bidding procedures, the status of the contractor and whether the contract is acceptable. Permits permeate down to each stage and detail. One will need to get a permit to excavate the land and then another to lay the bricks.

Other bureaux that enter into the equation include the environmental protection bureau, the zoning bureau, the fire bureau, the water, electricity and gas utilities, the safety at work bureau, customs, the quality control station, and the price bureau. Many urban areas also have an air raid shelter office. New public buildings are supposed to provide air raid shelter facilities. Few nowadays do, and a fee must be paid to the air raid office for the provision of alternative shelters in the vicinity. In practice, the air raid office has also abandoned building shelters. The fees, however, remain. Over the entire progress of the project presides the files bureau to make sure that all the proper records and files are kept.

In addition to the permanent bureaux there are a number of temporary offices that spring up to implement various campaigns. Prominent among these at present is the Spiritual Civilization Office. This was initially set up to balance the stress on the pursuit of material success, the attractions of 'getting rich is glorious', with socialist ideals in the hope of avoiding the spiritual decadence seen to accompany prosperity under capitalism. While almost all managers are, off the record, sceptical of the work of the

Spiritual Civilization Office, many nevertheless wish to attend its rallies to gain the attention of their superiors and to avoid charges of lack of enthusiasm being added to their sins should they ever run foul of the authorities.

While the maze of bureaux is not quite as Kafkaesque as it once was, many bureaux continue to wield considerable power through their ability to delay, hinder or stop projects and operations. In a situation where officials exercise substantial discretion, dealing with them successfully is an important art. Progress frequently depends on strings being pulled, and pulling strings must be done at the right level. To aim too high or too low can be so much wasted effort. One therefore needs to keep up to date with who does what in the bureaucracy and to cultivate the right people.

The bureaux can demand a range of fees and taxes, frequently of an *ad hoc* nature. They are often characterised as coming knocking with the attitude of 'You are a state enterprise, well, we are the state.' The firm is afforded little or no protection from the law, with the state virtually immune to legal sanction.

'Do not falsify accounts'

When Premier Zhu Rongji was invited to inscribe a motto for the opening of the new State College of Accountancy in Shanghai, he penned '*bu zuo jia zhang* – do not falsify accounts' (*Nanfang Zhoumo*, 7 June 2001). That he should have felt it necessary to make such an elementary point suggests that current standards in the field are somewhat less than might be hoped for. Yet for a market economy to function properly reliable accounts stemming from enforceable accounting standards are essential. Unfortunately, credible financial information in China is a rare commodity. Accounting standards frequently change and monitoring standards are weak. Yet without reliable figures it becomes impossible to allocate responsibility for poor performance and managers themselves may find it hard to ascertain the financial status of the firm. The laxity also encourages tax evasion and allows collusion with employees to raise incomes at the expense of the state.

Partly in an attempt to bolster their independence as a profession, accountancy firms are no longer owned by the state, but have been converted into private partnerships. Currently, however, they remain weak. Now having to fend for themselves, they rely on state enterprises

Box 2.6 Cooking the books

Our discussions about accounting practices with managers in the state sector produced the following comments.

The chief accountant:

> Oh, yes, I also have to fake accounts, quite often. The company wants to make a big investment, but fears the banks will refuse loans due to its weak financial position. So the bosses ask us accountants to fake the accounts to give a rosier impression. Things like this make being an accountant very difficult. When the bosses want you to fake, you have to fake, but when things go wrong, the accountants get the blame. Also, when the financial state of the company is bad, the bosses will blame the accountant saying that you are the accountant and you should have advised me. But when you advise them against bad practice, you are likely to upset them.

The general manager:

> Most companies have at least two sets of books, one to show the auditors, the other for internal use.

The chairman of the board:

> To evaluate the performance of a company and the senior management is a big problem, because almost all companies falsify their balance sheets. It is so easy . . . That is why Premier Zhu wants to have the accountants independent, because everybody is fiddling the books.

Fieldwork notes, 2001

for their work. Therefore, establishing a reputation for enforcing strict standards is more likely to earn them a bad name than a good one among prospective clients. No effective body has yet emerged to counter this.

Assessing the financial performance of state enterprises is made difficult by the understatement of liabilities due to low depreciation rates for equipment and plant together with valuing inventories at full price regardless of their real value or lack of it. Even without adjusting for this, Lardy (1998) places the average liability to asset ratio of state enterprises at 85 per cent, against an average of 50 per cent in advanced market economies. The figures suggest that a significant number of state enterprises are insolvent. Furthermore, many state enterprises show a continual rise in the ratio of liabilities to assets, suggesting that many firms operate continuously at a loss, subtracting value rather than adding to it, their output worth less than the cost of labour and material that goes into it. Liabilities rise in relation to fixed assets as loans are used not just for fixed investment, but also for paying wages and piling up inventories of unsold goods for which little effective demand exists.

Corporate governance

As mentioned earlier, in a fully developed market economy, agency problems in large companies are, in part, resolved by external monitoring facilitated by strict accounting standards and rules of disclosure aiding capital markets to funnel funds towards the successful and away from the unsuccessful. These controls are backed up internally by those exercised by the board. The exact balance between the different sources of control varies between nations.

Broadly speaking, there are two models for such corporate governance. The first is the Anglo-American model, based on an external market for corporate control through takeovers and mergers. The second is the model epitomised by Japan and Germany together with the rest of continental Europe. In these countries, there is no active market in corporate control, which is usually vested in large stockholders, including banks. In the case of Japan, the management is shielded by cross-shareholdings held with a group of allied companies, the keiretsu. The consequence of this is that, in Japan, 'the formal institutions of shareholder representation (board of directors and general shareholders meeting) do not serve any real function except to satisfy legal and regulatory requirements' (Tam 1999: 30).

In the move towards converting state enterprises into corporations, which started in the 1990s, China has managed a blend of both approaches. The outward forms of corporate governance and the rhetoric accompanying their introduction have been couched largely in terms of the Anglo-American model. This includes an expressed concern to protect minority shareholders. The reality, however, is clearly far closer to the opposing tradition of 'insider' control.

The path towards incorporation can be far from smooth. Initial disputes over dividing the shares in the reformed enterprise among the various local and national claimants frequently arise. This is particularly true in the case of large firms and those likely to receive an infusion of new cash if allowed to be listed on the stock exchange. These quarrels are frequently sidestepped by perpetuating the confusion over ultimate ownership by establishing a holding company that is not structured in terms of shareholding. This also often serves as a repository into which are shifted the less attractive aspects of the company, such as social services and support, a move particularly popular when a public offering is contemplated.

Most state enterprises that have adopted a corporate form of governance do not, however, list on the stock exchange. The right to offer shares on the domestic and international markets has been closely controlled by the government, with the result that only a small percentage of those enterprises that have transformed themselves into companies are listed. Little can, in any case, be hoped for from the domestic markets at present in terms of effective monitoring, as those markets are widely recognised as fuelled almost entirely by speculation and ridden with price manipulation. Even among those firms that are listed, the majority of shares remain untraded in the hands of government firms and agencies. Control remains firmly in the hands of the state. In such circumstances, listing becomes a rich prize fought over by officials at enterprise and ministry level as a means of raising money quickly with little thought of how it might entail attention to the interests of new shareholders. Should any small shareholders expect otherwise and choose to attend shareholder meetings they will regularly find themselves denied entry. These meetings are, in any case, simply a matter of ceremony, ratifying appointments of chairmen, directors and supervisors decided elsewhere by Party and state officials.

In China, the joint stock company reforms have enhanced the control of 'insiders' over resources without providing the institutional arrangements necessary to ensure they act in value-enhancing ways. This combination can lead, as it has done in Russia and other transitional economies, to asset stripping, poor investment, and decapitalisation through increases in wages and other benefits. Far from acting as a brake on management, the board of directors and senior managers are almost invariably the same people. As a survey of state companies by the World Bank concludes: 'In every case examined in this study, the majority of the boards of directors and the senior executives are one and the same. There is no real distinction' (World Bank 1997: 39). The new corporate forms adopted by enterprises may well serve a useful purpose under changed circumstances in the future, but for now little remains changed beneath the surface. Board, supervisory committee and shareholders meetings remain ineffectual with no clear division of responsibility, while managers often seem ignorant of the rules and regulations that supposedly govern the operation of their companies.

Figure 2.1 outlines the main players involved and sketches some of their relationships to one another. One difference from the Anglo-American system has been the addition of a supervisory board with the intention of providing yet another layer to monitor directors and managers, chosen to

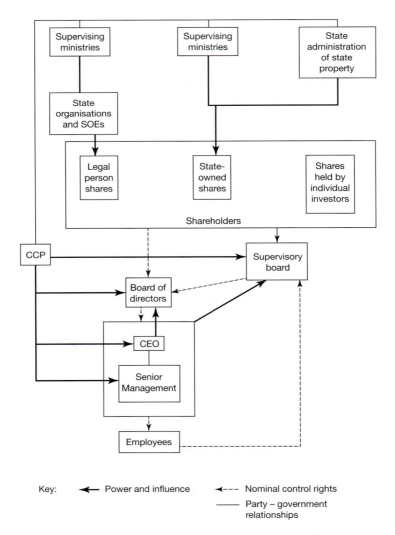

Figure 2.1 *Corporate governance (adapted from Tam 1999: 100)*

represent the interests of shareholders and workers. Most supervisory boards, however, have had neither the means nor inclination to launch independent investigations into company affairs. Interestingly, supervisory boards have also been added to companies in Taiwan, where they have proved equally ineffectual (Tam 1999: 86–87).

There is little sign of the board of directors and the supervisory board serving as an effective form of internal review in companies where the state remains the principal shareholder. The firm appears effectively in the control of insiders. However, these insiders are not entirely free of the various government agencies and Party organs to which they owe their appointment and future promotion prospects. The new corporate form has not severed these links between government officials and senior management. While some of these officials may now sit on company boards, their position as directors serves as a symbol of their power rather than being the source of their power.

Directors and managers of the corporate enterprises naturally favour insider control. Given the choice, most would prefer to have still more of the directors chosen from company executives. Where there is support for more outside directors, it rests on the belief that this will facilitate useful contacts rather than on any concern for checking the boardroom influence of managers. Officials of former ministries are popular for this reason (Tam 1999: 73–74).

While it was undoubtedly the hope of many that state enterprise corporate reform would remove the enterprises from political influence, the old links remain and have even become integrated into the structure of the new companies. The Party secretary will almost invariably hold one of the top posts in the company, either as chair or deputy chair of the board or as the chief or deputy chief executive officer (Tam 1999: 80).

Blending business with politics

As suggested earlier, it makes little sense in a situation in which the economy remains in large measure owned and controlled by the state to draw a sharp line between officials and managers and to view them as two distinct beasts. Instead, we find a situation in which government is involved in business and business in government. Mandarins and managers merge, the captains of industry are simultaneously cadres of the Party-state (Gore 1998: 201).

This intertwining means that business must attend to the concerns of government. From provincial governors and mayors of cities down to local county leaders, from ministers down through local bureaux to enterprise managers, runs a concern in operating state enterprises to balance economic efficiency against a range of political obligations. These include employment, welfare, price stability, and political monitoring. A large industrial enterprise can even find its younger workers being expected to train as a militia unit, the post of general manager combining that of commanding officer.

This blend of political and economic factors helps make sense of several of the peculiarities of Chinese management in the state sector. Officials on the spot face pressures to speed up the development of their locality, with success measured largely in terms of meeting planned targets for growth. This perpetuates a situation similar to that of the production targets of the era of the command economy, with the same incentive to falsify figures.

Output increases continue to be regularly lauded in the press, but they may at times be simply adding to the problems the state enterprises find themselves having. As mentioned earlier, producing in the absence of effective demand can only lead to piling up unsold inventories or inducing demand in buyers unlikely to meet their obligations. Anyone tempted to cut losses by cutting production puts their career at risk (see Box 2.8). It is far better, in a situation where government agencies derive benefits from investment projects while the costs and risks are spread over the entire system, to go for expansion.

State enterprises are also under pressure to rival one another in wages, benefits and social provision. Officials and managers have to ensure social stability and an aura of serving the people, as insensitivity and abuse of power pose a threat to the legitimacy of the regime. Consequently, the state builds into its personnel assessment criteria some measure of satisfaction from the masses. Fortunately for cadres, this can at times coincide quite well with their own economic self-interest. For, in the public realm, spending on general welfare is the only legitimate way for cadres to enhance their own welfare, a move at once both popular and ideologically acceptable. Deferred gratification is undoubtedly a Chinese virtue, one that accounts for the high proportion of income that is saved. However, while thrift may govern what happens to the pay packet once it reaches home, immediate distribution rather than investment is often more appealing to asset holding units. This is because the long-term beneficiary of investment in productive capacity is uncertain. Ultimately,

Box 2.7 Output targets

The auditors from the provincial government of Hubei found its municipalities and counties reported annual output figures at 80 billion yuan above what was actually produced in 1998.

The city of Dan Jiang, for example, reported a total output of over 10 billion yuan, making it one of the richest counties in the province. However, the provincial auditors using other measures rather than the figures reported by city and county officials calculated the figure to be less then 4 billion yuan, which placed Dan Jiang among the poorest cities.

Grass-root cadres complained that they have to report unrealistic figures because of quotas given to them by their superiors. As one explained:

> You are asking me why we report the figures when we know they are unreal? If you are in this position, and your yearly report does not show the figures your superior wants, your report will never be accepted. Every year, after every Spring Festival, we will be given all sorts of targets to fulfil within the year. The senior bosses want to show good performance to boost their political careers, so the juniors have to support them with high figures.

> We have not made much progress over the past ten years; we do not want to tell lies. But if we do not tell lies, we won't be able to keep our rice bowls. The targets are so high, there is no possibility for us to turn them into reality. So we have to lie, otherwise, our salaries will be cut or we will be sacked. We aren't paid much as junior officials, we can't afford to have our pay cut or our jobs lost.

> But the problem is we have to pay tax on the amount reported. So the more output we report, the more tax we have to pay. This means we have to levy extra taxes on the local population and people become still poorer. And the more output we report, the higher targets that will be given to us the following year . . . What can we do? It is like picking up stones to throw at our own feet.

Source: *Ershiyi Siji Jinji Baodao* (21st Century Economic Herald) 16 April 2001

the state, or any of a number of uncoordinated agencies acting in its name, may lay claim to the income generated.

Bureaucratic entrepreneurs

The role played by the state bureaucracy in the transition from a command economy to one employing market mechanisms is often

Box 2.8 The perils of cutting output

For a long time, the Long Rainbow Television Company held a position as one of the leading television manufacturers in the country. It contributes nearly half of the total output in Mianyang, the municipality in Sichuan where it is located. However, with about 70 television set manufacturers nationwide producing 40 million television sets per year and with only half of them sold, frequent price wars have undermined the company's profitability. In 2000, Long Rainbow's majority shareholder, the municipal government of Mianyang, decided to replace the general manager.

The new manager was a young man with novel ideas. Finding himself with a large stockpile of unsold sets, he decided it made little sense to incur the cost of adding to it. He cut production. This left the company balance sheet looking better, but made the municipality unhappy. Cutting production was lowering local output figures, a key measure used in judging the performance of local officials. Complaints also started to come in about lost orders from suppliers located in the city. It was feared this would contribute still further to the acute unemployment situation in Mianyang. Nine months later, the municipality decided to remove the new general manager and have the old one back.

The returned manager restored output and sparked another price war. His young rival found himself taken up into the council as a vice-mayor.

Sources: *Zhongguo Qiyejia*, (The Chinese Entrepreneur) No. 7, 2001;
Nanfang Zhoumo, (Southern Weekend) 18 April, 2001

viewed in largely negative terms. The expectation is that officials will largely resist the reforms as bringing changes that will deprive them of their power. In addition, the role of regulatory bodies in erecting obstacles to trade to enhance their income through fees and other payments is cited as further evidence of the deleterious effect of bureaucrats upon economic efficiency.

There is doubtless more than a grain of truth in this description. Yet, it is insufficient to do justice to the variety of reactions Chinese bureaucrats have proved capable of in rising to the challenge of the reforms. One particular sphere where this is particularly evident is in the variety of new businesses set up by civil servants to provide additional finance for their departments. From the end of the 1980s, many government departments (and, for that matter, other service arms of the state such as schools and universities) began to establish businesses to provide alternative employment for their staff and to share their profits with the founding department. Individually, these businesses tend to be small, but a department may have several such businesses in different fields. Usually they are in service industries. Typical examples include shops, restaurants, repair facilities and property development.

A variety of factors explains the emergence of this trend. The opportunities for establishing profitable enterprises offered by market reforms coincided with increasing financial burdens felt by the bureaux. For some, this was because old sources of revenue were lost. Commerce departments that previously had to coordinate the distribution of goods according to the plan found the market had removed much of their very reason for existence. Facing the very real possibility of being disbanded, many sought to establish other enterprises that would provide an alternative if the axe fell. For other departments, however, the reforms brought extra demands on their services without adequate expansion to

Box 2.9 Learning business

In 1999, negotiations took place between the Graduate Department of the Ministry of Education in Beijing and a British publishing company on setting up a joint venture in China.

The Graduate Department was, in the past, in charge of allocating students to jobs on completion of their studies. However, with students now having to look after themselves in the graduate labour market, the Department had become largely obsolete. Under government plans to streamline ministries, the Ministry of Education decided to get rid of a third of its existing departments, including the Graduate Department. They were given, however, a grace period of three years to find alternative ways to support themselves.

A number of service units within the Ministry had already converted into businesses. The canteens had turned into restaurants competing with each other and selling food to both staff and the general public. The travel arrangement office had broadened out into a tourist agency operating at the gates of the Ministry.

Some of these business, such as the tourist agency, were doing well, others, such as the restaurants, were not. This divided opinion among the staff at the Graduate Department as to the proposed joint venture. Some regarded the joint venture opportunity as crucial for the survival of the department so it should not frighten the British company away from the negotiating table by asking for too much. Some maintained that the department should not make any concessions because that would entail loss of face and there was always the hope that the government might change its mind about disbanding the department or turn it into some other department.

In the end, the latter group prevailed and the negotiations collapsed.

Fieldwork notes, 1999

their budgets. Such is the case with the Bureau of Industrial and Commercial Administration, which handles the registration and supervision of enterprises. This particular bureau has found itself faced with a growing number and diversity of enterprises needing attention.

As financial restraints tighten, the central government throughout the reforms has had periodic campaigns in an attempt to slim the ranks of a bureaucracy swollen by the planning needs of the command economy, needs that are now in many areas fulfilled by the market. The success of these reforms in slimming down departments depends partly on the opportunities departments have for opening businesses to absorb surplus staff. In Duckett's (1998) study of this practice in Tianjin, for example, she found that the staffing levels of offices of the real estate management bureau remained stable in the suburbs where little opportunity for opening business ventures existed. In the city centre, however, staffing levels in the offices had decreased, with staff being shifted to the successful ventures the offices had established. For the individual moving to such ventures, the break with the parent department is not always clear-cut. While they receive their wages from by the new enterprise, many seek to keep a grip on their old post for the fringe benefits and security it affords.

Far from being slavishly addicted to red tape and constitutionally averse to change, we see here civil servants sharing in a more general enthusiasm to 'take the plunge – *xia hai*' into business. For the bureaux chiefs it holds a number of attractions. They may stand to benefit materially through bonuses and improvements to working conditions made possible by the profits remitted by the enterprises. Successfully establishing commercial enterprises can also assist with their chances of promotion. Many leaders in local government look favourably on such displays of entrepreneurial dynamism, especially where it slims down employment in the bureau or part of the profits are used to support the work of the department.

This development can only be fully understood when set against both the legacy of the command economy and the direction it has taken under the reforms. Despite market reforms, bureaucratic involvement in the running of the economy remains strong, leaving officials with access to a range of resources and information. Bureaux are well placed to take advantage of this, both directly and through their connections when it comes to establishing and running businesses, especially in matters such as land development where administrative decision rather than market competition continues to play an important role. Limits on bureaucratic behaviour are still hazy in a situation in which Communist Party rule left legal structures to atrophy. An effective new legal system has not emerged to keep pace with the weakening of the old structures, controls and norms of the command economy era (Duckett 1998).

The reactions of the government to the entrepreneurial ventures of the bureaux have been mixed. Local governments often tend to support them as they help to ease the financial problems of the departments and to avoid layoffs, as well as adding to tax revenues and the vibrancy of the local economy. Central authorities seem more ambivalent. Periodically, national campaigns have appeared against them, but usually these have not been pursued with any vigour. Yet the ability of the central authorities to have their way on this matter should they really choose is clear from the way in which the army was forced to relinquish its enormous business empire in the late 1990s. There has also been a problem with some bureaux setting up subsidiary service providers in the areas they regulate and then pressing those applying for permits to use their services (see Box 2.10).

Box 2.10 Regulatory agencies

Enquiries at one construction project in 2001 revealed that the installation of most of the facilities had been contracted to companies owned by government regulatory bureaux. The municipal environment bureau was building a waste water treatment pool, the power bureau was building a transformer station, the water authority was laying the pipes, the public security bureau was designing and installing the security cameras and the fire station bureau was designing and constructing the sprinkler system.

'We did not award the contracts to them, they forced themselves upon us,' the project manager complained, 'otherwise they will not approve our design. In fact, they are bastards. They insisted upon us changing our design to use expensive systems the project does not need.'

Fieldwork notes, 2001

Paths to growth

The idea that success in powering a nation's growth depends on the state selecting and promoting key industries is, as Edward Steinfeld unsympathetically remarks, an 'idea that attracts politicians like spotlights attract moths' (Steinfeld 1998: 252). It is certainly a notion much to their taste in China where, in 1997, a national team of 120 large enterprise groups was chosen from sectors selected by the State Council as of strategic importance. The sectors included electricity generation, coal mining, automobiles, electronics, iron and steel, machinery, chemicals, constructions materials, transport, aerospace and pharmaceuticals. The aim was to foster international industrial giants with privileged access to bank support, building large corporations capable of competing in the global market.

The reform path from the 1980s has been a mixture of expanding enterprise autonomy with changes to ownership structure that have, in certain respects, proved more cosmetic than real. The central drive was to increase the autonomy of the operational unit, the plant, from the ministry. This meant giving increasing autonomy to what in the world's largest corporations would only be business units within a multi-plant company. If they were to stand any chance in competition with these, the state enterprises would need to amalgamate into larger entities. Two routes suggested themselves. The growth of large firms could be brought about by leaving them to their own devices, allowing market forces to stimulate mergers and acquisitions from below, or through state officials imposing regrouping from above.

The reforms found a number of major firms fortunate in possessing as leaders talented entrepreneurs harbouring large ambitions for their enterprises. Yet in this they seldom enjoyed the free hand of the western CEO in terms of capital market operations, including mergers and acquisitions at home and abroad, the disposal of unwanted businesses, downsizing and changes in remuneration systems. Ministries and bureaux at national and local levels retained an ambivalent attitude towards such firms, eager to garner the benefits flowing from greater autonomy, wary of allowing enterprises to slip from their grasp. For state enterprises, forging mergers across regional boundaries has often been made extremely difficult because of local protectionism. Overcoming these gave strength to the argument of those pressing for the gathering together of key enterprises under the auspices of the central state authorities. Here, though, one encounters once again the involvement of the political machine entailing considerations that may not necessarily enhance the ability of the firm to grow in a profitable manner. While state assistance can at times be vital in overcoming obstacles, at other times the eagerness of the state to take an active part in industrial restructuring can be less

Box 2.11 Top down or bottom up?
The case of Shanghai Petroleum

The situation in the petrochemical industry illustrates the tension between the top-down and bottom-up approach to building world-class enterprises. Sinopec was established in 1983 as a holding company encompassing all the state enterprises involved in the downstream processing part of the petrochemical industry. While formally it might appear that Sinopec controlled all its subordinate enterprises, the firms were independent legal entities responsible for their own financial affairs and a number of the more powerful of these took advantage of the new autonomy ushered in by the reforms to pursue independently their own expansion.

Prominent among these was the Shanghai Petrochemical Corporation (SPC), the most important subordinate enterprise within Sinopec, with total assets of 21.9 billion yuan and a workforce of 35 000. SPC, situated to the southwest of Shanghai and aided by strong backing from the Shanghai government, has pursued ambitious expansion plans through mergers and acquisitions, listings on overseas share markets, and international joint ventures with BP-Amoco and others. Its leadership clearly saw its mission as to form the basis of a petrochemical giant capable of holding its own on the world stage. In their eyes, Sinopec was not the motor of change, but was set to play a largely passive role. For a while in the 1990s, it seemed that the central authorities were prepared to go along with this strategy and give SPC free rein in pursuit of its ambitions. But opinion was never entirely in favour of such a market-based approach to achieving world-class companies in the industry. In 1998, policy took a sharp turn away from reliance on such a bottom-up approach towards forging large companies by administrative means. Sinopec was extensively reorganised and its authority over its constituent enterprises such as SPC reaffirmed and strengthened. A giant firm, fit to stand up against global competitors, was to spring from administrative fiat.

Many executives at SPC continue to chafe at the bit with regard to the increasingly active role Sinopec has taken in their affairs since the reorganisation. Sinopec has clearly some way to go in blending this and similar constituent companies into a unified firm. Nevertheless, it is clearly intent on doing so. Key figures in many powerful subsidiaries were replaced as Sinopec moved to consolidate its hold and in this SPC was no exception. Yet, some of its managers still compare Sinopec unfavourably with SPC in terms of the small size and lack of experience of its headquarters. One remarked optimistically that Sinopec's own flotation will give it a better appreciation of the rights independent joint-stock companies should be allowed to enjoy, but perhaps this was more with hope than conviction.

Source: authors' interviews and Nolan (2001)

welcome at the level of the firm. Some state enterprises, for example, may find themselves pressed into joining business groups that they would not if left free to consult their own economic self-interest (Keister 2000: 145).

Transforming the bureau

With the move from comprehensive planning to the use of markets to guide production, many government departments found themselves stripped of core functions. A variety of different attempts at reorganisation ensued in an attempt to accommodate the system to the changes that had taken place. The case of the transformed structure of the state-owned construction industry in Shanghai can serve to give a general idea of the trends at work.

Before restructuring in the early 1990s, the construction industry in Shanghai operated within a system inherited from the days of the command economy. As is illustrated in Figure 2.2, the Shanghai Construction Bureau was subject to the dual control of the centre and the locality, with the vertical line leading down from the ministry carrying somewhat more weight. The Construction Bureau had directly under its wing a number of central units and a series of localised construction units spread throughout the city. Elements of dual control continued down into

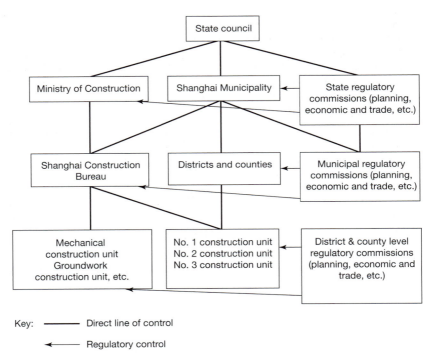

Figure 2.2 *Construction in Shanghai: before the reform*

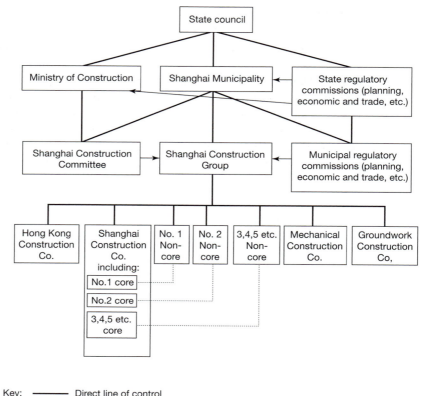

Key: ——————— Direct line of control

◄——————— Regulatory control

··············· Core and non-core share the same management and operation facilities.
Core and non-core support each other in various ways

Figure 2.3 *Construction in Shanghai: after the reform*

the localities, with districts and counties playing a part in the running
of the local units.

The reforms transformed the bulk of the Construction Bureau into the
Shanghai Construction Group (SCG), leaving behind a much reduced
Shanghai Construction Committee charged with regulatory functions (see
Figure 2.3). With the change, SCG itself was cut loose from its vertical
ties to the Ministry and was placed firmly under the leadership of
Shanghai. It now functions as a holding company for the assets of the
former Construction Bureau and has taken advantage of the greater
commercial freedom this afforded to expand through acquiring a
controlling share in a Hong Kong based construction company.

The formerly localised units of the bureau were cut loose from their local ties and now compete with one another for contracts. Each consists of a core and non-core element, the core containing the most profitable parts of each enterprise. Both core and non-core continue to work as one unit, sharing the same management and premises. The principal reason for the division was to gather the most appealing aspects of each under the umbrella of the Shanghai Construction Company to enable it to list successfully. As with other state enterprises, however, a majority shareholding remains with the state, allowing layers of coordination and dependence not allowed for in prospectuses to continue much as before.

3 Inside the enterprise

- Managerial appointments
- Management style
- The workshop manager
- Getting on track: formalisation
- The decision-making process: strategic investment
- Technology and the structure of the firm
- Breaking the iron rice bowl
- Trade unions and the Workers' Assembly

'What does the Party do in your enterprise nowadays?'
'Oh, not very much really.'
'So, it's no longer important?'
'Oh, no, it's terribly important.'

Comments such as this, taken from an interview with a manager from a state enterprise, are commonplace, especially in the case of larger companies. This seems, at first sight, to pose a conundrum. How can an organisation that has cut back on its activities within state enterprises nevertheless continue to enjoy considerable influence within them? For there is no doubt that, in terms of the experience of ordinary workers, Party-led campaigns have faded to a pale shadow of their former selves. Among ordinary workers the fear of falling victim to one or another of the endless political campaigns and study sessions that characterised the Cultural Revolution has gone. Party members are no longer called upon to fight one political battle after another, ferreting out class enemies. You Ji sums up the spirit of those times succinctly:

> Political drives were usually launched at the apex of power to purge a few designated members of the leadership, under the guise of abstract ideological rectification. At the grassroots, where the specific targets became remote, it was the task of Party cells to tackle the 'social base' of the disgraced Party leaders. So 'followers' of the erroneous Party line were ferreted out, often on the basis of a quota which factory Party cells had to fulfil. Because it was difficult to establish

the exact political and ideological crimes of those targeted, people who had either a 'bad family' origin or a bad relationship with Party cadres became vulnerable in these drives.

(You 1998: 92)

Little wonder that ordinary workers should lose what little appetite they may have had for political study after such a lesson. With the ending of the Cultural Revolution and the advent of reforms it has become increasingly difficult to inspire interest or even attendance at occasional political study sessions, where once weekly meetings had been the rule. When called, they may have dance parties attached to drum up interest, or those attending will be allowed to discuss whatever they wish once the Party documents have been read out. There seems little faith left in communist ideology among the mass of ordinary workers. Furthermore, it is a disillusionment shared by many of the full-time Party workers charged with spreading the word among them. The result is that they too would prefer to keep political meetings to a minimum. As one remarks: 'I am preaching something I myself don't have faith in. So you feel you cannot escape feelings of hypocrisy. The best way to avoid this embarrassment is to avoid study sessions where possible, or cut them to a minimum' (You 1998: 95).

Most of the lower level Party cadres in charge of full-time political education in state-owned enterprises would leave Party work if they were in a position to choose. In 1991, their pay levels were aligned with technical staff, itself a move resented by the latter for having their hard knowledge placed on a level with what many viewed as empty talk. At the same time, the settlement failed to please the Party's political workers as it left their pay still lagging behind that of managers. One summed up the situation as follows:

I'm aware that people like me are not welcome by workers and technical staff. But is it our fault? When I had just joined the workforce, I dreamed of becoming a technician. Yet Secretary Liu told me that because I had a 'red' family background and a high school certificate, the organisation [the Party] had decided that I should work in the Party propaganda department. All these years I have been playing with empty words, many of which seem odd today. Now I have a senior title as a political worker. However, besides talking about stuff which nobody listens to, I am good at nothing. All I can do now is to prevent any of my children from following my path but instead encourage them to learn a real skill.

(You 1998: 97)

Within many state firms there has been a shrinking in the size of the Party apparatus in terms of full-time posts devoted to political propaganda, although this varies with size and location. Some large state-owned enterprises still maintain the traditional panoply of departments and offices, with departments of propaganda, organisation, and united front work, offices of general affairs and of supervision, and the discipline inspection committee. Such enterprises approach the official standard of one Party worker for each hundred industrial workers. At the other end of the spectrum, small state firms do not keep any full-time Party officers, with Party work confined to activists outside work hours. Enterprises also vary with location, those in the capital and large cities being more likely to have full-time Party secretaries than similar sized firms at the county or township level. Departments with large numbers of younger members or intellectuals are also regarded as in need of additional attention.

These variations aside, at the shop floor level the presence of the Party has undoubtedly receded. This is not simply in terms of the political activities of the Party cadres. It is also in terms of ordinary rank-and-file membership among the workers. This has declined sharply. In a curious way, the retreat has helped ease tension between the Party and workers by removing the presence of Party members. The Party often lauded these as model workers. Their workmates, however, often failed to share this admiration, viewing them with distrust as the eyes and ears of management. The declining interest among ordinary workers in joining the Party results, in part, from work performance replacing political correctness as the arbiter of who gets what. It has been matched by the Party's dwindling interest in recruitment from the masses to a preference for recruiting from among better-educated staff.

Managers have matched the shift in recruitment interest of the Party with an equal enthusiasm for joining. Their enthusiasm to offer their services to the Party sits, as most are happy to admit, rather comfortably with promoting their own careers. General managers of state enterprises are, for the most part, members of the Party. It is common, in consequence, to hear vice-general managers who are not members comment on how this is likely to act as a bar to further promotion. Here, then, we have part of the answer to the puzzle with which we set out. The Party does do less within state enterprises, in terms of political propaganda, than before. For the ordinary workers it has become less of a presence. Yet, for the ambitious manager, gaining access to the Party gives a qualification that is often necessary, albeit no longer sufficient in itself, for scaling the heights.

Box 3.1 Forgetting one's lines

On one occasion the authors were offered a lift back home in a minibus with some middle managers, all Party members. We asked one manager, Wang Dong, who happened to be sitting close by, what the current Party policy was that he was implementing in his company. Unexpectedly this question roused the fellow passengers, who up until then had been dozing. Before Wang had a chance to answer, a manager at the back shouted: 'Why do you have to know these things? We have to live with these things, but surely you don't. Do you have Party lines in England too?'

This was interrupted by another manager: 'But let old Wang answer, I bet he can't remember.' Everybody laughed wholeheartedly at this. Wang laughed as well and said: 'But of course I can remember. It is engraved on my heart.' He then started to recite: 'According to the General Secretary of our Party, the Party should represent three things in the era of reform. First, it should represent the most advanced forces of production; second, it should represent the interests of the majority of the people; third, the third . . .' He faltered, which brought more merciless laughter from the others. One said: 'You can't remember it. You don't study as hard as we do, old Wang, knock some bonus off yourself this month.'

Fieldwork notes, 2001

This is, however, only part of the answer. The Party remains important within the state enterprise not only for the enhanced promotion possibilities membership confers upon ambitious managers. It is also important because a senior Party position can be the underpinning for exercising considerable power within the enterprise. To see how this is so we need to look at the relationship between the Party secretary and the general manager within the enterprise.

This relationship is one that, in the past, was often viewed as 'red versus expert', the ideologue concerned with promoting political correctness and fervour versus the hard-headed manager. Such tension as arose from this conflict has largely disappeared. The Party has long ago lost its taste for permanent revolution in favour of promoting development by any means other than those that pose a direct threat to its authority. At the enterprise level, this manifests itself in a pragmatic concern to raise production through whatever means prove most successful, a concern shared by general manager and general secretary alike. Propaganda is now directed towards promoting sales, raising the quality of products, reducing costs, and gaining acceptance of the need for inequality and competition among the workers. The cause of power struggles between Party secretary and general manager lies elsewhere.

The official purpose of the Party cells within state enterprises is to exercise supervision over management. Just what this entails is left vague, perpetuating a general confusion between the state and the Party and between the government and the enterprise. On the one hand, there is a desire to free enterprises to operate more efficiently as independent units. On the other, there is a reluctance to release control over the resources afforded by the enterprises. Similarly, the attitude towards granting general managers autonomy and control over the enterprise is equally ambiguous. It is recognised on the one hand that placing overall control in the hands of one person has positive advantages; on the other hand, this delegation is accompanied by anxieties about whether the person is to be trusted. The usual result of such fears throughout the Chinese system is to place one body side-by-side with another to watch over it. The supervisory function of the Party in the enterprise is one such mechanism.

The influence of the Party flows partly from the enterprise Party committee, which invariably includes a number of senior managers, including the general manager. At the same time, the Party secretary is likely to hold a prominent place in the management team. As noted in the previous chapter, where state enterprises have adopted the new corporate pattern the Party secretary will almost invariably hold one of the top posts, either as chair or deputy chair of the board or as the chief or deputy chief executive officer (Tam 1999: 80).

The existence of two power centres within the firm can frequently give rise to conflict, all the more so given the vague and sometimes incompatible regulatory framework within which their relationship is played out. The Enterprise Law, for example, vests the power of appointing personnel in the hands of the general manager. Party regulations, however, demur on this point, calling for the Party committee to be consulted. Strong managers have managed to press ahead with their appointments, treating such a consultation as a formality. Others have found themselves pulled into bargaining over appointments. In the case of Party members being considered for appointment to middle or senior management posts, Party control is greater and more convoluted. The general manager will need to approach the enterprise's Party organisation department to view the candidate's records. The Party organisation department will itself vet the appointment after consultation with higher Party organs. The Party organisation department rather than the general manager is then the first to inform the candidate of the results of these deliberations. The department, together with the Party discipline inspection committee, will continue to monitor the candidate's performance in the post. Fierce struggles over appointments often arise as both parties attempt to preserve and enhance their network of supporters within the firm. For, as You Ji notes: 'In China's state-owned enterprises the title of manager or Party secretary does not deliver authority automatically, and so titulars have sought to rely on the support of their own cliques' (You 1998: 61–62).

There is a variety of ways in which this relationship between the two centres of power can be played out. At its best, it can be a relationship of mutual support and cooperation, founded on mutual respect and friendship. The manager may, for example, turn to the Party secretary to lend support to his efforts to overcome resistance to the introduction of new working practices or payment schemes. In return, the Party secretary may find time being found for the Party's political propaganda work, and the Party's contribution to the success of the enterprise being highlighted by the management.

Alternatively, the two may be locked in struggle over control of the enterprise. One outcome may be the complete victory of one, who then exercises control with little attention paid to the wishes of the other. More generally, an uneasy and shifting balance occurs. Where this settles at any one time is determined by the local situation. The respective strength of character of those involved plays a role, as does length of service within the enterprise. The later will have enabled experience to accumulate. A Party secretary with technical expertise is held in far higher regard than one who is seen as a master of nought but empty words. Length of service at an enterprise will also have enabled the occupant of either position to build up informal cliques to provide support. In a similar fashion, how well connected either is in terms of their relationships with government and Party bodies beyond the enterprise will also weigh in the balance.

It is widely thought that, in the absence of friendly cooperation, the emergence of one clearly dominant centre of control is in the best interests of the enterprise. Unfortunately, other less optimal patterns can also emerge. One is based upon avoidance; with both manager and Party secretary steering clear of decisions over matters likely to provoke conflict. This naturally has a deleterious effect on the ability of enterprises to take timely decisions. The resulting lack of clear leadership where avoidance prevails also tends to undermine morale within the firm. Despite these drawbacks, this pattern is frequent (You 1998: 62).

Bad relations between manager and Party secretary can descend, however, into open warfare, with both sides seeking to frustrate one another at every turn. Where their respective forces are equally balanced, the ability of the firm to operate effectively can be paralysed. When matters reach this stage, the only solution is for higher authorities to intervene to remove one or the other of the two warring contenders. However, cranking up the apparatus to deliver judgement can be a convoluted process, given that the original appointments will have flown through different channels.

The resolution of one such conflict has been described by Steinfeld in his discussion of Anshan Iron and Steel, a steel producer located in Liaoning province in the north-east, heartland of China's 'rust belt' (Steinfeld 1998: 103–4). The Party secretary, Cheng Xichang, and the general manager, Li Huazhong, were unable to get along with one another. The management of the company suffered in consequence, but outside bodies were reluctant to intervene. Partly this reflected the differing external connections of the two. Cheng, the Party secretary, was widely looked upon as having strong backing from the local Liaoning Party authorities. Li, the general manager, owed his appointment to, and drew support from, the Ministry of Metallurgical Industry in Beijing. Eventually, however, a conference was convened between the province and the organisational department of the ministry. The result was the dismissal of Cheng and his replacement as Party secretary by a vice-minister from the ministry. The struggle was widely interpreted as a struggle between Cheng, the 'Liaoning man', and Li, the 'Beijing man', with the Liaoning faction within the enterprise being further watered down by Li taking on the role of vice-Party secretary in addition to his post as general manager.

As Steinfeld concludes, this incident illustrates how internal disputes within the firm can become embroiled with broader struggles between regional forces and the centre. The amount of comment the incident received in the industry suggests that such a decisive resolution of such disputes was unusual. For, rather than the appointment of senior staff resting clearly with one body, it was, characteristically, distributed throughout several bodies. In the case of a conflict between Party secretary and general manager, this called for cooperation between various agencies and levels of government that might well themselves be locked in a struggle over differing loyalties and conflicting ambitions.

Box 3.2 The Party steps in

Xu Yi was a young manager of a state-owned publishing house. When he was promoted to be the general manager in 1999, he started to introduce various incentive schemes in order to motivate staff members. This managed to upset some of the less productive employees who were paid less under these schemes. These employees complained to Xu's superior in the parent company. Xu's boss, however, supported him and encouraged him to try out more methods to revitalise the company.

In 2000, Xu's boss retired. His position was taken by an old cadre from the state bureaucracy. The new boss had different ideas from Xu on what was important for the company. He thought, for one thing, that it was more important to stop the complaints from the masses than to introduce more incentive schemes. He also disagreed with Xu on how to deal with the debts owed to the company.

Xu inherited many debts from his predecessors. These debts were incurred several years ago and they should, according to government regulations, have been written off. Xu's predecessors, however, preferred to sign agreements with the debtors extending the period for payment so that they could continue to calculate them as receivable. Xu, wishing to start with a clean sheet, decided to write these debts off. Xu's new boss, however, refused to allow him to do so.

In 2001, some disgruntled staff reported to Xu's boss the existence of a 'little gold safe' in the company. This refers to a separate account for income generated by off-the-record transactions, a commonplace phenomenon. Nonetheless, it is naturally frowned upon officially and this gave Xu's superior a reason to remove him from his post. The decision was not well received in the company. More than half of the middle managers handed in a collective letter of resignation in protest.

Upon this, the Party stepped in. Its intervention was characteristic. A team of Party cadres from the parent company moved in and had knee-to-knee talks with every Party member, urging them to stop supporting Xu. Any disobedience, they were told, would be dealt with as a Party disciplinary matter. The Party also rotated all the managers to remove them from their supporting subordinates. As for Xu, the Party decided to send him on a project to develop China's impoverished areas. He was to go to a remote countryside post in the west of China to help the local county government officials for three years. To pacify his supporters, the Party announced that this was a promotion for Xu, and that if Xu proved to be worthy of the Party's trust, he would be appointed to a more important position upon his return.

Fieldwork notes, 2001

Managerial appointments

Control over appointments remains one of the few forces sustaining the coherence of the present political and economic system. For this reason, despite modifications introduced in the pursuit of greater efficiency, the reins have never been allowed to slip through the fingers of the state authorities. Control over the career prospects of those in the state hierarchy ensures, in the last analysis, that the centre will get its way in matters that challenge the interests of those in power. Their ability to monitor those below may be limited, but where challenges or disturbances bring the attention of the centre to bear, the final say over career prospects remains to hand. Everywhere the beginnings of independent fiefdoms continue to spring up, but everywhere their walls can be torn down in the event of need. On the side of ambitious managers, this directs efforts upwards into attempts to win the attention of officials with eye-catching projects and displays of adherence to the latest policy and campaign pronouncements. It also diverts time and energy into the search for patrons in the bureaucracy to assist one's climb. The belief that managerial promotion depends not so much on what you know as on who you know is widespread in consequence. Competition for such favour is often intense within the firm, with the battle played out through the cultivation of cliques of supporters. Contenders remain locked in constant anxiety about what may happen in their absence, an anxiety phrased in characteristically Chinese fashion as concern over 'having one's walls undermined'. It is situations such as this, as much as any general cultural predisposition, that accounts for surveys finding Chinese managers spending greater time and effort on promoting relationships and less on task performance than do Western managers. A commonly heard refrain from state enterprise managers, making play on the slogans of an earlier era, is: 'We are not here to produce things. We are here to struggle with people.'

Under a long-standing principle, their supervisory bodies usually appoint the two highest levels in the hierarchy of a state-owned enterprise. Thus, the Party secretary and the vice-Party secretary together with the general manager and vice-general managers will be appointed by bodies overseeing the firm. This leaves the general manager not only having to cope with any division arising from the presence of the Party, it also means that he or she does not have the ability to appoint or dismiss immediate subordinates at the vice-managerial level. This leaves the general manager with only the post of assistant general manager within his or her gift as far as the immediate tier beneath is concerned. With no power to appoint or dismiss his vice-managers, the general manager is robbed of an important tool for enforcing unity of purpose and standards of managerial efficiency within the firm.

Box 3.3 Managerial appointments

The following comments about the system for the appointment of managers are taken from an interview with the chairman of the board and Party secretary of a major state-owned enterprise in Shanghai.

> The biggest problem is the nomination of senior managers of the holding groups by the government. There should be a promotion mechanism rather than the present practice of a red-letter headed [official] document. I like the private dot.com companies. They change CEO very frequently, and there are many debates in the newspapers over who will be the new CEO. This shows the dot.com companies have a transparent system. However, with state-owned enterprises, the municipal Party's Personnel Department will nominate the CEO. If a nomination is good, then the enterprise is lucky. If they make a bad decision, then the state enterprise will suffer. Although the Personnel Department also have some rules, for example, they will follow the mass line, talking to people, investigating and observing a cadre for a period, there is not a system, nor a standard. For example, in the past the nominee should not have participated in the 1989 demonstrations, now the nominee should be good at working for both spiritual civilisation and material civilisation. But these are very vague and ever changing. Also, those people who make the nomination do not carry any responsibilities if things go wrong. The small and medium companies do not suffer as much as we do, because the government largely leaves them alone, so they have now started to build up promotion mechanisms such as competition within the company or advertising publicly. For big businesses, the central government has a Big Business Office which nominates the CEO. And the cadres of the Big Business Office are nominated by the Party's Central Personnel Department. Most of the people in that department do not understand business.

> Another problem is that when a CEO is good, the government will remove him from the company to send him elsewhere not related to the original company. The original company suffers. But the government does not care. The government also sends bureaucrats to manage companies. These bureaucrats do not understand how business should be run at all.

> Interview, 2001

For large state-owned enterprises, control over senior managerial appointments remains in government hands regardless of the legal form assumed by the firm. This remains true for those that have converted into joint-stock companies. Appointments of the senior management team do no rest in any real sense with the board in such circumstances, although they may at one point or another go through the motions of endorsing such appointments. The power to appoint still lies in the Party and state

Box 3.4 The rise and fall of an industrial giant

Given the rich variety of forms encountered in China's organisational landscape, one can always find exceptions to the rule. Such was the case with appointments at the Capital Iron and Steel Company under the autocratic leadership of its Party secretary, Zhou Guanwu. Vice-general managers in large state firms are generally appointed by outside agencies and are thus not answerable to the leadership of the firm itself. Firms are, however, free to appoint one or two assistant general managers themselves. Zhou was able to achieve greater autonomy for Capital Steel by reversing the normal pattern, decreasing the number of vice-general managers and expanding the number of assistants.

That he was able to do so without objection from outside authorities was due to the unprecedented autonomy he had secured for the company under a 15 year contract with the State Council signed in 1982. The price paid was that Capital Steel was cut off from state financial assistance and required to meet stiff targets for profits. Forced to stand on its own feet, the tightening of the internal management structure went far beyond dealing with the vice-general manager issue. In most state enterprises, demotion is rare. Under Zhou's regime he not only appointed senior managers, but also removed them at will. Inefficient managers, while usually not dismissed outright, might find themselves reduced to the shop floor, an ever-present reminder to all around of the consequences of failure. In the first ten years of the contract, 1424 managers were promoted, 640 were demoted and 38 were dismissed outright (Steinfeld 1998: 205).

Running such a tight ship, Capital Steel prospered for a number of years. However, by 1995 it was revealed to be on the verge of financial collapse and Zhou Guanwu was forced into retirement. The reasons are instructive. What appears to have happened is that the firm became trapped between increasing diminishing returns and Zhou's ambition to make Capital Steel the largest steel producer in the country. In this, he was aided, and Capital Steel's fate sealed, by the softening of the hitherto hard budgetary constraints under which the firm had been operating. Following a much-publicised visit by Deng Xiaoping in 1992, the firm came to be seen as under his special protection. This perception was probably mistaken. Nevertheless, if a situation is perceived to be real, then it is real in its consequences, and this proved true with Capital Steel. The company found itself with access to state funds formerly closed to it. Regulatory bodies backed away from close monitoring of its affairs, which at this point included the establishment of its own bank, Huaxia. When soft budget constraints, diminishing returns and a contract stipulating annually increasing profit targets came together with Zhou's pursuit of unlimited expansion, nemesis followed fast behind.

Source: Steinfeld (1998)

apparatus beyond the firm. Hopes that the institution of a board would weaken such forces and lead to appointments more closely in tune with improving performance have frequently met with disappointment (see Box 3.5). Encountering a gulf between formal appearance and actual

Box 3.5 The red chip

One of the advantages reformers hoped to gain through transforming state-owned enterprises into joint stock companies was improved performance from managers. Theoretically, in China as elsewhere, the appointment of chief executive officer should rest in the hands of the board. In China, however, state agencies continue to exercise their former rights of appointment. The result can often be that, instead of clarifying lines of responsibility, the joint stock reforms have on occasion left them in a more muddled state than when they began. The Ma'anshan Iron and Steel Company is a case in point.

In preparation for its listing on the Hong Kong stock exchange the company was split, as is often the case, into a core of the best performing sections of the company and a holding company under whose direct control came all the ancillary facilities and services, including the bulk of the provision for retirement pensions. The core took on an appearance more likely to attract investment on the stock market, with a leaner workforce engaged in the core business of steel production, shorn of the traditional accumulated social welfare burdens associated with state enterprises. The new company was, however, to have a Party committee in addition to the board. While the stock market prospectus aimed at the Shanghai market was quite open about this, the Hong Kong prospectus and annual reports avoided all mention of the Party and Party position in reporting on appointments.

The government retained a majority shareholding in the new firm, the shares being vested in the holding company. This was reflected in the appointment of the general manager of the holding company, Hang Yongyi, to the position of chairman of the board of the joint stock company, and the appointment of the Party secretary of the holding company, Wang Wanbin, to the position of vice-chairman.

Tensions between the holding company and the joint stock company arose soon after the division between the two was made. In 1994, the new company announced dividends, but refused to pay those due to its holding company. It also failed to honour its contracts to pay for ore deliveries and the provision of services from the holding company. Given that the holding company had been left carrying the burden of the unprofitable parts of the original company, this only served to exacerbate its problems. There was, however, little that it could do to remedy the situation. The general manager of the holding company was indeed the chairman of the board, but he had no power to appoint or remove either the general manager or the vice-general managers of the joint stock company over which the board supposedly presided.

Part of the reason behind the joint-stock company's actions would appear to be the plummeting share price of the new company on the Hong Kong stock exchange at the time, in response to news of declining profits. With the high attention given to the flotation of the state-owned company, this was acutely embarrassing to managers owing their appointment directly to the government. The company could not be seen to fail, even if this meant pushing the burden for sustaining it back into the state system through enforced loans and subsidies from the holding company. In this respect, it is interesting to note that Ma'anshan made great play of its status as 'king of the "red chip" stocks' on the Hong Kong market. In Hong Kong, however, reference to the large Chinese state-owned enterprises that have floated there as 'red chips' carries a rather less complimentary air. It conveys the notion of a company that can be relied upon, however poorly it may perform, to pay out some dividend and always to be bailed out by the state rather than being allowed to go under.

Source: Steinfeld (1998)

practice in this area is commonplace. To take but one example: at one large steel company we visited, the power to appoint deputies was only granted at the level of department heads and below. Above this level managers had, in theory, the right to nominate their own deputies. In practice, the superior level, through the Party's personnel department, always nominated these. Nonetheless, the document announcing the appointment states that the immediate manager, who signs the document, appoints them.

General managers are not, then, free to appoint and promote managers at will. In the case of senior and middle level managers there is a standard procedure adhered to in most large state-owned enterprises. Managerial posts are increasingly advertised, but applicants will also be vetted in terms of similar criteria and procedures. Candidates are assessed in terms of four criteria: political correctness and moral rectitude (*de*), managerial capabilities (*neng*), hard work (*qin*), and record of achievements (*ji*). The ability to maintain harmonious relations with others is also taken into account. Information on this and the other criteria is available through annual evaluation reports, and Party staff gather further information in conversation with the candidate's superiors, colleagues and workers. The Party committee of the enterprise takes the final decision, with the general manager signing the letter of appointment on its behalf. On taking up their post, the successful candidate is briefed on the opinions that were expressed about him or her in the course of the selection consultations. These tend to be uncomfortably frank. They nevertheless accord well with the faith of those in authority throughout Chinese society – parents, teachers and bosses alike – on the benefits of reproof in moulding those under their care. It also chimes well with the communist tradition of willing self-criticism. Nevertheless, the frankness is at times mitigated by the caution with which colleagues and subordinates are prepared openly to discuss the shortcomings of those who may in the future be in a position to make life hard for them. The possibility that their words may get back to the person being reported on may well occur to those considering how candid they should be.

There are also mechanisms in place for the scrutiny of the performance of managers on a continuing basis. In the case of general managers and vice-general managers, this can take the form of an annual or end of contract visitation by cadres from the personnel department of the authority overseeing the firm. The cadres arrive and consult with middle level managers and workers on the performance of the firm's leadership. Opinions differ among managers on the impact of such exercises. Some managers feel that it is important to the general manager and vice-general manager to secure the expression of a good opinion from their subordinates and that this serves as a balance to their power. Others are more sceptical, suspecting that higher authorities make use of the results when they suit their purposes and ignore them when they do not. As with the selection procedure, there is a certain reluctance on the part of those taking this view to voice open criticism. As one manager remarked to us: 'There is no use to tell the investigators from the superior personnel department about your grievance. Actually, it is dangerous. I wrote a letter complaining about my boss, but the letter ended up on his desk. I was demoted immediately. The mass line is used to give them excuses to get rid of people they dislike or to promote people they like. If anything comes up from the masses that is different from what they have in mind they simply ignore it.'

Box 3.6 Management appraisal

A middle manager from a large state-owned company in Shanghai explained the importance of winning support from his subordinates:

It is very important not to do things that will upset one's subordinates too much, because every year before the Party makes decisions on which managers should be promoted, they will talk to a certain percentage of the employees and ask them to fill up questionnaires on the suitability of the candidates. If 60 per cent say they are not satisfied with a candidate, then no matter how much money he has brought to the company, he will not be promoted and his present position will be under threat. But this does not apply to the top managers. As long as they keep the government and the Party happy, they can do whatever they want.

Interview, 2001

In addition to such evaluations, the personnel departments of the supervising agencies are on the look out for talented young high-fliers to provide with training. Frequently these will go through a process known as 'picking up, putting down, and taking up again' (*ti shanglai, fang xiaqu, zai ti shanglai*). They will first be taken up into the bureau and given work to do, frequently in the youth league or cadres' department. During this stage, they will be given managerial training. If they prove good enough, after a year or two they will be sent down to act as general managers or vice-general managers in state companies. Those who do well there will be spirited back up into the bureaucracy.

At the other extreme, poor performance among managerial staff seldom meets with outright dismissal. Incompetent managers tend to reshuffled and sidelined, while retaining their rank and salary. The power to dismiss, like the power to appoint, is usually not in the hands of those most immediately involved. Those who do hold the power may well be those responsible for the appointment and they are sometimes reluctant to draw attention to their poor judgement by setting in train dismissal proceedings. Serious misconduct rather than mere incompetence will nevertheless bring demotion or even dismissal. Managers under a cloud often serve long periods of suspension, known as 'waiting for orders', when they hover around the office shorn of all power and with little or nothing to do. Whether their prolonged presence is deliberately intended to serve as a dreadful warning to others or is simply the result of bureaucratic delay is a moot point.

Retiring senior managers are often retained in an advisory capacity, possibly through appointment to the supervisory board. They may continue to occupy a desk at work and to attend meetings. This is a welcome position, bolstering pensions with further income. It is a reward from those they groomed as their heirs, and one not without advantages to the firm. The retired managers can provide the current leadership with valuable services through the connections they continue to enjoy. Where they have several managers who owe their current position to them, they can also at times exercise a mediating influence when rivalries threaten to get out of hand. This culmination of a career is often long-planned for in advance. Ensuring it comes about can condition the behaviour of managers, making them loath to make enemies of those who may, in future, be in a position to help them realise this ambition.

Management style

The role of senior managers in China is, in certain ways, similar to that of their counterparts in America (Mintzberg 1973). Like them, senior managers in China work long hours, often staying long after everybody else has gone home. Indeed, for Chinese managers, work does not end there. They will often get home to find one or two members of staff waiting to talk to them about some personal favour. Dealing with people in their homes has a number of advantages. Not only is it away from prying eyes and the constant interruptions encountered at work. It is also preferred precisely because managers will be less business-like when at home. With the boss surrounded by family, one hopes to benefit from a more warm-hearted atmosphere, one full of human sentiment (*renqing*). Employees also at times calculate on being able to capitalise on an element of embarrassment from the relatively sumptuous surroundings enjoyed by the manager. While at work there may be the excuse of 'look at the difficulties the company is in', this loses its force in surroundings that say 'look how well I am doing'.

Not only do managers find themselves cornered at home after work hours. They may find themselves propelled by the same logic into spending their evening paying visits to officials from whom they are seeking help for their firms (see Box 3.7). Work also extends into leisure through the time devoted to entertaining business associates in the evenings and at weekends. Business trips stretch out as hosts provide the customary additional day or two for sightseeing. Nowadays, such trips can also serve to strengthen ties favourable to business with another group of powerful patrons, the gods. With the revival of interest in traditional religion, many business people are happy to add to their agenda a visit to a local temple renowned for the efficacy of its resident deities. Chinese religion sits at ease with such a pragmatic approach to requesting favours. Indeed, the entire pantheon is modelled on the imperial bureaucracy, which bears striking resemblance to its contemporary successor. Knowing which is the best god in the heavenly hierarchy to address is much like the sensitivity needed to navigate one's way through its earthly counterpart in today's China.

It is the presence of this earthly bureaucracy presiding over the firm that points to one key difference between how Chinese and Western managers spend their time. For Chinese managers, a greater proportion of their attention is inevitably demanded by the agencies granted authority over them. These shower the firm with numerous regulations and policy

Box 3.7 Visiting the district governor

Two large state-owned companies ran into a serious dispute over a project in which they were jointly engaged. The district governor was instructed by the local mayor to visit the site every Saturday in an attempt to iron out the differences and to ensure progress on the project.

At one of these coordination meetings, a manager from one of the companies nudged one of the authors, who was observing the proceedings, and whispered: 'Notice the change of the district governor's manner towards the other company? He was shouting at them last Saturday, but now he is talking to them softly. They've got him fixed.'

After the meeting, a manager from the other company was asked what had been done to make the district governor change his attitude towards them. He laughed and replied: 'So you have noticed a change? We visited him at his home last night.'

When asked how they had managed to know the home address of the governor, he explained:

> We have an office in the company specialising in keeping good relations with government officials. People working in that office know many things about the local government; they are also on good terms with the administrative staff in the government. In this case, they know the General Affairs Office in the local district keeps details of its officials and their families, and they managed to get the address of the district governor from the office. They also told us he would be at home last night.

So was the governor surprised at their turning up at his doorstep?

> Not at all, people in their position are used to having others visit their home all the time. Besides, they can't turn people away, it would be far too impolite. We mainly wanted to let him know that although we are a big company, we also have our own problems. We wanted him to be more considerate towards us.

Did they take any gifts?

> How can you visit somebody's home with empty hands? We brought some gifts with us, but mainly fruit.

Fieldwork notes, 2001

directives. These can change frequently. Flowing from different sources, they can also be contradictory. One study by Boisot and Xing showed that 30 per cent of the mail received by senior managers in a sample of Chinese state enterprises came from government agencies, in contrast with just 6 per cent of the mail received by senior managers in America. Chinese managers, despite receiving much written instruction from on high, are themselves reluctant to reply in writing, preferring to communicate with their superiors in person. Thus, while they receive nearly five times as much written communication from their superiors as their American counterparts, they send back upwards less than one twelfth. The Chinese manager, on the other hand, spends four times as much time in direct personal contact with his or her superior than does the American (Boisot and Xing 1992: 170).

The reluctance to commit oneself in writing stems in part from a desire to avoid giving hostages to fortune. What is laid down in black and white may return to haunt one in a situation where official expectations are shifting and unpredictable. This reluctance of the Chinese managers to commit themselves in writing extends to how they manage their time – few keep diaries and those that do are unable to keep to them. Constant interruptions to whatever they are doing are the norm. Frequently, a general manager can be observed engaging in several different conversations at once or even attending several meetings simultaneously. The arrival of the mobile phone, seldom switched off, has only added to the seeming chaos.

That senior managers should feel impelled to participate in so many things at once reflects a reluctance to delegate. Many minor decisions are taken at the top rather than being passed down the organisational hierarchy. In part, this reflects a lack of trust in subordinates. This is partly due to a lack of faith in their abilities, with surveys revealing higher level managers estimating particular decisions as needing greater managerial skill than do their subordinates (Smith and Wang 1996: 331). Given the factionalism referred to earlier, the loyalties of fellow managers may also be suspect. For both reasons, the organisation cannot be relied upon by the general manager to carry out matters to his or her satisfaction. There is a constant need to reach into the organisation in order to keep in touch with what is going on, as reports that filter up attempt to bury difficulties. Meetings, for example, must be attended, as meetings seldom have minutes taken. Where they are taken, they tend to be extensively doctored to highlight the contribution of the principal actors and to protect them from future criticism. There is little sense of them being used as an instrument to record actions agreed upon and to monitor their implementation. Greater reliance is placed on unscheduled and informal meetings that provide a better atmosphere in which to cultivate good personal relationships. Managers are, in consequence, much given to dropping in on one another for a chat and a cigarette to keep in touch, whether or not any specific task is on their mind. Such social visits contribute nonetheless to cementing the network of good personal relationships seen as central to carrying out one's work and advancing one's career.

If the general manager has little faith in the organisation to deliver, then neither do others. Consequently, everyone wishes to deal with the person at the top personally, so that he or she could not delegate even if the wish were there. Both employees and those beyond the firm look to the general manager to provide guarantees that their interests will be attended to. The uncertainties and divisions introduced into the firm by its institutional setting work against structured working methods and delegation.

Nonetheless, the general manager cannot be everywhere at once. Some delegation has to take place. Size matters here, of course, with those at the top of smaller firms managing to keep the reins more firmly in their hands. The nature of the decisions involved and the conditions under which they are carried out will also shape the outcome. In the early years of reform, buyers operating far from the firm in other parts of the country were given great freedom to act on their own initiative simply owing to the poor state of communications. Nowadays, fax machines and mobile phones have left them less freedom to act without consultation. The move back towards the centre has been prompted by the widespread practice of giving kickbacks, leading managers to take a keener interest in how the matter is conducted now they have the means to hand.

One popular way of regulating delegation has been to extend the 'one manager responsibility' contracts down into the company. Contracts are drawn up with divisional, factory and workshop managers, setting a range of targets that they undertake to meet. One factory manager's views on how this operates in practice is given in Box 3.8.

Box 3.8 The factory manager

The following remarks are taken from an interview with a factory manager. The factory is situated alongside several others belonging to the same diesel engine company, at its main site.

In the past, under the collective leadership, it seemed that everybody was taking responsibility, but in reality, nobody was held responsible for anything. Our company started the 'one manager responsibility system' last year. The system applies to division managers, factory managers and workshop managers.

Under the system, as a factory head, I sign a contract with the division head promising to achieve targets in revenue, profit, cost, inventory, and keeping the machines in good working order. The profit targets are not real, the factory does not sell the products to the company, we simply deliver the products to other departments. But the prices of the products are estimated according to the market.

In exchange, I am given power in making decisions regarding finance, personnel and production. But in financial matters, the company has many rules and conducts frequent checks. For example, the company states clearly how much cash flow a factory has to keep. And any cost exceeding 2000 yuan will have to be approved by the company, anything purchased exceeding 2000 yuan will have to be registered with the company as fixed assets.

Production is relatively easy. At the beginning of the year, the company gives me a plan. I simply follow it while trying to keep costs down. After completing the plan, we are encouraged to find orders for ourselves on the market. We are allowed to use the resources of the company for this purpose. We have our own salesman and can sign contracts with the customers. But the company handles the financial side of these contracts. The company also arranges our production plan for these orders. The company deducts the cost from the revenue of these extra orders and gives a third of the profit back to us. And we can distribute that as bonuses.

The procurement department of the company purchases materials for the production of the planned and extra-planned products. The factory pays for these materials to the procurement department through the company's internal bank. However, the price we pay is higher than the market because the procurement department has higher overheads. But to procure internally has the advantage of making sure of quality. Besides, the company will not let the factories handle financial matters.

I make suggestions about who should be the deputy factory manager and workshop managers. I submit my suggestions to the human resources department in the company. They then conduct all sorts of checks on these people and finally they nominate. But I can sack workers now without authorisation from the company.

It is very difficult to obtain permission to recruit people. The government regards our industry as energy consuming and environmentally polluting. So they will not allow us to expand. The company has already laid-off a third of its employees. I will need to apply for a quota from the human resources department. This quota will have to be approved by the government labour bureau.

Whether the one-manager responsibility system will lead to dictatorship depends on the individual. It also depends on the nature of business. If the business is mass production, then it will be difficult to be dictatorial. Sometimes the system can also lead to corruption, which is why the company keeps tight control on finance. There is still some participation in the management from the workers. In the 1980s, the policy was that everybody should participate. So everybody was given a role, such as family planning person, quality person, safety and security person, political stability person. Quality and safety are now taken over by the managers, but the rest are still taken up by the workers. These workers are compensated spiritually. For example, they are given titles such as 'civilised worker' and 'model worker'. There will be some bonuses for their work, but not much.

If the workers do not like the manager, they can complain to the manager at the next level up. Workers do not complain about business decisions, they complain about how you treat them. The workers evaluate the manager with three standards. First, whether the manager obeys the rules he has made himself. Second, whether the manager is using the workers to their full ability. And third, whether the manager emphasises quality control.

There is a lot of responsibility and pressure under this system. We have difficulties to pay for the laid off workers and provide welfare for the workers, including kindergarten fees for the children of employees. I would prefer not to have to pay for them, but this is a state-owned enterprise, if we don't pay then the state will have to pay. It is from the same pocket. The worst thing about the job is to have to deal with people and the greatest pressure is how to win the liking of the workers.

The compensation is not equal to the pressure I am under. But the company is not rich and we Chinese pay more attention to what people think of us. I will wait until the company is richer, then I will ask for more pay.

Interview, 2001

The workshop manager

Despite the reluctance to delegate, centrifugal forces are also at work, pushing in the opposite direction – taking power away from the top of the firm. Reforms to the industrial wage system have shifted a certain amount of power down into the hands of workshop managers. With the reforms has come a move from a standard wage system to one in which payment is more closely tied to output. Within many factories, workshops are allocated a flexible amount of wages related to output, and they then share this according to various criteria among the workers. As a result, the focus of worker interest and bargaining over wages has shifted to the workshop level, both in terms of the total allocated to it by the firm and the way in which this total is divided among the workers. This has changed the role of the workshop managers, placing them under increased pressure from both above and below. On the one hand, they must strive to satisfy their workers if they are to secure their cooperation in meeting the production quotas on which their own hopes of higher income rest. This leads to attempts to grant more money to the workers, even if this means finding ways around state and factory regulations. On the other hand, they face pressure from above. Senior managers, faced with budget constraints and the need to satisfy the bodies to which they owe their appointment, exert varying degrees of restraint. Workshop managers in this situation frequently find themselves in difficulties when general managers break wage deals that are proving more expensive than they had anticipated (You 1998: 139–40).

The closeness of the workshop managers to the shop floor often places their sympathies and interests on the side of expanding payment to their team. Securing worker cooperation is likely to loom larger in their minds than worries over labour costs or overall profitability. Yet at the same time as they are under pressure from their workers to meet with their demands, the managers' new powers over wage issues has strengthened their authority over the workshop. While dismissing workers may remain difficult, their ability to tighten work discipline and control absenteeism has increased alongside greater authority over setting pay.

Many workshop managers have also gained access to independent financial resources through having the workshop engage in moonlighting. This work can range from producing small orders to disposing of equipment belonging to the firm. Such activities are frequently carried out off the books, giving rise to numerous secret accounts, 'little gold safes', to strengthen the hand of the workshop manager.

Box 3.9 The little gold safe

At the accounting department of a major state-owned company, one of the authors asked the accountants about the practice of keeping a '*xiao jinku*' (little gold safe). The accountants all laughed. The chief accountant later explained:

The *xiao jinku* is a very sensitive topic. Everybody knows of its existence, but nobody talks about it. Only you come to ask us about it. The money for the little gold safe comes from several sources. For example, we actually employ less people than the figure we tell the government. These non-existent employees are paid salaries and bonuses every month. And this money goes into the *xiao jinku*. Or when we take money out from the official account to bribe officials, we write it down as entertainment costs. But occasionally the bribes are returned. But we cannot put the money back into the official account. So that also has to go into the *xiao jinku*. But the biggest chunk comes from the proceeds from our sideline businesses that the government does not know about. Also, a lot of business is done in cash without receipts, especially when we deal with private businesses. Proceeds from these deals go into the *xiao jinku* as well.

But we have good reason to keep the *xiao jinku*. The government has strict rules over bonuses, tours and other fringe benefits in order to protect the assets of the state. Companies have to find ways to get around this, so that everybody can have a good time. Also, when government officials come to visit the company, they expect to be treated well. But the state puts limits on how much we can spend on entertainment. So for occasions like this, the little gold safe is utterly necessary. Usually the *xiao jinku* is not kept in the accounting or finance department. The general manager will entrust it to a trustworthy person.

Fieldwork notes, 2001

On the other hand, centrifugal forces have at times proved stronger than many in the workshops and departments may have wished, as some large state enterprises have experimented with spinning off peripheral units in cost saving exercises, most notably those involved in the provision of services. Box 3.10 provides an illustration.

Box 3.10 The transport unit

Baosteel, a large state-owned steel manufacturer situated in Shanghai, has been trying, in accordance with suggestions from the government, to shed its service units such as the baths, dining halls, clinic and internal transportation. The reform started with the transport units. The transport units are under Baosteel's logistics company. This was instructed to shed its transport companies by simply giving the existing assets, the vehicles and the offices, to the companies and telling the managers and workers they must now shift for themselves. However, the Baosteel logistics company will continue to pay the companies to run a shuttle bus service within the plant. On the other hand, there will no longer be any shuttle buses to send staff and workers back and forth between home and work. The staff and workers are now given travel allowances and told to make their own arrangements.

The transport companies are expected to find other business, for example, shuttle services for other companies, or trips for schools. However, they cannot compete with public transportation because they do not have licences. In addition, the companies' staff and workers, as state employees, are paid much higher than is the norm in the Shanghai transportation industry. The Baosteel logistics company has little hope that the transport companies can make any profit. They cannot get anybody to lease the companies. Therefore, the target is for the transportation companies simply to support their staff. The companies have already shed 20 per cent of their workers by lowering the retirement age (females from 50 to 43; males from 60 to 52), although they still have to provide pensions and various other benefits to these workers. The transport companies are just managing to struggle along, mainly through relying on subsidiaries of their own, such as garages, which are making money. Given the difficulties experienced in the transport sector, the reform of other services has been put on hold.

Fieldwork notes, 2001

Getting on track: formalisation

From the late 1980s, an increasing number of firms within the state sector have refashioned their organisation along the lines of models drawn from abroad. Behind much of this adaptation has been an explicit desire to 'get on track' with international business practice, to follow the ways of companies operating in advanced market economies. At the level of corporate governance, this takes the form of adopting a company structure resembling that found in capitalist economies, complete with shareholders and board. Internally it has taken the form of greater formalisation, the drawing up of explicit rules and procedures to guide the running of the firm. Thus, some state firms have drawn up sets of organisational rules and established job descriptions, appointment procedures, promotion tests and grievance procedures. Nowadays, enquiries about whether a company has established such formal procedures will, in those state firms that pride themselves as being most 'on track', have the manager swivelling his computer screen towards you to scroll through one example after another.

Yet, many state enterprises appear quite content to continue in their old routines without the benefit of drawing up such explicit rules and procedures. What leads to this difference? Exposure to how foreign firms operate undoubtedly plays a part, with those state enterprises engaged in joint enterprises tending to pick up some of their practices and for these to spread to their other operations. Similarly, those state firms actively courting foreign joint venture partners often consciously seek to present themselves as suitable partners by adopting a structure and mode of operation that makes them appear to be on the same track. The educational background of the general manager is also of importance. State enterprises in which the general manager has an education in economics or business are more likely to introduce such formal procedures (Guthrie 1999).

Where it is occurring, however, the convergence with western practice may be less complete than it appears at first sight. The rules may appear similar, but their application differs. This is because, to take a distinction made by Max Weber, different forms of rationality are at work, one formal, one substantive (Weber 1978). Formal rationality entails the impersonal application of a rule applying equally to all within its scope. The aim is to keep exceptions to a minimum and to judge these by reference to earlier applications of the rule, to decide by reference to precedent. Substantive rationality is distinguished by a desire to judge each individual case on its merits, the rule serving merely as a rough guide in the hands of someone who should take full account of the specifics of the situation. Here, power lies not in the rule but in the person interpreting it. While all societies, institutions and organisations contain elements of both types of rationality, in China the balance has traditionally leaned more heavily than in the West toward substantive rationality and in many ways continues to do so. In such an atmosphere, the introduction of formal rules into a firm may serve not to replace the cultivation of personal ties and conflict between cliques, but for the rules to be pressed into the service of these cliques.

The decision-making process: strategic investment

Whether it is the differences between managerial practices in China and the West or the similarities between them that comes most readily to mind depends in part on the level of generality at which one operates. For all the cultural differences between the two, it is still possible, for example, to trace striking parallels in the process of decision making in the area of strategic investment. Strategic investment relates to such matters as introducing changes in existing capacity, technology, and product mix. In contrast to resources aimed simply at keeping the existing operation going, strategic investments will involve large amounts of capital and are generally viewed as open decisions within the company. Easterby-Smith and Gao (1996) have outlined these similarities in terms of the vision, the mechanism and the logic lying behind such decisions in the oil, chemicals and steel industries in Britain and China.

In large companies, all strategic investment decisions will need to pass through formal procedures to secure approval. Nevertheless, before this stage commences, the proposal will have undergone extensive informal discussion. By the time it is raised formally, it will form part of a consensus that will have emerged among senior managers concerning where the company should be headed and what it is going to do. After somebody in the company starts the initial idea, it will need to spread if it is to take hold and eventually to make its way to the attention of top management. Its spread can take place through channels ranging from informal chats and gossip through to notes and memos. The time it takes will be determined partly by how far the original source is from the centre: the lowlier the status of the originator, the longer the process of gestation. No matter which route the idea travels, however, it will be reshaped on its journey. In both China and Britain, it was found that managers involved in this stage of the process:

> do not simply pass on whatever they receive, they normally add their own views, preferences, interpretations and judgments, and delete the parts they do not like; they may also impede, or simply stop, the transmission. It is a process of screening, enhancing, refining, and altering the original proposal . . . this process is the main reason why investment proposals are rarely turned down by the formal examining procedures: an inappropriate proposal would have been killed well before any formal discussions on it had started.
> (Easterby-Smith and Gao 1996: 111)

For those ideas that survive this initial process, the next stage is to pass through the scrutiny of formal examination. This procedure may be written down or it may simply follow accepted convention, but in either event a definite routine will have been established. The course followed will, in part, be decided by the size of the investment. Each operating unit will have a certain ceiling on the amount of funds it can allocate to investment on its own authority: the larger the investment, the greater the likelihood that a higher level, the division, group or bureau to which they operating unit belongs, will have to give its permission. These limits are set so that mistakes by the organisation would not cause it more damage than it could sustain. They tend to be subject to frequent adjustment by higher authorities.

Outside contacts may have already been made on an informal basis during the earlier gestation period of the planned investment. Nonetheless, in China as in Britain, the project usually originates in the operating unit. Its managers assume responsibility for pushing the proposal along through all the intermediate levels until it reaches the person or body with the ultimate authority to give permission to proceed. The different levels apply different criteria as the proposal proceeds on its way up the hierarchy, with increasing consideration given to its broader principles and less to its technical aspects. Nevertheless, functional departments and their staff are active participants in the process, with senior management relying on their advice to judge the feasibility of the proposal. In this sense, they remain important gatekeepers, and power descends into the technostructure of the firm. As a manager of one of the Chinese oil companies included in the Easterby-Smith and Gao study put it: 'These functional departments are more serious than the ministers. If they don't say good things about your project, then the project cannot proceed' (Eastery-Smith and Gao 1996: 114).

Despite the established path followed once the formal proposal is floated, in both countries use of informal channels continues to be made by those responsible for pushing the proposal along. Use will regularly be made of informal and individual contacts to elicit opinions and to keep others on board. As one of the managers of a British chemical company explained:

> There is a general rule that you make sure that people feel that they have the opportunity to make comments and have influence, that you don't give them any surprises or put them in any embarrassing position . . . We involve them all as early as possible, even when it is still a vague idea. It is courtesy, good practice and strategic influencing at its best.
>
> (Easterby-Smith and Gao 1996: 114)

Attention also needs to be paid to formal standards laid down by higher authorities, parent companies in the case of the British operating units, and national regulations in the case of the Chinese. The low rate of rejection of proposals is largely due to the care taken to tailor the proposal to meet the requirements of the authorising bodies.

Just as the initial informal emergence of the vision and its subsequent formal assessment share common characteristics in China and Britain, so does the logic by which the investment projects are judged. In both cases, financial return is a key consideration. It is not, however, the only one. In addition, the attention of managers is taken up with three other considerations. These are company strategy, the technology involved, and the public relations image the plan projects.

Investment projects will be formed and shaped by how they contribute to the overall long-term growth and development of the organisation. This may be through the contribution the investment will offer in such areas as increasing market share, enhancing position in the industry, or removing external constraints. Shifting definitions of the business interests of the broader group within which the operating unit is located will shape the fate of investment proposals competing with those from other units. In addition to questions of strategy come technological considerations. With so much investment in industry driven by technology, contributions from the technical side of the business assume great importance in shaping the fate of a proposal. Technological considerations intertwine with others throughout the process of decision-making.

Companies in both China and Britain are also concerned with promoting a good image. Investment opportunities can be one means of achieving this. Quite just whom they are trying to impress and how they do so varies, however, from one country to another. In Britain, typical concerns are to impress customers with the appearance of a new plant, or by showing concern for the environment that goes beyond the standards set by regulatory bodies. Over half the cost of one investment proposal of a British chemical company reviewed by Easterby-Smith and Gao, for example, was made up of a treatment plant for discharged wastewater, even though the firm had permission from the water authorities to discharge this directly into the river. This, nevertheless, was thought to fall beneath rising public expectations. In the case of Chinese firms, the image held of the firm in the eyes of the government looms larger. As one manager in the case of a firm in the Chinese oil industry remarked on an investment project: 'The project is not very profitable for our company. But firstly it is of benefit for the state . . . the country needs the product, and secondly it is good for society in terms of employment. There are therefore invisible benefits' (Easterby-Smith and Gao 1996: 118).

Only those proposals that satisfy such strategy, technological and public relations criteria will make it through to financial evaluation. Taken together, however, the criteria are in the minds of managers right from the inception of investment proposals, filtering out weak ones and shaping the others as they progress through the system.

In broad outline, then, the process of decision-making follows a similar route in both China and Britain. It is only when we focus on specific details that differences begin to emerge. While managers in both Britain and China make use of informal and personal contacts with those at higher levels, Chinese managers employ them to a greater extent. Apart from any cultural predisposition in this direction, part of the difference is related to differing career patterns. British managers are subject to frequent moves, so that changes in the team promoting the project are more likely, leading to the need to rely more on formal channels. Chinese managers, in their turn, have often had experience working within the supervising bureaucracy and will have built up connections that can be called upon (Child and Lu 1993).

Technology and the structure of the firm

Gu (1999) has outlined the technological and market forces that have been at work in shaping the internal restructuring of firms in China. Gu identifies three internal structures: the U-form (Unified form), the H-form (Holding-company-like form) and the M-form (Multi-divisional form). In the first, the organisation has a centralised structure and divisions are not delegated the power to dispose of company assets. An H-form structure, in contrast, is decentralised, with the centre having little control over the divisions that control the corporate assets. In an M-form structure, the internal organisation is decentralised, but the centre retains effective strategic control over assets, protecting them from abuse on the part of the divisions.

Gu focuses attention on the interplay of two factors that draw a firm in the direction of one or another of these three forms of internal organisation. These factors are the number of market niches that the firm enjoys and the technological activities conducted to service them. Their influence is illustrated in Figure 3.1. Low diversification and technological processes that are highly interrelated are associated with U-forms. High diversification combined with little interrelation between processes favours H-forms, while a high number of market niches combined with a high level of interrelatedness between them exercises a pull towards M-forms.

The existence of these relationships is borne out by Gu's work on the restructuring of the machinery technology institutes in China, but the same considerations apply equally to other sectors of industry. Movement

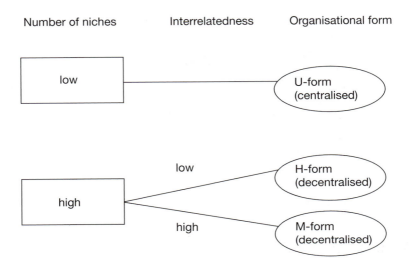

Key: U-form: Uniford form
H-form: Holding-company-like form
M-form: Multi-divisional form

Figure 3.1 *Alternative forms of internal organisation: influence of the number of niches and their interrelatedness (adapted from Gu 1999: 339)*

from one form to another is not always easy, however. In his study, Gu (1999) notes the difficulty experienced by a number of institutes in attempting to move from an H-form to an M-form. Part of this rests on a lack of the necessary internal accounting techniques, and part on resistance by departments used to greater independence under the previous H-form, a difficulty similar to that encountered by Shanghai Petroleum and Sinopec (Box 2.11).

Breaking the iron rice bowl

The reform of the employment system in state-owned enterprises has aimed at ending lifetime employment and cradle-to-grave welfare provision by the work unit. This was felt to have resulted in a number of problems, which the reforms hoped to address. The 'iron rice bowl' security of employment was linked to low productivity and lax labour discipline. Locating responsibility for the provision of a range of benefits, including housing, health care and pensions within the enterprise resulted in their bearing a burden often out of proportion to their performance.

The provision of such services by the work unit also made the prospect of shedding staff all the more difficult to contemplate.

State-owned enterprises under the planned economy did not recruit their workers. Instead, the enterprises were allocated an annual intake from the local labour bureau. They now enjoy freedom in their choice of new workers, but frequently continue to rely on drawing candidates from those recommended by the labour bureau. Many large, long-established state enterprises have vocational schools attached to them providing technical training for their workers. These schools also enrol children of employees and are expected to offer them work with the company if they successfully complete their education (Warner *et al.* 1999).

Command economies are characterised by a frozen wage structure, and the Chinese command economy was no exception. Low wages were, in part, compensated for by the provision of a broad range of welfare provision by the enterprise. With the reforms, however, providing these benefits became an increasing burden as wages began to rise. This was mainly the result of increased bonus payments tied to the performance of the firm and the individual worker. The aim was to replace Mao's faith in the power of ideology with Deng's recognition of the effectiveness of material incentives. This shift brought growing disparities in income between workers, in contrast to the more uniform and equal pattern of the past. Workers' incomes and the benefits the firm could afford to provide became more closely related to financial success. In his study of state enterprises in Shanghai, for example, Guthrie found the average annual salary of workers in the troubled electronics sector standing at around 7000 yuan in 1995, in contrast to those in the garment sector, where the average annual salary stood at over 11 000 yuan (1999: 80).

The reforms have also loosened the tie between the worker and the work unit. The guarantee of lifetime employment has increasingly been replaced by fixed term contracts. Contracts signed for one-, three-, or five-years leave the enterprise with no duty to renew beyond the stated period, although continuous employment for over ten years does entitle the worker to permanent status. In some cases, the introduction of contracts has been more symbolic than real, with workers being rarely, if ever, fired at the end of a contract or for failing to comply with the contract while it is in effect. Some of the managers in Guthrie's Shanghai survey reported this to be the case, but the great majority, over 86 per cent, claimed that they were now able to dismiss workers in such circumstances (Guthrie 1999: 94).

Box 3.11 Put out more flags

Despite the move from ideology to material incentives, mass mobilisation campaigns have by no means completely disappeared. Government officials and state enterprise managers often fall back on this method when facing difficult problems as one method with which they feel familiar.

Therefore, when government officials realised that the deadline they had set for the construction of a key project was not going to be met, and that, in addition, the quality of the work and safety measures had greatly deteriorated, they ordered a campaign to be waged on the site. The drive was to encourage harder work, while at the same time promoting greater attention to quality and safety standards.

A campaign office was set up on the site with all the senior managers of the project acting as the heads. Two middle managers were assigned to the routine work of the office. They contacted the municipal campaign office to obtain various guidelines on how to conduct the campaign. After a month of hard work, the rules and procedures of the campaign were drafted and approved by the municipal office and a date for the inauguration of the campaign was decided upon.

There was much preparation for the inauguration. All the construction teams had to raise banners with slogans on the site. The content of the slogan had to be approved by the site campaign office. The media were invited to broadcast the event. At the inauguration, government officials from various offices delivered speeches. Managers of the construction teams took turns to take pledges stating that they 'herewith promise to the government and the people, that the project will be built before the deadline set by the government, with international quality and a good safety record'.

However, despite all of this, nothing much followed after the inauguration apart from a wall chart reporting performance on the construction site. The wall chart contained the names of the construction teams, and each week the teams were given flags of different colours indicating how the teams were doing in areas such as speed, quality, safety, and willingness to help other teams. There were three different flags: red for excellent, yellow for good and green for normal. For the first month, the chart had many red flags, some yellow flags and one or two green flags. This did not mean that everything was going well on the site. On the contrary, quality and safety continued to deteriorate, and there was no sign that the deadline could be comfortably met.

Government officials called more meetings to push things along. One of the officials noticed that almost every team was given either a red or a yellow flag on the wall chart. He shouted at the manager in charge of the campaign, saying that the chart was not reflecting the real situation on the site. He wanted to see teams not performing well to be shown on chart, so that they could be taken to task. People at the meeting all laughed, including the official. The manager in charge of the campaign promised that black flags would be given.

The next week, there was a black flag on the chart, but the flag was not given to any team, it was in a note of warning only. For the rest of the campaign, every team continued to have many red flags, some yellow flags and one or two green flags. At the end of the first leg of the campaign, every team was given a bonus, totally unrelated to their performance and flag rating.

Fieldwork notes, 2001

The greater freedom that many state-owned enterprises have enjoyed recently in adjusting the size of their workforce has been reflected in the increasing number of workers who have been made redundant from state enterprises. This figure grew throughout the 1990s to reach a peak in the three-year programme that was aimed at turning round loss making state-owned enterprises and which began in 1998. Redundancies from state enterprises have swollen the unemployment total. Just how large this total is, is impossible to state with any confidence given the widely acknowledged gross inadequacy of official statistics on the matter (Solinger 2001). The World Bank, without citing sources, estimates 21 million state enterprise workers were laid off between January 1998 and September 2000. This needs to be set against a background of 110.4 million employed in state-owned urban enterprises in 1997 to gain an idea of the scale of the redundancies (World Bank 2001a). Just where the axe falls is not determined by financial performance alone. Some enterprises are seen by the government as being too big to be allowed to fail. Others can be closed with less risk of sparking social unrest. The textile industry in Shanghai, for example, was an early target for drastic downsizing, a fate not unrelated to its largely female workforce.

For those unfortunate enough to become unemployed, the range of help they can expect varies enormously and has little to do with their needs and everything to do with the nature of the work unit from which they came. Workers laid off by state firms, for example, fare better than those from collectives. An official in Wuhan explained this to Solinger as due to state firms being able to rely on the state to subsidise them, as they are its property. Collectives, on the other hand, belong to the 'labouring masses', who, evidently, can shift for themselves (Solinger 2001: 684).

In accordance with this logic, the best treated among the unemployed are those entitled to permanent status with a state enterprise, who have nonetheless been laid off or 'stood down' (*xiagang*). The work unit continues to exist and is regarded as having some continuing responsibility towards these workers. If it is prospering, they will receive a substantial severance payment or monthly allowance. They also have the right to enter a re-employment centre that provides training and assists with finding jobs. They will also have preferential treatment in obtaining permits should they wish to set up in business on their own. For those from state enterprises that are losing money, the situation is bleaker. Allowances from such firms are smaller or non-existent. In the latter case they may be able to get unemployment assistance, but only if their firm has contributed to the local fund.

Lower down the line there are those whose firms have gone bankrupt. These are the officially registered unemployed. If their firm did not contribute to the unemployment insurance fund, they will not receive any unemployment pay. Consequently, they will not be counted in the unemployment figures. In a worse position still are those laid off from 'double-stop' firms, firms that have stopped production and stopped all payments. These, however, are not officially recognised as having closed. They are not allowed to go bankrupt, as priority on any amounts realised goes to providing for the workers, present and retired. Debts owed to other state institutions such as the banks would have to be written off. In such circumstances, the authorities may prefer to leave the defunct firm in suspended animation rather than allowing it to be wound up. The workers have no work to do and no salary but, still having a work unit, are not unemployed and cannot claim unemployment benefit. At the bottom of the heap are the migrant workers from the countryside who have no entitlements whatsoever. This profusion of different categories means unemployment serves to perpetuate divisions between different types of worker, rather than drawing them together in their common plight. Added to considerations of cost, the prospect of conjuring up such unity may well deter any attempt to unify a system that sits at ease with a broader cultural tendency to treat people on the basis of their affiliations rather than as isolated individuals.

Redundant state enterprise workers who are lucky enough to secure re-employment elsewhere will often find themselves in occupations very different from the factory work they were used to. Most end up in the service sector, often in temporary or insecure positions. Many take to street trading. Re-employment centres follow a similar strategy. A popular job creation project for the re-employment centres in Shanghai, for example, is to equip their clients with tickets and to assign them a stretch of the street to patrol as wardens collecting fees from cyclists for parking their bicycles.

Trade unions and the Workers' Assembly

Within state enterprises, there exist two bodies charged with representing the interests of the workers, the trade union and the Workers' Assembly. An idea of how they fit in with the leadership system of the enterprise is presented in Figure 3.2. The relationships are complex and can only be suggested in rough outline in such a form. The standing of the various

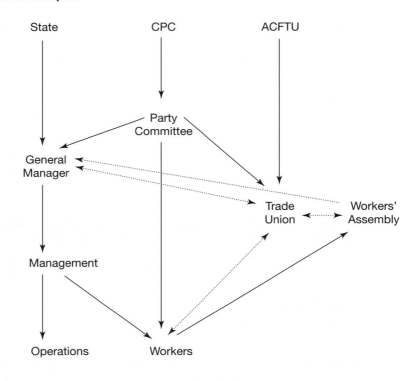

Key:
    ——▶ Indicates an authority link.
    ┈┈▶ Indicates similar links but of a weak or unclear kind.
    ◀┈┈▶ Indicates reciprocal links of authority or influence.

CPC: Communist Party of China
ACFTU: All-China Federation of Trade Unions

Figure 3.2 *Leadership in the state enterprise (adapted from Child 1994: 67)*

bodies *vis-à-vis* each other is liable to shift from one enterprise to the next. Nevertheless, the chart is interesting in a number of ways. In its initial form, it was taken from the work of Child (1994). This was shown to the managers interviewed by the authors in China in 2001. All immediately recognised it as representing a close approximation to the situation prevailing in their enterprise. This was as true of those enterprises that had adopted a joint-stock form as those that had not, suggesting that the newly adopted forms of governance had not altered the basic underlying structure of the enterprise as much as might be supposed. In the course of our discussions, the managers suggested a number of modifications to the original version of the chart and we have incorporated these into the version presented here. In particular, they frequently suggested moving the Party committee away from its original position of parallel with the general manager to a position above him or her. They explained that, although the position of the Party had declined during the earlier years of the reform from above the general manager to being level, in recent years it had regained a degree of its former pre-eminence.

While there are a number of different trade unions organised according to industry, all operate under the control of the All-China Federation of Trade Unions (ACFTU). The purpose of the trade union within the state enterprise is not solely, nor indeed primarily, improving terms and conditions of employment. In addition to safeguarding the rights and interests of workers, the unions are also required to take into account the interests of the country as a whole. Other aims are helping members to participate in the running of their work units, mobilising the workforce to raise productivity, and educating the workforce to be better members of society. Like so many other bodies in China, the ACFTU also runs its own enterprises, employing over one million workers (Ng and Warner 1998: 39–40).

Union membership is concentrated in the state-owned enterprises, where membership is more or less automatic. While the unions take an interest in the everyday welfare of their members, they do not bargain freely on their behalf to settle wage levels as they do in Western countries. Welfare takes second place to fostering a commitment to production among the workforce. As a result, the workforce expects little of the unions. White (1996), for example, found only a low level of trust in the trade union on the part of factory workers in the north-east region of the country. Only 13 per cent saw their union as representing their interests, while 41 per cent saw it as an instrument for ensuring compliance within the workplace. Alternatives, however, are unavailable, as independent trade unions are outlawed by the government, possibly mindful of the example set by Solidarity in Poland. The docility on the part of their union has, on occasion, provoked workers to various forms of indirect and unofficial action on a local basis in support of claims. As Naughton remarks, managers have found themselves at times 'nearly helpless if a group of disgruntled workers chose to disrupt production through slowdowns or industrial absenteeism' (Naughton 1995: 105).

Another avenue to which workers can resort to settle grievances is to take the matter to the local Labour Arbitration Committee. In 1999, these committees handled 120 000 cases nationally, involving over 473 000 workers, an increase of 28 per cent over the previous year. Thirty-seven per cent of the cases related to pay, 24 per cent to breaches of contracts, 24 per cent to welfare provision, and 7 per cent to laid off workers' living allowances (State Development Research Centre 2000). Younger workers appear more ready to make use of the Labour Arbitration Committees. Principally this stems from their being more likely to be employed under a fixed-term labour contract. Another reason is that, having been brought up during the period of reform, they are also more aware of the legal shifts and innovations that have accompanied the introduction of the contract system. The banners one sees in workshops exhorting the workers to 'Study the Labour Law' have evidently borne fruit in this group (Guthrie 1999: 70).

The Workers' Assembly was set up to give the workers a voice in the running of the enterprise. The workforce freely elects its members, although sometimes with fixed quotas for the number of representatives to be drawn from different sections, such as women, and old and young employees. Almost all state enterprises have an assembly, but the frequency with which it meets and the influence it enjoys varies. In smaller firms, meetings tend to be called rarely, if at all. In other enterprises, they may be scheduled at one, two, three, or even, in a few cases, four times a year. The meetings serve for general managers to report on the business plan and finances of the firm and anticipated changes to its structure. For the representatives of the workers the meetings serve as a forum to voice their concerns, especially in areas such as terms and conditions of employment. Some have votes on matters such as organisational reform, but these are rare. In theory, the Assembly has a right of veto, but in practice this is never exercised and the extent to which its views are solicited and listened to depends largely on the attitude of the general manager.

Box 3.12 The trade union official

The following is taken from an interview with a part-time union official.

How did I get elected as a trade union official in the company? Well, one afternoon I received a call from the head of the trade union in the company. He said that a former colleague in our office had been acting as a trade union official. Now that he had left the company, could we choose another person from our office instead? I asked around and one colleague said, why don't you do it yourself? I thought I wouldn't mind, there is nothing much to do, after all. So, that's how I became a trade union official. For the election of the trade union in our parent company last year, the company asked one or two representatives from each office and sent them to the parent company. They were given a list of names, about 12 or 13, and they were asked to choose ten. We were not consulted about that list. But the head of the trade union has to be a Party member, we all know that.

I am now in charge of the finance. It is very simple. I collect the membership fees, but that's not difficult because they are deducted from the wages automatically every month. At the end of the year, I tell the union how much we have and the union will decide to buy things like cooking oil and shampoo to distribute to the workers. That's about all we do really.

The Workers' Assembly is relatively more important than the trade union now. When we have problems, we now go to the Worker's Assembly instead of the union. For example, when we wanted the company to have a security guard and to employ some cleaners for the company's housing blocks, we went to the Workers' Assembly. They talked to the management directly. I heard in some factories, the Workers Assembly can have a say about the content of the labour contract. The company has an office called the Associations Office. The Workers' Assembly is under the leadership of the office, together with other associations such as the youth league, women's association, the United Front, and the trade union.

Interview, 2001

4 Taking the capitalist road

- The return of the entrepreneur
- Red hats and roundabout investment
- Family business
- Finance
- Subsidiaries and diversification
- Creditable conduct
- Government relations
- Business associations

No neat divide exists in China between the public sector of the economy and the private. Hybrid forms of ownership span the two domains. Private firms pretend to be public and public firms spawn private offshoots. The scene has changed dramatically from the pre-reform era. Then, those bold enough to engage in private trade might find themselves reviled as 'capitalist tails' – leftovers from the days before nationalisation had severed the head of capitalism in the 1950s. 'Better socialist weeds than capitalist flowers' was the proud boast of slogans.

Much of this has melted away. Now members of the public sector, frequently with the blessing of the authorities, weigh the merits of leaving to join private enterprises or to start their own, with many going on to take the plunge into the turbulent waters of commerce (*xia hai*). Shifting attitudes were endorsed in 1999 by a constitutional amendment that gave recognition to private enterprise as a legitimate and important contributor to the economy, albeit one not completely on a par with the public sector.

And of growing importance it undoubtedly is. Judging the exact size, character and performance of the private sector is, however, far from easy. Official figures often fail to distinguish between sectors in any clear fashion – an understandable vagueness in the face of the ambiguity in property rights that exists on the ground. In addition, a large black economy escapes the official trawl. Given this situation, any figure must be at best a rough approximation. One of the best figures in recent times comes from the analysis conducted by the International Finance Corporation (IFC), the wing of the World Bank charged with promoting private enterprise. It calculated that the share of gross domestic product generated by the officially registered self-employed and private businesses amounted to 13 per cent in 1998. To this, however, must be added some allowance for enterprises registered as collectives that nevertheless are run substantially as private concerns. The IFC estimates that these account for a further 13 per cent of gross domestic product, bringing the figure of private enterprises up to 26 per cent. Adding to this the output generated by foreign-owned enterprises provides a further 6 per cent, resulting in an overall percentage of gross domestic product attributable to the private sector of 32 per cent. Debatably, this could be expanded still further by adding the percentage of output from agriculture, a figure of 18 per cent, on the basis that most farming has, following the end of collectivisation, been placed in the hands of individual farmers. This would raise the amount of output flowing from the private sector still further to roughly half of the gross domestic product (International Finance Corporation 2000: 18). This leaves China with what is very much a mixed economy, but mixed, as we shall see, in a manner quite its own.

The return of the entrepreneur

The pronouncements of the Chinese Communist Party's Central Committee in December 1978 are widely taken as the starting point of the reform movement. This event marked a clear shift in emphasis towards economic growth by means of market mechanisms and individual incentives and away from a reliance on inspiring ideological commitment as a source of economic development. While not mentioning private enterprise specifically, it gave the green light to experimental moves that had already started in this direction. Nevertheless, many regarded private enterprise as of dubious morality and its scope was limited accordingly. Small individual businesses (*getihu*) were confined to employing no more than seven workers.[1] Such sole proprietorships did not enjoy limited liability and were forbidden to pool their capital. It was not until 1988 that regulations legalised limited-liability privately owned companies (*siying qiye*) that had no limit on the numbers they could employ.

In the interim, private entrepreneurs had developed a number of ways to get round the restrictions limiting their size and sphere of operations.

Some were simply given permission by local authorities to overstep the limits set to *getihu*. Others paid an administrative fee to a state or collective unit, sheltering under their name to circumvent government restrictions on private firms and political harassment. This practice continues to this day, despite central directives ordering private enterprises to 'take off the red hat'.

The growth of the private sector has not been smooth. Often it grew in directions unanticipated and ignored by official regulation, only to be met with rectification campaigns aimed at tightening control over it. It also suffered in the clampdown following the suppression of the pro-democracy demonstrations in 1989. Private enterprise found itself subject to close scrutiny. This was not only because it was suspected of lacking loyalty to the regime, although there was an element of this. More salient was the support for the demonstrations that arose from popular discontent with growing corruption; a practice widely associated in the public mind with private business. As a result, political and economic restraint on private business was tightened and the number of registered private companies (*siying qiye*) declined from 90 600 at the end of 1989 to 88 000 by June 1990. Some firms were transformed into collectives, while others had the numbers they employed reduced to below eight.

This proved but a temporary reversal. The 1990s were to see a dramatic surge in growth, most notably in the immediate aftermath of Deng Xiaoping's southern tour in 1992, in which he spoke out in favour of pressing forward with reform more boldly. Between 1991 and 1997, the average annual growth rate in the number of private companies was 46 per cent. Over the same period, the numbers they employed rose at an average annual rate of 41 per cent, and their output by an annual average of 71 per cent (see Table 4.1). This growth has been propelled in large measure by management characteristics shared with successful Chinese business systems overseas, most notably in the retention of control by owners combined with extensive informal networking between firms (Montagu-Pollock 1991).

Red hats and roundabout investment

As mentioned above, private enterprises have often found it to their advantage to register as having collective ownership rather than as privately owned businesses. This wearing of a 'red hat' has provided them with several advantages. It brings with it, according to the particular

Table 4.1 *Private firm development 1991 to 1997*

Year	Number of firms (thousands)	Number of employees (thousands)	Value of output * (RMB billions)
1991	107.8	1839.0	93.7
1992	139.6	2318.4	116.0
1993	237.9	3726.3	260.1
1994	432.2	6483.4	551.7
1995	654.5	9559.7	1005.3
1996	819.3	11 711.3	1592.3
1997	960.7	13 492.6	1983.7

* In 1995 constant prices
Sources: International Finance Corporation (2000: 11); *Yearbook of China Industrial and Commerce Administrative Management, 1992–1998; China Statistical Yearbook, 1992–1998*

arrangement arrived at, a degree of local government involvement in the enterprise, which can be beneficial in terms of access to land, assets, finance and markets. Concessions on local taxes and fees available to collectives also become available. On the other hand, there are drawbacks. Too close integration can, at times, entail the enterprise taking on some of the negative aspects of state-owned enterprises, with the entrepreneur taking profits in the event of success, but with the local authority saddled with the losses in the event of failure.

At times, however, the degree of involvement can be remote. Private enterprises may simply pay a management fee to an established collective or local state firm that takes no active role in the enterprise operating under its aegis. This 'getting backing' (*guakao*) is often done to gain the right to engage in business monopolised by the state sector (see Box 4.1). Alternatively, collective firms may simply be rented out in their entirety to private entrepreneurs, who then proceed to operate them as their own.

The division between the private and the public sector is thus at times obscure, and often intentionally so. Some private firms seek to dress themselves in the aura of public bodies, giving themselves titles such as 'service department' and bringing on board local cadres as advisors or board members. The level of domestic private investment is also clouded by the practice of 'round tripping' by which private entrepreneurs set up firms outside the mainland through which to funnel investment back into

Box 4.1 *Guakao* – the art of getting backing

No walls can resist a penetrating wind.

Although the private sector is forbidden to operate in a number of restricted areas, ways can usually be found to get round such barriers. One way is through the practice of *guakao*, of getting backing from a state unit that faces no such restriction. Publishing, for example, has for long been jealously guarded as the 'throat and tongue' of the Party and placed off limits for the private sector. Nevertheless, even here ways can be found for private companies to run papers.

According to one private owner of a highly successful job recruitment paper, the trick is to *guakao* with a state unit that has a licence to publish a journal, but is unable to make any money out of it. As he explained:

> Our *guakao* unit is a ministry of the central government. As part of its function, it runs a newspaper for the returned overseas Chinese. Of course, they cannot make money out of it in spite of their state subsidies. So they were delighted when we approached them. The arrangement is very simple. We pay them an annual fee, and for that they allow us to publish our paper as a supplement to their paper. We can have our own name for our paper, but we have to state that we are a supplement, though in small print.
>
> Two years ago, we wanted to sell the paper because we had made a lot of money and we wanted to do e-commerce, more interesting than advertising jobs. A British company wanted to buy the business. We had many rounds of talks. But they could not make up their mind because we did not have a licence. We told them most people do not have a proper licence and that if the ministry chucks us, we can always find somebody else to *guakao*. In China, if you are bound by the regulations, you end up doing nothing. But they could not understand this and we could not understand why they were so afraid.

> Fieldwork notes, 2001

the country. This enables them to benefit from permission to set up joint ventures with state enterprises and also to benefit from the tax concessions these enjoy.

Family business

It is generally observed that as firms grow in the size and complexity of their business they tend to adopt more formal modes of operation. This can affect a range of legal, financial, governance and market matters. Small firms at start-up require little in the way of such formal arrangements. What is notable about Chinese private enterprises is that they tend to retain the informality that characterises this stage as they grow and mature. This has a number of benefits in the Chinese context, although it is not entirely without cost.

Chinese private firms pose few agency problems in terms of the separation of ownership and control. The owner continues, in the great majority of cases, to play an active role in the management of the enterprise as its chief executive. As the business grows, however, there comes the point at which some delegation of managerial authority becomes unavoidable. With it comes the inevitable possibility of a rift in interests between the owner as principal and the manager as agent. As one might expect from the centrality of the family to Chinese society, this problem has been regularly resolved by appointing family members to key management positions. One medium-size private firm encountered in a survey of firms in Wenzhou typifies the pattern. With a turnover of 300 million yuan a year, it makes analytical devices for the chemical industry. 'The father is the chairman of the board, the mother is the office manager, the eldest daughter is the general manager, the son is the vice-general manager, the second daughter is the financial manager, the second son-in-law is the sales manager, the sister-in-law is charge of general affairs in the office, and the nephew is the purchasing manager' (International Finance Corporation 2000: 23).

Family members are usually brought on board in an order of precedence based on degrees of proximity and trust. For the smallest firms this will be limited to immediate family, parents and children. As the demands on management grow beyond what the nuclear family can provide, the next preference is to make use of siblings. Married sisters, however, tend to be suspect. Having 'married out' they are considered to now owe allegiance to the family of their husband. Bringing in nephews, nieces and cousins may prove necessary as the firm grows, but it is a move best avoided if possible. Lacking the incentive that sons have to add to the family wealth, these relations are widely viewed as likely to prove idle spendthrifts (Wank 1999: 101–2).

The potential for using this device, so characteristic of Chinese capitalism overseas, will in the future inevitably be held in check within China itself by the effects of the one-child policy. While it is possible for richer entrepreneurs to circumvent the policy, their ability to do so is nonetheless limited. Consequently, growth must be restrained or outside managers employed. Even where they are, however, the owner is likely to remain an active participant and to retain control over major decisions. Professional managers in family firms may well find themselves relegated to the middle levels and are not expected to exercise initiative to any marked degree.

With regard to their relationship with their employees, many entrepreneurs will actively seek to cast themselves in the role of benevolent father or concerned elder brother. This may take the form of celebrating festivals together, or displaying concern for an employee's personal affairs. Such behaviour is not entirely founded on disinterested benevolence, however, as the entrepreneurs themselves are quick to admit. Cultivating a family atmosphere is openly advocated as good for business, increasing loyalty and diminishing friction. Public displays of concern for an employee can also be manipulated to give face, cultivating a sense of gratitude and obligation.

The treatment accorded to the workforce tends, however, to distinguish between locals and those from elsewhere. The effect is partly one of divide and rule, separating the workforce in terms of sympathies and putting local supervisors over migrant workers to guard against complicity between the two. Just where the line falls between *us* and *them*, insiders and outsiders, can vary, and vary in a way that once again reveals the element of calculation behind what seems at first sight pure sentiment. In trade, for example, the definition of who is an insider and who is an outsider is narrower than in manufacturing, where workers are less likely to have money passing through their hands.

Migrant rural workers are generally allocated the most strenuous work and given the poorest pay. They also often frequently have to make do with poor accommodation in cramped dormitories within the factory grounds. Their poor conditions of service are partly accounted for by their high turnover rate and lack of skills, but they also reflect the fact that, in the event of them lodging complaints about the company, the local authorities are unlikely to take their part against the local business. Entrepreneurs are more concerned to maintain good relations with their local employees, however, as few are in an entirely unimpeachable position with regard to tax and other matters. Antagonised local workers are more likely to resort to complaints than simply to pack their bags and move on. They are also likely to be better placed to make their complaints strike home.

Reporting of business irregularities is also a danger faced from disgruntled neighbours and former colleagues spurred on by envy at an entrepreneur's success. The 'red-eye disease' is particularly characteristic of small towns among those who have not benefited from the market economy and who have felt themselves pushed back in the face of their neighbour's success. It is also bolstered by the egalitarian ideology common to communism and peasant society. Given the fragile position of private enterprises in relation to many of their official obligations, this envy can pose a very real threat, one to which the prospects of vandalism can be added. To meet this, one finds in some localities entrepreneurs taking on neighbours and former colleagues in a part-time capacity (Wank 1999: 105–7). Where this happens one often finds the close relationship to such workers enshrined in the language. They are 'neighbours' (*linju*) and their work is referred to as 'help' (*bangmang*). Full-time migrant workers, in contrast, are simply called 'workers' (*gongren*) and their work counts as 'labour' (*zuo gong*).

Finance

Private companies in China are widely believed to keep three sets of books: one for the tax authorities, one for the bank, and one for themselves. To be fair, it must be acknowledged that the popularity of the manipulation of accounts in this manner is not confined to the private sector. As mentioned earlier, the state sector is far from immune. However, this in part accounts for the practice of negotiating tax bills, for given that the returns tax offices have to work with are assumed by all concerned to be unreliable, some more realistic figure has to be arrived at. Unfortunately, this results in a vicious circle. Firms fear the tendency of the authorities to pick upon those firms known to have resources, ratcheting up demands for taxes and targeting such firms for a variety of *ad hoc* fees and fines. Local Industrial and Commercial Bureaux, for example, have quotas for fines. As the period for these to be fulfilled draws near, those businesses thought to have resources are more likely to find themselves having infringed one requirement or another than their less wealthy neighbours. In some localities, return visits are not unknown if it is felt the business can bear the weight. Given the power of the Bureau to grant or withdraw licences, there is no option but to pay unless one can call upon the right connections. In the face of such a regulatory environment, managers view manipulating accounts to hide company resources as a necessary defensive strategy.

The unreliability of accounts also explains the reluctance of banks to make advances to firms without government backing, for they have little

Box 4.2 The White Gang and the Black Gang

Mr Gu, the owner of a retail chain in Shanghai, had this to say on the topic of taxes and fees:

> I have to pay 1.5 per cent of my revenue as a management fee to the local council and a profit tax, which is 6 per cent, and all sorts of other fees and levies. I can't remember all the names, but adding them up they can amount to a lot of money: flood control fee, air raid fee, voluntary army service fee, education fee . . . The voluntary army service fee is quite a lot, 5 per cent of the profit. We call tax and levy collectors the White Gang. In the past, when the White Gang visited, they would demand you fed them and gave them gifts. Now, though, this is much better. There is also the Black Gang. They demand protection money. . . .
>
> Because of the economic downturn now, all of us are having a hard time. So if everybody paid tax according to the state regulations, then nobody would earn enough to live on and would have to close down. The government knows not everyone is reporting truthfully. They still ask us to report our revenue and profit, but will send officials round to fix a tax rate according to the business size and the number of employees. But everybody *tuoshui taoshui* (evades tax). The local bureaux know all about it. It is a compromise on both sides.

Interview, 2001

reliable data on which to assess risk or performance. Even when accounts are audited, the auditing profession in some areas stands in such low regard as to be discounted by banks for doing little more than acting as a rubber stamp (International Finance Corporation 2000: 53).

The misreporting of such matters as financial flows, assets and employee numbers has advantages in the form of evading not only tax, but also restrictions on registration under different categories of incorporation. The resulting lack of any formal structure makes it difficult to identify who owns assets, who controls the firm, and how management decisions are made. It gives to private enterprise a continuing air of shady practice that adds to the reluctance of banks to advance credit, especially as credit officers are held personally responsible for the loans they agree. To have a loan go wrong to the private sector risks greater suspicion as to why it was advanced in the first place.

On their side, private businesses can be deterred by the time and cost involved in applying for bank loans. Sound prospects seldom speak for themselves. Typically, relationships need to be cultivated and favours given to a number of branch officials. A welter of official documents has to be gathered and the associated fees paid. In the absence of collateral, guarantors have to be sought and recompensed. Start-up capital is, in consequence, almost invariably from principal owners, start-up teams and their families. One study puts the figure at 90 per cent of the initial capital coming from such sources, leaving self-financing in China higher than other transitional economies, and much higher than the United States. The same study showed that, as one might expect, the amount of bank loans to private firms in China as a proportion of additional finance following start-up did increase with the size of firms. It rose from under 4 per cent for those with less than 51 employees to 25 per cent for those with over 500 (International Finance Corporation 2000: 48–49). Much of this increased access to bank loans can be attributed to the greater collateral available to larger firms that have acquired long-term land use rights.

The current climate in China still leads private firms to seek loans from sources other than the state banks. Most have at one time or another made use of the informal market for loans, usually relying on family and friends, where reputation and relationship can substitute for collateral. It tends to be of a short-term nature, often allowing the purchase of materials for an order followed by repayment upon settlement. An advantage over bank loans is the greater flexibility of informal loans in terms of duration and the possibility of a grace period. They are also far easier to arrange and charge interest at much the same rate as official institutions. On the negative side, once one moves beyond one's immediate circle, problems of default and cheating rise sharply.

Another avenue for finance has been the semi-formal credit associations organised by local governments. These attracted savings through higher rates of interest and offered loans to local firms, but many directed these more according to local political pressure than sound financial assessment. The resulting problems led to an edict from the national government ordering the closure of these associations. They manage to survive nonetheless in some localities where they have established a sound track record, such as in Wenzhou. As mentioned earlier in discussing the banking system, semi-official banks have also tended to spring up with the support of local governments and because of the unfulfilled demand for loans. They lead a somewhat precarious existence, facing the likelihood of closure should they attract the attention of the banking authorities.

Box 4.3 The Tailong Credit Association

In 1993, a 28 year old, Wang Jun from the Luqiao District of Taizhou City in Zhejiang province, managed to gather one million yuan with a group of partners to start a credit association in two rented rooms with seven employees.

Before this, Wang had worked first in a pawnshop and later in a state-owned enterprise. His first job had made him realise the desperation of private business owners in his home district for bank loans. His second job made him understand the deficiencies of state-owned enterprises and gave him the confidence to compete with them.

Wang's credit association tries to do what the state banks do not care to do: target small businesses; provide loans no matter how small; make quick decisions on loans; link loan performance with staff payment; and dismiss inadequate employees. Wang insists his staff stand to serve in order to break with the off-hand manner with which clients are treated in state banks. Customers can also come to see the bank manager after supper. Wang has a 10 per cent share in the bank. 'It's our own money,' he remarks, 'so naturally we take good care of it and find good ways to make it grow.'

In six years, Tailong has made 6.2 billion yuan worth of loans, which is 17 per cent of the local market share, and made a profit of 62 million yuan.

Wang Jun has high ambitions. 'If I am allowed, I should like to do business beyond this district, for example, to expand my business to Taizhou city. Give me two years and I could increase current deposits from 2 billion to 10 billion . . . I want to do business in Shanghai in four years' time. Now, I cannot compete, I need to train the staff. If only I am allowed.'

Source: *Nanfang Zhoumo*, 7 December 2000: 10

Seeking finance through listing on the stock exchange has been extremely restricted as far as private firms have been concerned. Many would wish to if possible. Those in hi-technology firms, in particular, see it as a means of providing incentives to key employees and managers in an industry that is knowledge-intensive. More generally however, the domestic stock market is eyed by private entrepreneurs much as it is by state enterprises, as a source of windfall finance from an institution characterised by price manipulation and speculative swings that makes little in the way of demands on those listed. So attractive has this proved that some firms have sought to circumvent barriers to entry through purchasing their way into state companies that have already listed, 'borrowing the shell for the egg'.

Subsidiaries and diversification

Private business in China shares with a number of state industries a tendency for firms to grow into conglomerates spanning a number of related and unrelated businesses. This can be seen in the results of the national survey of private firms conducted by the International Finance Corporation. Of the firms surveyed, 28 per cent had one subsidiary, 22 per cent had two, 27 per cent had three to five, and 24 per cent more than five. Thirty-eight per cent said that there was no connection between the goods or services produced by themselves and those of their subsidiaries. Thirty-three per cent reported that they were part of a conglomerate. The portrait of the average conglomerate to emerge from the survey was of one that employed 1127 workers, and achieved revenue of 150 million yuan (18 million dollars) and a profit of 20 million yuan (2.4 million dollars), making it roughly equivalent to an average size state-owned enterprise (International Finance Corporation 2000: 27–28).

As is the case with Chinese enterprises overseas, all these different activities of domestic private enterprises tend to be organised into separate legal entities rather than as formal subsidiaries or divisions of the parent company. Family ties rather than legal definition mediates control and coordination. This renders the structure and finances of the organisation more difficult to penetrate. It also makes takeovers more difficult as parent companies do not exercise legal control over subsidiaries. At the same time, it makes unbundling of activities easier.

In the case of the private sector, diversification is traceable to a variety of factors. One is the attempt to lower exposure to economic and regulatory risk. Rapid changes in market conditions and government regulations expose firms to different risks in different sectors of the economy. The lack of complete correlation between these makes it possible to reduce risk by operating in different areas simultaneously. Where the climate for business is less certain, diversification seems more prevalent. This may partly explain why private enterprises in China seem to diversify more widely than is typical of Chinese businesses in Hong Kong (Redding 1993).

Another factor in diversification is the failure of markets. In the capital market, such failure invites ventures into unrelated businesses as opportunities arise. Diversification also allows the matching of a business with uneven cash flows, such as property development, with one with a more steady income, such as a department store. In an atmosphere where market transactions can be costly in terms of reliability and risk, extending vertically to incorporate units upstream or downstream is also encouraged. A degree of vertical integration is also frequently encouraged through inviting suppliers or customers to invest in the company.

Creditable conduct

Many private enterprises are unwilling to advance credit to one another due to the difficulty in establishing creditworthiness. There is a natural move in such circumstances towards establishing stable long-term relationships between suppliers and customers. While private business relies heavily upon the faceless market to find customers and suppliers, there is a natural desire to move towards cementing stable long-term relationships to safeguard transactions. With great reliance on trust inescapable, there is a preference to follow lines laid down by prior connections, to make connections vouched for by introductions through family and friends.

The need to establish trustworthiness is further strengthened where resorting to the law to seek redress is not viewed as a viable option. Partly this lies in distrust of the courts and their impartiality, especially if the dispute should happen to involve government agencies (see Box 4.4). But partly it flows from a sense among those involved in business that to become entangled in the law is to risk being branded as unable to deal with people in a proper manner (*budongde zenme zuoren chushi*). This approach, with the implication that to become involved in a dispute is blameworthy in itself, regardless of the merits of the case, is characteristic of Chinese attitudes to conflict. It finds expression from the earliest years in the way parents punish their children for any involvement in fighting, regardless of whether they were the attacker or attacked.

The weakness of the law means less reliance is placed on universal rules applicable to everyone regardless of background. This supports a greater attention to placing trust in particular ties, to preferring insiders before outsiders. Here, family ties take precedence, but other bonds based on being schoolmates, colleagues or compatriots can also serve to enhance feelings of mutual trust and obligation.

More generally, bureaucrats and business people alike are more likely to judge conduct not in terms of whether it is legal (*hefa*) but whether it is

Box 4.4 Going to court: a case study

The local district court is situated in a large city in southern China. It has about 350 staff members and handles about 50 000 cases a year, 20 000 of which are commercial disputes. The court has three departments handling each stage of the case from lodging a complaint through hearing the case to executing decisions of the court. For the hearing, judgement can be delivered by one judge if the case is minor, or by one judge consulting with two lay assessors when the case is complicated. Any judgement delivered by a judge has to be approved by the head of the court, sitting separately. Recently, to fight against corruption in the legal profession, the court added an additional department to supervise its staff and has changed its practice from allowing one judge to handle a case in its entirety to a system under which a case is handled by several judges from different departments. Apart from the campaign to fight against corruption, the court has also started to strengthen the execution of its judgements. Nevertheless, in the year 2000, according to one court official, only half of the judgements were successfully enforced.

However, in spite of its efforts to make the court more accessible, effective and fair, the court is still reluctant to handle cases against government bodies, despite the growth in legislation regulating administrative procedure. An illustration of this is provided by the case of two farmers who were trying to sue a government agency.

Six years ago, the two farmers signed a contract with a state-owned company. According to the contract, the farmers leased their allocated land to a company that wished to build a garage. The initial lease was for three years. In the event of the lease not being renewed, the land was to be returned to the farmers in its original arable state. Three years later, the company decided not to extend the lease and returned the land to the farmers. They failed, however, to honour their agreement regarding the demolition of the garage and the restoration of the land to its original state.

The farmers filed a case in court and won. The company was ordered by the court to remove the garage and to return the land in its original arable state. However, the company failed to implement the court's ruling. The farmers decided to appeal to the local land management bureau, a state agency with the task of protecting arable land. Despite this, one official told them that it was not the business of the bureau. Now the farmers wanted to sue the land management bureau for its failure to take any action to protect their land.

The judge at the local court, however, told them the case could not be accepted: 'I remember you from last week. I told you to go back home. You did not have evidence. Why you are here again?'

'We have the evidence now. We recorded our conversation with the official at the land management bureau.' The farmers presented the tape.

'What did he say?' the judge asked.

'He told us to go back home and not to bother him any more,' said the farmers.

'You can't sue the land management bureau simply because one of their officials refuses to handle the matter. I told you the same thing last week,' said the judge, waving aside their tape.

'But what can we do? Please tell us what will make you accept our case, otherwise we will have to come here again and again' The farmers were persistent. This is a time-honoured response to official refusal in China, one expected on all sides. The judge sighed.

'Write a letter addressed to the land management bureau and when the bureau write back refusing to help, then you have the evidence against it.'

'But they will not write back to us. We have been writing letters to every government department we can think of, we even wrote to the mayor, but nobody replies to us. Please accept the case. We know we may not win, but this is the only thing we can do now.'

But the judge was firm: 'I cannot accept the case because you do not have enough evidence, you should go next door to the department in charge of executing court orders to ask for help.'

'But we have been there dozens of times, all we got was being shouted at and told to get out of their office.'

The farmers pleaded repeatedly and told the judge that they would not go back home unless their case was accepted. Eventually the judge grew tired of them and stopped talking. However, the farmers took this as a sign of consent and, pushing the tape and the complaint form forward in front of the judge, left.

After the farmers' departure, the judge remarked: 'You see how stupid these peasants are! They try to sue the government. I cannot accept this case even though they do have one. We have to be very careful when deciding what cases to accept, the bosses will think we are no good if we take cases that are awkward. We have to protect ourselves.'

Later the judge recounted how he used to work in a textile factory and was selected to be a cadre by the party in 1970s. 'At that time nobody wanted to work in the court, everybody wanted to work in big state enterprises. So you see I do not have any legal background. Recently the court sent us to night school to study law, but I do not like legal theories. They are useless for my everyday work. I get all my knowledge from handling actual cases.'

Fieldwork notes, 2001

reasonable (*heli*). Indeed, anyone attending local courts will find the judges themselves preoccupied not with the legality of an act, but with considering whether or not it is reasonable, with *heli* before *hefa*. This outlook is general and predates communism. It is a preference with deep roots in Chinese history, echoing arguments advanced by Confucians against Legalists from over two millennia ago.

Government relations

In many countries experiencing the transition from a command to a market economy the approach of bureaucrat to entrepreneur is one of 'reaching out the grabbing hand'. The government in such circumstances consists of a large number of substantially uncoordinated bureaux and bureaucrats pursuing their own interests, including taking bribes. They remain largely independent of the courts, and are free to impose a variety of restrictions on business and to extract *ad hoc* fees as they occur to them. Russia is a case in point (Frye and Shleifer 1997).

The grabbing hand is not entirely alien to Chinese bureaucracy. In the case of China, however, a helping hand is equally apparent. Compared with Russia, the Chinese state remains more stable and decentralisation has long given localities an incentive and need to promote business development for tax revenue and to sustain local employment. Corruption remains, but in a relatively contained and more organised form. Both for the public good and private benefit, the goose needs to flourish.

Private entrepreneurs are keen to cultivate patrons in local government for the help they can provide. Government officials, in their turn, are equally eager to establish such relationships for the benefits they can bring. The support they can offer in return can broadly be divided into providing access to the resources controlled by the local bureaucracy and local units on the one hand and protection from bureaucratic interference on the other (Wank 1995).

Local cadres can grant favourable access to resources and opportunities in a number of areas. First, there is the large amount of real estate in the hands of public units. Preferential access to this can be arranged or leases renewed on favourable terms. Second, there are a number of restrictions on the areas in which private firms can operate, such as a prohibition on foreign trade and the provision of certain goods and services. Local authorities are sometimes able to lift these in the case of specific companies. Alternatively, a public unit may allow a private firm to trade under its name in such areas for a consideration. Third, public units are free to decide where to dispense custom. Often, private firms prefer public firms to fellow private firms as clients. Their larger size and readier access to bank loans make them more attractive customers, as does their greater reliability in terms of being unlikely to disappear or go bankrupt. Fourth, protection for firms can be provided by restrictions being placed on the entry of competitors. This can extend from local

Box 4.5 The brothers

Family occasions, such as wedding and birthday celebrations, are often used to cement business relationships. One private entrepreneur we met in the course of our interviews, a Mr Wang, kindly invited us to his daughter's wedding. During the course of the wedding banquet, he was constantly calling out to one brother or another, and we remarked to his wife how fortunate it was for people of her husband's generation to be able to have so many. She laughed and said that those her husband had been calling brothers were not related to him at all. They were 'business friends'.

We later learned more about them. One was from the Bureau of Industry and Commerce, which issues business licences. When Mr Wang started a restaurant, he registered his business as catering. However, since then he has converted the rooms above the restaurant into a small hotel with a karaoke bar. According to regulations, Mr Wang should have had to apply for separate licences for the hotel and the bar and to pay additional management fees and taxes. However, having a 'brother' at the bureau meant Mr Wang was spared this particular trouble.

Another hailed as 'brother' was from the street station of the local public security bureau. The police regard hotels and bars run by private business as more likely to house illegal activities than those run by the state. In this atmosphere, his patron at the police station has served to protect Mr Wang's hotel from surprise checks and raids. In addition, due to this contact, the police branch in charge of residents' registration overlooks Mr Wang's forgetfulness when it comes to registering his migrant workers.

A further guest was from the hygiene department of the district community, which conducts inspections at the local restaurants on a monthly basis. Mr Wang said in the past he was often fined large sums by the inspectors, but since adding this new member to his 'family', these have vanished.

Mr Wang is currently looking for ways to cultivate a friendship with someone from the local tax bureau. This, however, might prove difficult. As Mr Wang put it: 'They have grown big heads, because everybody wants to make friends with them.'

All the invited officials presented the bride with the traditional red envelopes containing money. Within the family circle it is polite, in the case of certain relatives, to return these offerings unopened. Mr Wang duly returned the envelopes to the officials, but not before putting more money inside.

We said that it was a pity we were not also in a position to help him with his business ventures. Mr Wang was sanguine. 'But the book you are writing will make you important, you will know other important people then. You can introduce them to me.'

Fieldwork notes, 2001

protection up to national regulations limiting foreign involvement in a specific industry. Fifth, official support can facilitate the provision of loans. Sixth, private entrepreneurs may enter into a variety of joint public–private enterprises. These include the 'red hat' practices referred to earlier. Such alliances provide a variety of benefits, enabling private firms to share with other public units greater freedom in the range of activities they can undertake, lower taxes, easier bank loans, greater respectability, and less bureaucratic harassment. Seventh, local regulatory bureaux have a wide discretion about whether to initiate or pursue enquiries and what, if any, penalties to impose. Finally, there is the

Box 4.6 A fixed line: private business and government support

Huawei was founded in 1988 by Ren Zhengfei, a former director of the Information Engineering Academy of the People's Liberation Army's General Staff Department. The academy is responsible for telecommunications research. In 1984, Ren left the academy to work for the state-owned Shenzhen Electronics Corporation. Four years later, he founded Huawei with 14 colleagues and a loan of 70 million yuan (8.5 million dollars) from a state bank.

Since then Huawei has evolved from a small reseller of foreign equipment into China's biggest telecom-infrastructure company, employing 16 000 people with an annual revenue of 993 million dollars in 1999 and a net profit of 182 million dollars.

Many observers within China view the rapid rise of Huawei as an indication that China has the ability to produce contenders in the information technology realm capable of competing on a level playing field alongside international rivals. Despite its success, however, Huawei still remains small in comparison with global competitors such as Cisco and Lucent in terms of profits and research and development. Much of its success to date can be attributable to government support in the form of government restrictions on the import of networking equipment, the procurement policies of state units and state mandated bank loans.

Behind the Chinese government's financial and political support has been the desire to promote Huawei as a national champion to ward off foreign domination of the telecom equipment industry. Here, its status as a private company has not stood in the way of it receiving preference over other up-and-coming equipment makers from the state-owned sector, such as Zhongxing Telecom. Many have attributed this to the good connections with high officials in the government and army that Ren is known to enjoy.

These connections have given rise to a stream of visits to the company from army commanders and government leaders. With such friends in high places, little has been allowed to stand in its way. The state banks have proved generous with loans to the company and credit to its customers. Big contracts have been provided by ministries, provinces, and state-owned conglomerates.

The local government, Shenzhen municipality, has made the company one of its key development projects. When local peasants protested against a company construction project because it did not allow them sufficient time to move ancestral graves, the company was able to call on the police to make arrests and local Party officials to persuade the peasants to desist, even though such issues are often approached with greater caution.

In return, Huawei has gone to great lengths to maintain a politically correct image. Unusually for a private company it has an active branch of the Communist Party, which organises regular staff meetings to propagate the party line.

Based on Gilley (2000c) and Nolan (2001)

opportunity for a degree of insider trading when new regulations are in the pipeline and have yet to be announced.

Businesses also seek to cultivate ties with officials to avoid the difficulties and disruption that stem from government action. Their first need is to deflect official harassment. Displeased officials may seek to hobble an enterprise in a number of ways, such as strict application of the rulebook and orchestrating inspection visits by other departments. The intention is to make the poor victim 'wear small shoes' (*chuan xiao xiezi*). Cultivating ties with officials is aimed at warding off such a plight. Second, entrepreneurs also feel the need for protection against the arbitrary imposition of sanctions. Fines and the seizure of goods can take place with or without infraction, often serving as a source of income for the agency concerned. Cultivating sympathetic inside informants can also provide forewarning of raids and enforcement actions, allowing time for evasion. Third, central state policies can change suddenly, with what was encouraged one day becoming anathema the next. Well-disposed local officials can, however, soften the impact through slack implementation. Finally, central authorities are also the source of periodic campaigns launched against particular malpractices. Once again, timely warning of these can assist in escaping attention.

To gain such favours, an entrepreneur will seek to cultivate ties with officials in a number of ways. Some entrepreneurs are lucky enough to be able to rely on previously established ties of family or friendship. Where the bonds of sentiment are weak or absent, however, more material means may suggest themselves. In the case of lower level officials, this may well take the form of pay-offs. These can include kickbacks to buyers from public units, 'donations' solicited in the name of various community projects, hospitality and gifts – with the last often being prompted by hints. With middle-level officials, ties can be forged through offers of employment, as with taking on those recently retired as 'advisors' for the value of their connections. Non-officials may be employed for their connections with officials, such as the classmates and teachers of officials in strategic positions. Backing may also be sought from top level officials through offers of shares in the company, known as 'power shares' (*quanli fen*) to distinguish their contribution as other than financial.

The strategy used by private businesses to influence officials appears to shift as the firm grows in size. Wank (1995) in his study of private enterprise in Xiamen, outlined the path that tends to be taken. The growth of a business is usually matched by a move to establish ties with more highly placed officials and towards ties of a more enduring and less openly calculative nature. Lower level officials, after all, have few assets at their command and their protection extends no further than protection from their own depredations. Not only do higher level officials have more within their power, cultivating numerous low-level officials is not cost-effective in terms of time when one could be cultivating their boss.

Purchasing official assistance on a case-by-case basis with individual cash payments is also less appealing than establishing a long-term relationship based on gifts. The latter has several advantages; promoting feelings of gratitude that will be at work in unforeseen circumstances and smacking less of outright corruption. Once again, family ties show themselves to advantage here in terms of their endurance and strength of sentiment. Carrying this logic to its extreme, it is easy to see why the best position of all for engaging in business is enjoyed by the 'princes' party' (*taizi dang*), the children of the country's leaders. Having such a parent casts a spell, opening doors and attracting favours even in the absence of any action, or even foreknowledge, on the part of the parents. This is, of course, not unique to China, and politicians there as elsewhere may at times feel their offspring the source of occasional political embarrassment as well as of parental pride. Nevertheless, China's way of conducting business and public affairs renders such embarrassment less pressing at the same time as it bestows on the children of the elite a particularly lustrous mantle as they make their way in the world.

Box 4.7 '777'

Localities differ in respect of their supportiveness towards private enterprise. Typically, the helping hand has been more evident in southern China, an area where there were few large state-owned enterprises for local authorities to lean upon. Even there, however, private businesses can find themselves squeezed by public authorities acting to favour the interests of large state-owned enterprises, as the tale of '777' reveals.

'777' was at one time a household name in Guangzhou. It was founded by seven brothers who set out with the ambition of owning 777 petrol stations in seven years. By 1999, they owned 17 petrol stations with annual sales exceeding 100 million yuan and a majority market share in the district in which they were located.

However, state policy changed in 2000. Entry was tightened and all existing petrol stations had to re-register. Certificates from the Industrial and Commerce Bureau, the Environmental Protection Bureau, the Fire Station and a number of other state agencies were necessary for the re-registration.

'777' managed to obtain these certificates. However, when it went to re-register with the government, it was told a long-term supply contract with one of the two state-owned petrochemical conglomerates, either Sinopec or CNPC, was also needed for the new business licence.

Government officials explained this necessity as a means of guaranteeing the quality of the petrol to be sold to consumers. However, '777' and other private petrol station owners saw this as part of a government strategy to help Sinopec and CNPC to grab the lion's share of the market before foreign competitors are officially allowed to own petrol stations with China's entry into the WTO.

Although '777' had always bought petrol from Sinopec, Sinopec refused to sign the supply contract. Instead, Sinopec wanted to buy the petrol stations owned by '777'. '777' refused. Shortly afterwards, one of its petrol stations was shut down by a government bureau. The bureau's reason for the shutdown was that the petrol station was too close to a property development.

A manager from '777' said: 'We got the hint from this, so we approached Sinopec and sold them all our petrol stations without being able to make any profit.'

The petrol station that was closed down was reported as opening again shortly after the transfer deal was signed.

Source: 21 *Shiji Jingji Baodao*, 30 November 2000

Business associations

China has a long tradition of business associations stretching back to the guilds of imperial times. Despite this history, these associations have never managed to achieve independence from state involvement in their affairs, except at times of transition from one regime to another. This was as true of the rule of the Kuomintang as it was to be of their communist successors.

Today, there exist two government-sponsored organisations for private entrepreneurs, the All-China Federation of Industry and Commerce (ACFIC) for large *siying* enterprises, and the Self-Employed Labourers Association (SELA) for small businesses. There is, in addition, a third association that caters for an important emerging element of the new Chinese business elite, the Chinese managers employed by foreign enterprises. This is the China Association for Enterprises with Foreign Investment (CAEFI).

The All-China Federation for Industry and Commerce has, as its proclaimed role, the protection of the rights of its members and to benefit them through the provision of information and training and advice on improving quality and standards. At national level, it has spoken out in favour of more favourable treatment for business. At a local level, branches engage in a variety of activities on behalf of their members. In Tianjin, for example, the local branch reports trying to negotiate lower municipal fees for members and attempting to locate sources of credit for them. In keeping with what we have seen earlier, however, what success it had in this area is often more attributable to the personal and former institutional connections of its officials than to any weight it carried as a body (Pearson 1997: 132).

The top leaders of the federation are active or former officials of the government, which provides a substantial source of its revenue. Its main tasks are set by the Communist Party Central Committee, and include informing members about government policies, tax regulations and drives against corruption. Like so many other government agencies, the federation also runs its own businesses, including glass and technology companies, a telling difference from its Western equivalents where such ventures by the organisation's officials might well be viewed askance by members. To the extent that they make use of the federation, members find the local chambers provide useful places to interact, but there is a general tendency to regard the federation as not particularly important for business people, either individually or as a whole.

The Self-Employed Labourers Association is similar to the ACFIC in claiming to represent the opinions of its members to higher authorities. It is also supposed to assist them with solving business problems and to

Box 4.8 The small-scale business association: a case study

The state-sponsored association established for small businesses goes under the name of the Self-Employed Labourers Association (SELA), a title harking back to an earlier era. In the Pudong district of Shanghai, the SELA has 40 township branches, with a medium size town having about 600 members. Although membership of the township SELA is, in principle, voluntary, in reality, all private businesses are persuaded to join and those who refuse are treated as troublemakers.

The deputy head of the Industry and Commerce Bureau (ICB) of the Pudong government chairs the district SELA. The chairman has five deputies elected from the membership. When asked why the chairman is an official rather than a private businessperson, one of the elected deputies replied: 'It is a government regulation. In any case, we feel we need the officials. They can give direction to the association.' SELAs at the township level have a parallel arrangement, being chaired by officials of the township ICB.

Under the chairman and the deputies, the district SELA has a standing committee with around 40 members, half of them from the ICB and the rest elected from the membership. The ICB also provides the general secretary of the SELA and all the staff in charge of daily affairs. Their salaries are paid by the ICB, in part from member-ship fees.

The district SELA is similar to a government unit or a state-owned enterprise in its organisation. Under the standing committee, for example, there are subcommittees common to such organisations, such as the Youth Committee, the Women's Committee, and the Committee for the Promotion of Spiritual Civilisation.

The role of the SELA, according to one of the deputies of the Pudong SELA, is *Shang xing xia da*, a well-worn phrase meaning to inform the members on government policy and to report the opinions of the masses to the government. 'The Association,' he explained, 'works side-by-side with the ICB to manage individual trades and private businesses.' The district SELA organises many Party-inspired campaigns for the township SELAs to implement. Such campaigns range from raising donations to help people in disaster stricken areas and to assist bankrupt private business people, to campaigns against the banned religious cult, Falung Gong. During the annual campaign of 'learning from Lei Feng to serve the people', members and their workers are mobilised to sweep streets and to clean buses, or to provide their services free. The SELAs also organise training courses on management, business law, and the international and domestic economic situation.

Every year, as with government units and state-owned enterprises, the SELAs are given quotas from the government for the number of people to be awarded titles as models of exemplary conduct. These titles are highly prized by some members. According to one informant 'It is good for business, you get invited to all sorts of meetings, so that you can meet people and higher level officials who can be of great help for business.' One antique dealer donates genuine articles to government museums and government agencies in order to win titles such as Patriotic Private Businessman of the City. He displays these awards in his shop to win the trust of customers purchasing articles of less certain antiquity.

The SELAs at both district and township level have a disputes settlement committee. Grievances are seldom brought before it officially, though this does not deter some committee members from volunteering their services informally, seeking to persuade those in dispute to see reason and to follow the right path (*shuo ming daoli*).

Fieldwork notes, 2001

support their rights against arbitrary impositions by officials. To the extent that it does so, it is reliant on the strength of the connections of its local officers. In general, however, there is little hope placed in receiving much help from this quarter and the SELA appears less energetic in promoting its members' interests than is the ACFIC. The government controls the organisation more closely, with no attempt to disguise this fact, unlike the ACFIC, which claims to be a 'non-governmental' (*minjian*) organisation. The SELA states directly that it is a mass organisation under the leadership of the Communist Party and it is clearly viewed as a means of propagating government policies. Its top positions are filled by government bureaucrats and most of its funding comes from the Bureau of Industry and Commerce, its supervisory agency.

In many ways, the control that the SELA attempts to exercise is reminiscent of the patronage exercised by the Party under the old *danwei* system. Membership is compulsory and, from this membership, a select band who show particular loyalty will find themselves rewarded with privileges. They may be chosen, for example, to form a delegation to explore opportunities for members to do business abroad, a somewhat remote possibility given the nature and size of most *getihu* enterprises. At the same time, the mass of ordinary members, summoned to meetings at times when the authorities feel the need to cajole them into supporting government measures, may show their displeasure through passive resistance. Openly voicing criticism of officials and official policy at such meetings is avoided as too dangerous, but in its place speakers may find themselves struggling in the face of an audience that makes its complete lack of interest embarrassingly plain (Bruun 1995).

Box 4.9 Building a fortune: a case study

Wu Dong turned himself from a penniless young village lad into a wealthy man within ten years. He attributes his success to two events in his life. The first occurred in 1986, when he passed the college entrance examination. This enabled him to leave his poverty stricken hometown in the countryside to come to Shanghai to study at a construction college. 'Had I not passed the examinations, I would still be planting rice in a paddy field,' Wu reflects.

The second event was his meeting with Mr Miao, the manager of a state-owned construction company. 'Without him,' Wu says, 'all this would not be possible. He has taught me so many things about construction. He is like a father to me.'

The two met in the late 1980s. At that time, state-owned construction companies were laying off their construction workers and contracting work out to migrant work teams. Wu joined a migrant team that was working for Miao's company. One year later, it occurred to Wu that he could start a team of his own rather than labouring for other people. He returned to his village and persuaded a dozen young men to follow him back to Shanghai. They formed a team, with Wu as its leader. It happened that Miao's company had just won a job to erect a massive imported steel structure factory for American Standard. However, no managers from the company nor any of the migrant labour teams had erected a steel building before.

Recalling the situation, Wu remarks:

> I still do not know why I took the job. It was such a risk. I suppose I had
> nothing to lose then. But I had no clue about how to put the steel pieces
> together, I had only learned how to build things with bricks. The managers
> from Mr Miao's company had no idea either. We had several supervisors
> from the company that exported the factory. But they did not speak any
> Chinese. All the installation instructions were in a foreign language as well.
> The schedule was very tight. I had to take sleeping pills most nights.

Despite the difficulties, the factory was built and Wu's team became the first team in Shanghai to specialise in steel factory buildings.

Miao's company managed to get more steel buildings to erect and subcontracted them all to Wu. Now Wu has more than 250 people and experience of building complicated projects, such as the Shanghai 80 000 seat stadium. However, Wu said: 'I am more careful now. But then I can afford to be more picky now. All this money did not come easy. I have to be very careful not to lose any of it.'

All his workers are young men from his village and neighbouring villages. Unlike the old days when Wu spent day and night on the work site with his team, he now has five managers doing this work for him. All of them were among the group that followed him from his first recruiting trip. Each of the managers handles a whole project, including project management, procurement and site management. Wu himself manages them from his newly acquired home in an expensive area of the city centre and seldom visits the sites.

'Unlike other businessmen, I don't like managers who cannot solve problems and constantly report them to me,' Wu remarks. He runs his business entirely through his mobile phone. He does not have an office, office hours, secretary, computer or a business diary. He is very proud how efficient and lean his company is.

> Each of my managers works more efficiently than five managers in a state-owned company. Managers from foreign companies are not willing to take responsibility, either. A lot of the time I suggest to them good ways to save labour and money, they don't want to listen. Perhaps they are afraid of losing face listening to a subcontractor from the countryside.

> I came here driving my new car; things like that still make me feel as if I am in a dream! But I still have to work hard and not to take risks. Lots of my workers are my relatives, friends or neighbours, I have the responsibility to make them rich as well. But I am also very strict with them, they work from dawn to dusk. If a worker is no good, I send him home immediately. This is very effective because they do not want to go back home. It also makes their family lose face.

There are no set working hours for the workers. They normally work when there is enough daylight. And if the schedule is tight, they work at night as well. Several years ago, all the workers slept on the site. However, as this is now forbidden by state regulation, they now sleep in bunks in a house rented by Wu, usually 20 men in one room. He employs women from the village to cook for the workers and one of the few times he found himself on the verge of a labour dispute was when the young workers became discontented because he was not feeding them enough meat. They are paid 200 yuan as a monthly allowance, which they usually spend in cafes and bars in the city on Sunday, their day off. At the end of the year, Wu gives each of them a bonus of around 8000 yuan and returns to their hometown with them in glory.

> I spend two thirds of my time building good relationships. Mr Miao's company gives me almost all of its steel building projects. Mr Miao and other managers of his company are very clean, they have never asked for any money from me. But I still have to find ways to thank them for being so nice to me. So for example, at a business lunch, one manager said his daughter had never tasted the big yellow fish we were eating. After lunch, I went to the fish market over the other side of the city and bought the biggest yellow fish you've ever seen. It cost 600 yuan. I took it to his home. He was not there, only his wife was at home. She didn't invite me in. I was hurt; people look down upon me because I am from the countryside. I also take them out for good meals and when we are on business trips together I usually invite them out to enjoy the night life in the local bars.

> Mr Miao's state company is very poor because they don't want to sack people, they are afraid that if they do not take care of their people, others will not take good care of them in the future. So the company often owes me money. I do not mind. I always tell them they can pay me when they have it. The long-term relationship is more important.

Fieldwork notes, 2001

5 A shift in complexion: the emergence of new organisational forms

- Changing pockets
- High-technology spin-offs
- Learning and organisations
- Privatising the professions
- The changing balance

In 1995, 72 per cent of the smaller state-owned enterprises under the direction of local authorities were in the red, compared with 24 per cent of the centrally held firms (International Finance Corporation 2000: 14). In response, the Chinese government devised a policy towards state enterprises of 'keeping the large and letting go of the small'. This entailed keeping under the ownership of the central government a core of between 500 and 1000 large state enterprises. Local authorities were instructed to put the state enterprises remaining in their care through a process of reorganisation. This would include a raft of measures including mergers, acquisitions, leasing and sale.

Letting go of the small state enterprises was bound up with changing their ownership structure (*gaizhi*). Just what this was to entail has varied greatly from one area to another. At one extreme, there was straightforward privatisation, although authorities that have pursued this in an across-the-board fashion have drawn reprimands from the centre (World Bank 2001b: 4). At the other extreme, there were enterprises in such a sorry state that no one wanted them. In between, there has been a range of measures that resulted in a variety of forms of organisation, mixing public and private elements.

Most changes left an element of public ownership, sometimes large, sometimes nominal. Some local authorities addressed *gaizhi* as one more administrative task to be achieved within the time set and simply changed the titles of firms and little else of substance. Others made more extensive use of the established practices of leasing and contracting state enterprises to managers.

Another adopted method of restructuring was to introduce ownership in the form of employee shareholding. Enterprises restructured in this way are still regarded as a form of collective firm and, as such, subject to local government involvement in their operation. However, initial moves in this direction were sometimes reversed in favour of other ownership forms due to a number of difficulties they encountered. First, employees were sometimes reluctant to buy shares in the firm owing to lack of resources or faith in its future. Second, the management was still in the position of agent, preserving difficulties in ensuring their interests coincided with those of the owners. Third, spreading shares among the workers did not solve the free-rider problem, as individual employees would continue to receive dividends regardless of personal performance. Finally, uniform shareholding did not help to establish clear authority in the firm.

For these reasons, local governments often sought other solutions. Listing was highly sought after, but at the same time highly restricted. More available were the possibilities for management buy-outs. While competitive bidding is allowed, in practice firms have gone to the incumbent managers. Once again, however, it was quite usual to find local government involvement continuing alongside developing management ownership over a fixed or indefinite transitional period. Where considerable net assets were involved, buy-outs have tended to be replaced with forms of leasing to managers.

Changing pockets

The growth of hybrid forms of ownership has been pursued with an eye to the dynamism it is hoped they will breathe into firms. However, the increasing intermixture has also had consequences of an unintended and less welcome kind. If the move towards privatisation by managers and officials in their official capacity has at times been cautious, the enthusiasm of some for the process of transferring state assets into private hands through other paths has more than compensated. Asset stripping has emerged as a regular feature of transitional economies, and China is no exception. Known as changing assets 'from one pocket to another' (*huan kou dai*), the practice thrives on a lack of transparency, and those involved make full use of the hazy boundary between the public and the private to slip resources from one to the other.

Estimates of the amounts involved vary. Research into the area appears to have been discouraged following some rather alarming findings in the early 1990s, which put the figure being drained from state firms at between 50 and 100 billion yuan (6 to 12 billion dollars) per year. This further undermined the performance of the state sector, adding to its debts and diminishing its share of production (Ding 2000: 1–2).

At its most straightforward, backdoor privatisation has taken place through managers of state companies setting up their own companies in the same line of business. They then divert resources to these in the form of machinery, materials and loans drawn from the state company at little or no cost. Orders from the state firm may also be diverted in favour of the second business.

Such 'one manager, two businesses' arrangements can be highly profitable, but are clearly risky. In breach of Chinese law and Party discipline, gross offenders have on occasion been shot, especially those unfortunate enough to have their case come to light during one of the periodic campaigns against corruption. It is not surprising, therefore, to find a variety of strategies being adopted to avoid detection. To hide their direct involvement, managers may place the ownership of their firm in the hands of relatives or trusted friends. To escape the attention of the local supervisory body, the shadow factory may also be established far away in another province. For companies involved in trade, the second company may well be a hollow shell used to divert funds through such means as fictitious commissions, and transactions easier to hide from view than the transfer of physical assets.

Workers naturally resent such misuse of funds by managers, for it undermines the stability of their own enterprise. It is a situation frequently complained of in terms of the adage 'the temple is bankrupt while the abbot grows rich' (*miao qiong fangzhang fa*). For this reason, some managers prefer routes to divert state assets that can secure the cooperation of the workforce rather than alienating them. One of these is to establish subsidiaries of the state firm. These, as we have seen earlier, are popular among state enterprises and non-commercial state units. At their most benign they can be a means of generating work for redundant workers and additional bonuses for staff, often through ventures into the service sector. However, they can also take a more malign form.

In this, parts of the state firm are spun-off and established as what appear to be independent units. In reality, they remain tied to the firm in a parasitic relationship under which they obtain inputs and outlets for their products and services from the state firm on terms better than those available on the market. At first sight, many of these moves seem to mimic the attempts to increase efficiency seen elsewhere, by concentrating on core activities and spinning off others. A transport unit, for example, might be transformed in appearance from an internal department to an external subsidiary. If the new firm were indeed independent in its operation and was only awarded contracts based on market competition it might well improve the efficient allocation of resources. However, if the transport unit continues to have its equipment provided by the state firm and is awarded work by its parent regardless of price, assets can be transferred into the new subsidiary and beyond the ready grasp of the state. What is established is a process akin to the use made by multinationals of transfer pricing to shift resources across borders.

Such subsidiaries usually operate as collectively owned, 'a category full of ambiguity and confusion in the ownership classification of the transitional Chinese economy, spanning the vast grey area that is neither strictly state-owned nor clearly privately owned' (Ding 2000: 6–7). Transferring assets into this grey area is to remove them one step further from the control of the state, particularly as most of these offshoots are closer in operation to the private than to the public end of the collective spectrum. Tellingly, turnover of the top personnel of such subsidiaries tends to be frequent, reflecting the zeal with which the managers of the parent company are prepared to enforce their rights against anyone suspected of undermining them.

New firms established on the basis of partnerships between state-owned enterprises and non-state-owned enterprises or non-commercial government units (*lianying*), constitute a hybrid form of organisation, which grew in number throughout the 1990s. Many such organisations were deliberately created for the opportunities to weaken the grip of the state upon public assets, with funds being shifted into independent bodies whose ownership is ill-defined. Supervision by the state was further weakened when these organisations were set up at a distance, in parts of the country noted for their relatively slack regulation. This goes a long way to explaining why a large proportion of such consortia organised from Beijing finish up being established at the other end of the country, in Shenzhen, moving from a city noted for its close bureaucratic supervision to one noted for its absence (Ding 2000: 12).

Box 5.1 Changing pockets

The following examples of asset stripping are two of the many unearthed by Ding in his investigations in China (Ding 2000).

One manager, two companies

In 1990, the director of a state-owned lighting factory in central China set up a private company in secret. The company was located in a coastal city in the south, hundreds miles away from the site of the state factory. Unable to be in the south in person, the director entrusted the daily operation of his company to friends. The private company also produced lighting facilities. In time, the director made it a major subcontractor of the state factory, with most of its investment, raw materials and workforce training provided by the state enterprise. The state enterprise also paid for its orders in advance, with no penalty against late delivery or low quality. In addition, the director made frequent trips to the private company on expenses drawn from the state company. In 1994, the manager was offered promotion to head the industrial bureau. He declined, fearing that the profitable connection might be disturbed if he were to leave the state firm.

Organisational proliferation

In the mid-1990s, a state-owned energy equipment manufacturing company established three auxiliary businesses with 200 employees. Of these, 120 were unemployed family members and the remaining 80 were staff from the company. Although the 80 staff members were transferred to the auxiliaries, they remained on the payroll of the state company. The business of the auxiliaries was mainly to undertake operations such as purchasing, marketing, engineering and transport for the parent company. These tasks were formerly carried out by internal departments of the company, but now the company paid the auxiliaries to do them. For example, when the company wanted to purchase office facilities, instead of buying directly from the market, it contracted the purchase to one of its auxiliaries, paying 15 to 20 per cent more than the market price. Partly as a result, the company ran losses of between 10 to 30 million yuan per year. Despite this, its employees and the employees from the auxiliaries were reputed to be among the best paid in the area, enjoying numerous fringe benefits, while the managers were able to take trips abroad in rotation.

Source: Ding (2000)

The more that setting up such new firms means sending assets originating in state-owned enterprises across administrative lines, industrial sectors or ownership types, the weaker the ability of the state authorities to keep track of them. This means that the money injected into the consortium by the state firm eventually ends up in private holdings. Initial investments can be understated or are simply not recorded, a possibility enhanced by the loose management of assets in state firms, where some assets may not appear on the books. Where the new firm is established far away, the supervisory authority has little chance to act out its role as the custodian of public policy. Where records are left incomplete and personnel changes frequent, some state firms lose touch with their distant offshoots. Those managers involved in their foundation frequently have better memories, however; going off to join them on retirement. Returns from the venture may be ploughed back into developing still more layers of subsidiaries and partnerships, making financial flows still more difficult to trace and further diluting whatever element of public ownership remains. Through one route or another, the managers of the state enterprise who organised the initial investment are frequently able to contrive to be its chief beneficiaries.

High-technology spin-offs

Many of the more successful firms within China's high-technology sector are the offspring of state institutions. Prompted by the decline in central government funding that has been part of the decentralising direction of the reforms, universities and research institutes have had to become increasingly self-financing. This has led to them establishing their own commercial ventures, a move encouraged by the government as a means of drawing the academic and business worlds closer together. It is a move that has also been encouraged by the frailty of patent protection. This has meant a reluctance to rely on others to remit royalties when putting inventions into production.

Establishing such spin-offs has proved a highly successful policy, serving, for example, as the launching pad for Legend, one of China's largest and most profitable computer companies. Contrary to those who argue that clearly defined property rights and a secure rule-based environment is necessary for the growth of business, such companies have flourished in an atmosphere of ill-defined and poorly secured property rights relative to their parent organisations.

What lies at the root of this? In her study of high-technology spin-offs, Francis (1999: 230–34) points to four factors fostering this lack of clarity. First, the law fails to allot any special rights to the founding agency, leaving its status ambiguous, an ambiguity added to by state policies that veer back and forth between encouraging the formation of spin-offs and insisting on founding agencies cutting their ties with such enterprises. Second, it is difficult to draw a dividing line between the contributions attributable to the founding institution on the one hand and the business ventures on the other. Employees often remain with their institute and continue with their job while at the same time engaging in the commercial activities of the offshoot. This leaves them free to continue to enjoy the full facilities of the parent organisation. Dividing responsibility for the founding of the offshoot in terms of ideas and support is also difficult. The period of product design, market research and capital accumulation often takes place within the founding institution before the offshoot is formally established. Third, the lack of developed markets for labour, technology and capital often make the valuation of inputs difficult to specify. Typically, technology inputs from the founding organisation tend to be overlooked by members of an offshoot in discussing the contribution of the parent body. Finally, the absence of clearly defined property rights between a parent organisation and its spin-off is regarded as perfectly normal and accepted with equanimity by all involved. This, it is often felt, is best left to being worked out by negotiation as matters proceed rather than being settled in advance. This is because much remains uncertain, including the prospects for success, the contribution of the parties, the regulatory environment and the enforceability of contracts.

In the place of any clear contractual relationship set out between the parties, numerous issues between parent organisation and spin-off are settled by bargaining. Profit sharing arrangements are often not specified in writing, but worked out through discussion. Even where these are spelled out in a contract, the agreed arrangement is often subsequently ignored. Repeated renegotiation of terms is commonplace and meets with no surprise. Likewise, procedures for the appointment or removal of general managers are left vague. As long as the founding fathers remain involved, their value to the enterprise in terms of their talent and drive often renders their position secure, whatever tensions may arise with the parent organisations. Even where they do not hold a formal position in the company the prestige and position of some founders is such that their presence continues to make itself felt over appointments and policy through less formal channels. This pattern of continuing influence independent of formal position is one familiar to many Chinese universities, the originators of many of the spin-offs, as well as in the highest reaches of the Chinese state.

As with all bargaining, the outcome of these continuing negotiations over who gets what is shaped by the changing balance of power between the parties. The contest is shaped by the relative size and centrality of the sponsoring unit's initial input and continuing support in terms of finance, technology and personnel. The reputation and links of the founding unit may also be of importance in securing outside finance and assisting with marketing and distribution. The position of the spin-off is strengthened where success is clearly more attributable to the knowledge and drive of its founders than to the 'hard' inputs of the parent. The nature of the administrative machinery set in place by the parent company is another factor weighing in the balance. Some set up and maintain close supervision from the beginning. Others take little interest in the affairs of their offshoots at first, only to find that later, when success prompts greater involvement, it is too late to assert control as the venture has secured effective independence (see Box 5.2).

Box 5.2 Power struggles in the world of high-technology spin-offs

The comparison by Francis (1999) of two Beijing high-technology spin-offs and their relationship to their parent institutions offers a fascinating insight into the forces shaping contests over their control.

The story of Legend, one of China's most successful computer companies, presents an example of a high-technology spin-off that managed to achieve considerable independence from its parent institution, the Institute of Computer Technology of the Chinese Academy of Science. Legend was founded in 1984 by a group of researchers from the Institute, which provided 200 000 yuan to help launch the venture. While Legend agreed to pay a certain percentage of its profits to the Institute, by the late 1980s its general manager, Liu Quanzi, had grown dissatisfied with this arrangement and called for it to be lowered. The Institute refused and a struggle commenced in which Liu sought support from the public through interviews with journalist friends and through going over the head of the Institute to officials at the Chinese Academy of Science. The Institute threatened to dismiss him, but he in turn threatened to resign. In the end, he simply refused to hand over the level formerly agreed upon. The Institute felt unable to remove him and was left with no alternative to submit, given the independence of Legend, which was not reliant on the Institute for human, technological or financial resources.

By way of contrast, Beijing University managed to retain greater control over its offshoot in the field of computer technology, Beida Founder. From the inception of Beida Founder, the university had played a greater contribution than had been the case with Legend and the Institute. Beijing University invested an initial 400 000 yuan in the project, and later helped to raise a further 4 million yuan, 1.5 million of which came from the university itself. The university provided the key technology for Beida Founder, related to the saving of Chinese characters in computer memory. This was the result of many years work by a large university research team. The university's name and contacts also made access available to crucial markets for the product. It also provided a continuing source of personnel, unlike Legend, which recruited from the market rather than from its founding institute. The university has also taken a more active role in running its offshoot from the very beginning, and has intervened to remove a general manager on more than one occasion. Legend was left far more to its own devices from the beginning, and while the Chinese Academy of Science did establish a management company in 1992 to secure more effective control over its offshoots, this was not extended to those older companies such as Legend that had already achieved sufficient strength to assure their continued independence.

Source: Francis (1999)

The balance, then, rests on the extent of mutual reliance. In general, the larger and more profitable spin-offs enjoy greater independence and bargaining power relative to their parents. In addition to a growing reliance on the part of their parents for support, this also stems from increasing complexity making it difficult for outside bodies to manage the spin-offs in detail. The speed needed to adapt to changing market circumstances may also bar measured bureaucratic deliberation as too inefficient.

High-tech spin-offs from research institutes and similar bodies constitute China's hope of being able to forge ahead in a sphere in which entry barriers are low and adapted to small and medium size enterprises, being knowledge intensive rather than capital intensive as in the case of heavy industry. While this may prove over-optimistic (Nolan 2001), the firms that have arisen in the area, such as Legend and Stone in the field of computers, provide examples of new organisations emerging in China that are in many ways quite unlike traditional state-owned enterprises, locally owned collectives or traditional family firms.

Learning and organisations

China entered the reform period with a wealth of resources in terms of the knowledge and talent contained within the research institutes, universities and other state bodies. These had proved themselves highly successful in terms of managing large-scale military projects, such as the development of the nuclear bomb and missions such as the development of a satellite launching capacity. China's science and technology sector was, however, ill adapted to meeting market demand.

The reasons for this were woven into the fabric of the command economy. Organisational barriers stood between those doing the research and those running production. Universities and research institutes, such as those of the Chinese Academy of Science, often pursued research in an ivory tower; remote from what little commercial reality pervaded the world of business at the time. Even those research institutes within industrial ministries had their contact with enterprises funnelled up and down through the bureaucratic hierarchy. Incentives to push innovations through into production were also low among the research teams. Typically, research projects were self-contained, often leading no further than the production of prototypes that were never put into mass-production. Successful peer evaluation secured the favourable commendations that alone were necessary to a researcher's career. As for the state-owned enterprises, they had neither the resources nor the incentive to engage in innovation, especially product innovation. They were there to fulfil the plan. As such, enterprises functioned more like a production unit within a larger organisation than an independent firm. Strategy, planning, financing were all in the hands of the bureaucrats who wove plans in happy innocence of market forces.

What was needed was to find a way of directing the intellectual resources built up in the institutes and universities into commercially viable activities. The solution lay in organisational innovation and its success was to be seen in companies such as Stone, Legend, Founder and Great Wall. All operate in the area of computers. Stone was the first of the new form of enterprises to be forged within the high-technology field, basing its success on the development of a Chinese word processor. Legend was a spin-off of a research institute and grew to become the largest manufacturer of personal computers in China and one of the world's leading suppliers of motherboards and add-on cards. Founder was an offshoot of one of the country's leading universities, Beijing University. It grew to become the country's leader in the field of electronic publishing systems. Great Wall was a spin-off of the Computer Industry Administration Bureau and grew to become the largest supplier of computer parts, components and peripherals in China.

What all shared in common was, in the words of Stone's charter, a commitment to 'independent management and financial self-reliance' (Lu 2000: 22). The former of these has rested, in large measure, on the latter. Typically, the seed money provided by the founding institution was relatively small, often in the form of a loan that was to be repaid over a set period. Financial resources came at an early stage from reinvestment, frequently with funds generated by trading and support activities in the initial phase. These resources eventually built up to provide the basis needed for manufacture. This accumulation was aided by strict limits set on the amount of profits that could be dispersed to the staff and the necessity of funding innovation if the firm was to survive in a rapidly changing industry. Stone, for example, operated from soon after its founding in 1984 with a distribution of profits that was divided 50 per cent towards enterprise development, 30 per cent towards an employee welfare fund, and 20 per cent towards a staff bonus fund. Even then, the staff bonus fund was itself allowed to accumulate and provide loans for the firm rather than being dispersed. This policy stemmed, in part, from local authorities pressing Stone not to excite wage demands elsewhere and, in part, from a highly progressive income tax.

All the firms were technically neither state nor private, belonging to a broad category that is applied to a variety of mixed forms, known as *minying*, people-owned. This left greater security for accumulating resources within the firm through ploughing back profits, a path often shunned in state-owned enterprises in favour of distribution. As noted in earlier chapters, this tendency towards distributing profits as soon as possible results partly from a fear that a string of predatory state agencies will arrive on the company doorstep intent on plunder with an attitude of 'you are a state company, well, we are the state'. Shorn of this excuse, the legitimate claim of the state was limited to taxes, and tax exemptions in this area were very much the rule given government policies aimed at promoting the area's development.

The management of the new high-technology enterprises was thus free to make investment decisions and increasingly held the financial resources to enable them to do so. Equally importantly, they also had access to the accumulated knowledge, trained personnel and technology of the research institutes. The founding fathers of such companies invariably came from this circle and many did the initial work on the projects they were later to develop in their companies. In the process, they had acquired not only capabilities but also contacts, which were to prove of great use later. The new companies benefited not only from being able to make use of the facilities of the institutions in which they had their roots, they also benefited from being able to make use of a wide variety of highly skilled people working in government research and educational institutions. Many were keen to moonlight for the new companies. Given the low wages of their state positions, companies such as Stone could afford to double or even triple their salary and still obtain their services at negligible cost in relation to the value they produced. Later, with increasing competition for staff from foreign companies setting up in China, this was to change, but in the initial period of their emergence, the low cost of talent helped ease development costs considerably.

For the organisations we are considering, the speed of change in the high-technology realm meant that innovation was essential. To achieve this, the organisations had to prove themselves capable of learning, thus acquiring new capabilities quickly and thoroughly. As we have seen, in this they suffered no shortage of highly intelligent and talented staff. Furthermore, the age range in the field, as everywhere, tilts in favour of youth and an accompanying openness to exploring new ways of doing things. Learning, however, needs not only the capacity to change. Learning needs motivation. This, too, the organisations provided through a combination of hard budget constraints and the personal and financial commitment of those who pioneered the enterprises and carried them forward.

Learning also rests on the free flow of information, on being able to tap the experience of others. Here, the need to keep abreast of world trends in their field had cultivated a willingness to learn from abroad, an openness of mind that was to stand them in good stead when it came to forming international alliances. They not only had a keen sense of their capabilities, they were also equally aware of where their development was lacking in comparison to others. This greatly encouraged the desire to forge international strategic alliances and joint ventures. There was with this, a keen sense of what could be digested and what could not, given the stage of development they had reached. This could serve as an advantage in preserving independence when collaborating with a more advanced partner. Stone, for example, when collaborating with a Japanese partner on the development of their Chinese word-processor refused to use the more advanced testing equipment available at the headquarters of the Japanese partner. It did so for fear of seeing control slip through its fingers. Instead, it insisted on making use of a modified form of its own equipment. This caused additional difficulties, but these were thought worth the price for maintaining more equal control (Lu 2000: 44).

The ability of these high-technology organisations to learn from overseas in the technical sphere was evidently transferable to the organisational sphere. It was here that the organisations were often groping in the dark, with no background in business to guide them. Yet, here too they proved themselves quick to see the relevance to their needs of information gleaned from every corner. This could be true, for example, even in the case of abortive joint-venture negotiations, as can be seen in the case of Great Wall. Although it was eventually to enter into a joint venture with IBM, its first attempt to do so was a failure. The negotiations themselves, however, proved of unexpected worth. As one of the negotiating team recalls:

> The negotiation was a detailed and painstaking process. At the centre was how to divide the profits. We had to go step by step through each stage of the value chain to see each partner's contribution. So we went through each and every aspect of the business process, including R&D, purchasing, production and marketing. This way we learned how IBM organised its business. It was the first time we learned first-hand that there were different ways of organising a business.
>
> (Lu 2000: 152)

In the case of Stone, their Japanese partner brought them face to face with the necessity of considering cost in design. With their background in research institutions, the staff at Stone had been purely technical; aiming at creating the best possible product regardless of cost and the impact this might have on sales. At one time, the Chinese side, for example, were pressing to design the word processor so that it would meet high American standards. This was done with a view to being able to sell it to the United Nations headquarters. The Japanese managed to convince them that the additional cost this would entail would not be worthwhile without the justification of a larger market (Lu 2000: 44). As they moved on to a joint venture with their Japanese partner, more formal training was provided to Stone's staff by the Japanese, including placements in Japan. The result was the acquisition of a Japanese model of management, including such elements as just-in-time production and quality control standards and inspection.

Privatising the professions

The presence of independent auditors is widely recognised as playing an essential part in resolving the principal–agent problems that arise alongside the separation of ownership and control. In the China of the command economy era, independent auditing of accounts did not exist. The reforms, however, produced a pressing need for them with the need to develop a capital market and to attract foreign investment. In addition, the reforms also promoted the need for review by independent accountants through the greater autonomy they gave to managers of state-owned enterprises. Accompanying this went various bonus schemes linked to performance in an attempt to address the emerging principal–agent problem. As performance was usually measured with accounting information, it became crucial to discourage the managers from manipulating the figures to their advantage, a practice that appears not uncommon (Tang *et al.*, 1999).

In order to address such needs, auditing firms were established under the sponsorship of various government bodies. Their lack of independence, however, led to a number of imperfections in their operation. Auditing firms under a government department, for example, might be directed to audit enterprises under the control of the same department. Similarly, a local authority was able to enforce local protection through demanding that local companies used local auditing firms. Government control over accounting firms also sheltered them from litigation and disciplinary action.

Concerns over these issues were among the reasons why the accountancy firms were ordered to commence disaffiliating themselves from their sponsoring units. This process began towards the end of 1996. By the time it was completed at the end of 1998, the firms had transformed themselves into private practices, either in the form of partnerships or as limited liability companies. This, it was hoped, would ensure that they would feel freer to exert a critical eye over company accounts. Furthermore, partners would have more of an incentive to be rigorous in discharging their duties, as they would be exposed to personal loss resulting from action taken against their practice for failing in their duties. Partners face unlimited liability, and this also remains true of the partner in charge of an audit in a limited liability firm, the limited liability here extending only to the other partners. Finding themselves placed at such risk, it was felt, would concentrate the mind and harden the judgement.

Indeed, there is some evidence to suggest that this is the case. This comes from the figures on the appearance in audit accounts of non-standard opinions. A non-standard opinion indicates a problem or potential problem with financial statements. These vary in intensity, but all are unwelcome by the company being audited and hence indicate a degree of independence on the part of the auditors. Using audit reports for the companies listed on the Shanghai and Shenzhen stock exchanges, Yang and his colleagues reveal that a clear increase took place in the number of non-standard opinions expressed as the privatisation of the accountancy firms progressed, rising from 9 per cent in 1996 to 18 per cent in 1998. This may well have been stimulated by a new found zeal for launching lawsuits against auditors and a greater readiness on the part of the Institute of Certified Public Accountants and the Securities Regulatory Commission to issue warnings, impose fines, and withdraw or suspend licences (Yang *et al.* 2001).

Similar motives to those outlined above lay behind privatisation moves in other professions. This has been successfully carried through in the legal profession, for example. Elsewhere, however, as with case of quantity surveying reviewed in Box 5.3, the process stalled.

Box 5.3 Privatising the surveyors: a case study

Tiandi Quantity Surveying Company was formerly a small department of a large state-owned design institute in a major city on the eastern coastline. Under the planning system, the department did not have much work to do, as the days of the construction boom had to await the arrival of the reform period. What building there was, was accomplished through administrative orders rather than through contracts.

However, by the 1990s, the city had entered a period of rapid expansion. Contracts were also widely introduced into the construction industry, even among state-owned enterprises. Consequently, the department found its services in greater demand.

In response, the head of the department, Mr Zhen, decided to expand the department into a company, a plan welcomed by the institute. With a problem of overstaffing, the institute saw the new company as a way of providing for some of its staff, and possibly for some of their children as well.

The institute contributed 65 per cent of the initial investment in the new company, named Tiandi, with the remaining 35 per cent contributed by the employees as a condition of joining the company. Profits were to be divided equally between the institute and the company. The institute allowed Tiandi to share its office building, Party organisation and trade union. This enabled Tiandi to cut down on its overheads. The institute appointed Zhen as the chairman of the board of directors and the general manager of Tiandi.

Tiandi proved a success. By 1999, the company had developed to include 80 members of staff and enjoyed a revenue of 15 million yuan and a profit of 500 000 yuan. Zhen had relinquished his position as general manager to Mr Mu, but remained as chairman of the board to see the company awarded a prestigious 'A' grade by the government. Such a high grade was crucial for Tiandi to bid for large-scale projects. Tiandi's success was also partly rooted in its relationship with the institute. As the institute's spin-off, it was in an excellent position to get quantity surveying contracts in projects the institute designed. Tiandi also enjoyed a similar advantage over other quantity surveying companies with regard to contracts in projects designed by foreign architects. Under state policies, foreign architects have to employ state-owned design institutes as consultants on Chinese building regulations and codes. The institute made use of this work to guide contracts towards its subsidiary.

Tiandi's success was also due to its emphasis on staff training and development. Zhen has a friend in Hong Kong managing an American-owned quantity surveying company. The two companies launched a joint staff development programme, with Tiandi sending three young members of staff every year for training in the Hong Kong based company. The seconded mainlanders are normally set to work on projects related to China. The programme enables the mainland staff to be introduced to international standards and practices, while their Hong Kong counterparts are informed on regulations and codes in China.

The company was still expected to take on children of the staff members and contacts of the institute, even though some of them were not qualified. The company spent a considerable amount getting them trained.

In 2000, Tiandi was suddenly faced with a crisis.

As part of Premier Zhu Rongji's move to privatise all the professional bodies, such as law firms and accountancies, the Ministry of Construction published a policy ordering state-owned quantity surveying companies to privatise, severing their links with state bodies. This also applied to companies such as Tiandi with mixed ownership. The companies could be re-organised into either partnerships or limited companies. In the latter case, shares were not allowed to be owned by any state unit. Instead, only staff members who were certified quantity surveyors or who held equivalent qualifications could hold shares. The policy also stated that a privatised quantity surveyor could employ nobody over the age of 60. The privatisation had to be completed by the end of 2000. Any companies failing to privatise would lose their current grading certification.

Opinions were divided among the managers and the staff as to what Tiandi should do. Older managers and staff members in fear of early retirement wanted the company to return to the institute and operate as a department as before. They argued that although this would mean the loss of the current grading, they would still be able to win projects under the institute. They worried about whether and how the company would compensate them if they were forced to retire. The state policy did not give any clear guidance on this issue, it simply stated that 'proper arrangements should be made for those over 60'.

Most of the younger managers and staff members had mixed feelings. On one hand, working for Tiandi had the benefits of working for both the private sector and the state sector: the company paid well with many additional benefits, but without any strict rules or discipline. On the other hand, the younger managers and staff members were excited about the opportunities lying ahead. They wanted to own part of the company and make more money.

First, however, there was the question of how the existing assets were to be divided among the staff members, since each of them has contributed to the start-up cost of the company. They also wanted the intangible assets such as the 'A' grading to be valued and payment made to the employees by the new shareholders. The last thing the younger ones wanted was the company to be privatised with the new shareholders alone reaping all the benefits, or that much of the money the company had accumulated should wind up being used to compensate those who had to take early retirement.

As for those who had joined the company because of their connections rather than merit, they were strongly against the impending privatisation, fearing they would lose their jobs.

As for Zhen, he was very keen on the idea of privatisation. He was, however, worried that there were only 15 people qualified to hold shares according to the state policy. This would mean each of them would have to invest a large amount of their own money, if the company decided to distribute all its assets to the employees.

Zhen had many discussions with key staff members, seeking to persuade them of the necessity for more shareholders. He pointed out that the policy mentioned that people with equivalent qualifications to a state certificated quantity surveyor could also hold shares. This would mean, for example, that Mu, the general manager, would also be allowed to hold shares, since he was certified in Hong Kong. Zhen also held discussions about potential candidates for the board of directors.

Zhen's talks aroused discontent in the company, especially among the younger staff members. They suspected Zhen of wanting to have his own people controlling the board so that he could continue to be the head of the company. Some young staff members drafted a letter to the management of Tiandi and the institute demanding the management publicise the privatisation procedure. The letter also demanded participation in the privatisation process by the ordinary members of staff. The majority of the employees signed the letter.

The management bent to the demands of the employees and decided to organise a team to deal with the privatisation matter. The members of the team were to be elected by all the employees. The vote was taken, with half of the team elected consisting of younger staff members. Zhen was not elected. Mu, whose right to hold shares Zhen had been championing, gained the highest number of votes and became the head of the team. Unfortunately for Zhen, once Mu was on the team, he decided to ally with the younger generation, rather than putting his weight behind Zhen in his desire to be remain as chairman of the board.

However, the democratically elected team still could not reach agreement on the major issues in dispute. Meanwhile, similar situations were being experienced by other quantity surveying companies across the country. Many complaints were made to the Ministry of Construction and the State Council as to unfairness in the privatisation process. Finally, the government ordered the postponement of the privatisation.

Zhen seized upon this opportunity and allied with the older members of Tiandi who would lose their jobs if Mu and his younger supporters had had their way. Zhen talked to the institute and initially succeeded in persuading the institute to take Tiandi back as a department.

At the time of writing, the privatisation of the industry has resumed. Tiandi has not yet returned to the institute, if it ever will. Zhen has for the moment managed to keep the grading of the company without privatisation.

Fieldwork notes, 2001

The changing balance

The course of the reform programme in China over the last 20 years has moved China away from an economy in which traditional forms of public ownership and state planning monopolised the landscape to an economy with far greater diversity of property forms. These now operate under market conditions, however imperfect these markets may sometimes appear. The reforms did not set out to replace the traditional state firm with completely privatised firms, but produced a variety of hybrid forms between the two extremes. Overall, there has been a shift in the centre of gravity of the Chinese system of ownership towards the more private end of the continuum between private and public forms of property, a move illustrated in Figure 5.1. It has been a move that has been accompanied by granting those managing enterprises a greater right to the profits they produce and greater responsibility for any losses they incur.

It is possible to think of this change in terms of a shift in property rights. These rights cover a number of areas, with rights in one area not always being accompanied by rights in another. Broadly, we can distinguish between rights over the control of assets, rights to the income of assets, and rights over the transfer of assets. The first of these three concerns managerial control over what the assets should be used for and how they should be used. This covers major decisions concerning investment down to day-to-day operational matters. The second concerns who has the right to the income generated and responsibility for any losses incurred. The third concerns who can transfer such control and income rights, and who benefits or loses as a result (Walder and Oi 1999).

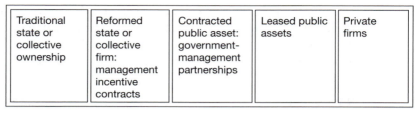

Figure 5.1 *Types of ownership (based on Walder and Oi 1999)*

In the case of the traditional state or collective enterprise operating under the planned economy of the pre-reform era, government bureaux decide what to produce and how to produce it. They are responsible for allocating inputs in the form of capital, materials and labour to the firm and allocating the resulting output. The government takes all the profit and absorbs any loss. Officials acting on behalf of the state appoint managers on a fixed salary.

With the start of the reforms came a move away from the traditional state or collective firm. Under an array of different management incentive contracts, managers – while remaining state employees – gain new rights of control over product mix and production processes, the purchase of supplies and the marketing of products. They also gain new income rights through incentive schemes allowing retention of a percentage of the profits above a certain threshold. The different uses to which retained profits may be put are stipulated by the government, but include allowing a proportion to be spent on bonuses and welfare benefits for managers and workers.

While incentive contracts have typified reforms in urban areas, partnership contracts have been widely used in the countryside since the middle of the 1980s. These are drawn up between local governments and managers acting in an entrepreneurial capacity. The enterprises in question tend to be relatively small in scale, but not always so. In comparison with the incentive schemes of the larger public enterprises, these partnerships grant greater freedom and responsibility in the area of control and enjoy a larger share of the profits with fewer restraints on how this share may be used. Profits, however, are still shared, giving this form its distinctive partnership rather than leasing quality. Contracts tend to be longer than under incentive schemes, which are apt in practice to be annually adjusted. Typically, contracts last for three to five years, with no readjustment allowed for during that period. The entrepreneur-manager also bears greater risk in terms of job insecurity in the event of failure and loss of whatever money they have brought to the enterprise or reinvested rather than distributed.

With leased public assets, the leaseholder takes over all control and income rights for the fixed term of the lease. Disposal is limited to within the terms of the lease. Leasing has proved particularly popular in disposing of less profitable firms for which an outright purchaser cannot be found and has often served as a step towards privatisation. Privatisation itself brings us to the end of the continuum. With private ownership, the owners assume full rights of control, income and transfer within the limits set by government regulation and taxation.

In the next chapter, we look more closely at this shift in balance relating to the control of industry as it has developed beyond the urban heartlands of the state-owned enterprises. We turn to consider a unique Chinese phenomenon, the township and village enterprise.

6 Managing a surprise:
the township and village enterprises

- Comparative organisational strengths
- Enter the manager
- Contracts and collectives
- A helping hand

> What took us completely by surprise was the development of township and village industries. All sorts of small enterprises boomed in the countryside, as if a strange army had appeared suddenly from nowhere. This is not the achievement of our central government. Every year township and village enterprises achieve 20 per cent growth. This was not something I had thought about. Nor had the other comrades. It surprised us.
>
> Deng Xiaoping, *People's Daily*, 13 June 1987

Deng Xiaoping and his comrades were far from alone in their surprise at the explosive growth of rural industry in China. It was equally puzzling to those Western observers who held that the only way to rescue command economies was to privatise the economy as quickly as possible. Only by wrestling enterprises from the dead hand of the government bureaucracy could there be any hope of instilling dynamism into the economy. For such observers, a thorough movement to capitalism appeared the only answer, as gradual moves away from communism merely prolonged the agony through allowing officials to continue with their interference in matters beyond their competence. Local opposition to such plans was to be expected and consequently a clear national policy was required to push it forward.

In China, however, the rapid growth of enterprises in the countryside came about in the absence of privatisation or any national blueprint for reform. Far from acting as restraints on growth, the rural cadres brought it about through their management of public enterprises. This initially took place on their own initiative. Indeed, it was, for a short while, opposed by the central authorities for fear it would pose a threat to established state-owned enterprises. The dynamic role the local cadres played in promoting economic development stands in marked contrast with the conduct familiar from local officials in other transitional and developing economies.

Townships and villages are administrative areas that emerged out of the abolition of the communes and brigades into which peasants were organised during the Maoist era. They number over 48 000 towns and over 800 000 villages. Townships are the lowest rung of local government administration and are staffed by full-time paid career officials. Villages, on the other hand, are not part of the administrative hierarchy. Leaders at the village level are not paid as full-time officials, but do receive various expenses. The leader of the village is elected by the village, although at both township and village level the Communist Party committee or branch is the real seat of power. Confusingly, the term township and village enterprise is used in two different senses, one broad, and the other narrower. In its broader sense, it is roughly synonymous with rural industry, encompassing both collective enterprises owned by the townships and villages and private enterprises operating within their boundaries. In the narrower sense it is used to refer to the collectives alone, creating confusion that mirrors the ambiguous and shifting nature of the beast. Table 6.1 presents the official figures for the relative size of the different sectors in 1998.

In terms of ownership, the township and village collectives are described officially as belonging to all the members of the local community, and there is indeed often a proprietorial attitude towards them on the part of local people. This makes itself felt, for example, when it comes to expecting better conditions of service than are accorded to migrant workers. However, whatever the *de jure* position, *de facto* power rests in the hands of local leaders.

The onset of the reforms found these leaders stripped of many of their functions and powers in relation to agricultural production. As the communes were dissolved individual families took over responsibility for farming. They decided on land use, labour allocation and the distribution of revenues, all functions formerly in the hands of the local cadres. While the ownership of land passed in formal terms from the team to the village, in practice families acquired succession rights over the land they

Table 6.1 *The performance of township and village enterprises in 1998*

	Collective enterprise	Private company	Individual household	Total
Number of enterprises	1 065 825	2 222 037	16 751 491	20 039 353
Number of employees	48 286 279	26 204 029	50 875 150	125 365 458
Output (thousand yuan)	4 329 773 370	2 129 860 990	3 209 731 250	9 669 365 610
Sales revenue (thousand yuan)	3 828 407 120	1 887 026 460	3 219 667 820	8 935 101 400
Net profit (thousand yuan)	169 778 130	103 361 710	190 390 680	463 530 520
Total wages paid (thousand yuan)	248 299 810	129 392 120	247 494 290	625 186 220

Source: *Zhongguo Xiangzhen Qiye Nianjian 1999* (China Township and Village Enterprises Yearbook, 1999)

farmed and even limited transfer rights, enabling them to redistribute within the family and to subcontract use rights and quota obligations to other families. Stripped of their control over agricultural production and revenue, local leaders found themselves hard pressed for resources and consigned to a far less significant role than formerly. Cut off from their management role in farming, the promotion of industrial development beckoned as a way to restore their position. Collective enterprises would provide the means.

Pressure from both above and below added to the attraction of this course of action. The career prospects of local officials depend on increasing economic growth, both for its own sake and as a means of providing the revenue with which to achieve further goals. Leaders in the villages are not immune to career ambitions, with younger village heads cherishing hopes of being elevated to full-time government service. From below comes community pressure to provide employment and rising expectations fed by the new-found success seen in neighbouring communities. Living in the local community, leaders are often made acutely aware of such comparison and their failure to equal other communities in industrial development can result in painful loss of face. Conversely, those presiding over areas whose economic development outstrips their neighbours reap the benefit in terms of drawing local praise and official attention.

The reforms to the taxation system that took place in the mid-1980s gave further incentive to the drive to promote industry by rural officials. The reforms had the effect of making each district responsible for raising the funds needed for public services, rather than having these dispersed by the central government. The Chinese system of state revenue has always relied on industry rather than agriculture as its principal source of finance. Those areas with little or no industry now found themselves with a pressing need to develop it once they were cut off from the redistribution of funds from more industrialised areas provided by the state under the earlier taxation system. With industry of their own, not only would they be able to retain an element of the tax levied, but also further non-budgetary revenue would be generated in the form of profit remittances and fees.

Local officials are heavily dependent on the development of local industry to achieve a high rating when it comes to having their work appraised under the cadre evaluation system. Chen (2000) details one list of criteria employed for cadres in Qingyunpu Township in Jiangxi province in 1993 (see Table 6.2). This judges performance under the headings of economic development and the promotion of spiritual civilisation, with points divided equally between the two. The former includes such measures as the increase in the value of industrial output and profit, the increase in grain output and grain sales to the state, and the increase in rural per capita income. In terms of how they had advanced spiritual civilisation, the officials were judged according to the quality of cadre supervision, the maintenance of law and order, the development of education and family planning targets.

Achieving the economic targets set out under the cadre evaluation scheme clearly relies heavily upon industrial development. Furthermore, other targets are partly dependent on such development for success, for they rely on it to generate the funds needed to achieve their own success.

In addition to helping speed promotion or safeguard against relegation to some out-of-the-way posting, the success of township and village enterprises can be the source of numerous personal benefits to local officials in the form of bonuses and improved conditions of service. Perks proliferate. Officials not allowed to spend public funds on luxury cars, for example, may well find that they can borrow these for indefinite periods from enterprises under their wing.

Table 6.2 *Performance criteria for township leaders (Qingyunpu Township, Jiangxi Province), 1993*

	Points
Economic development	
Increase in township and village enterprise gross value of output	15
Increase in gross value of industrial output	15
Increase in industrial profit	10
Increase in gross value of agricultural output	10
Increase in grain output	10
Grain sales to the state	5
Increase in per capita net income of rural residents	10
Township fiscal revenue	10
Accomplishment of agricultural capital investment	5
Others (totalled)	10
Total points	100
Spiritual civilisation	
Cadre management and supervision	20
Political propaganda	10
Public order (crime and conflict control)	20
Education (completion rate for compulsory education and funds dedicated to education)	15
Family planning (birth control)	15
Other (totalled)	20
Total points	100

Source: Adapted from Chen (2000: 38)

Comparative organisational strengths

For much of the reform period, township and village enterprises have outpaced state-owned enterprises. Views differ on why this should have been the case, but Walder (1995) suggests that the key lies in moving away from considering the state as one monolithic entity to paying more attention to the various divisions and levels that exist within in it. While the central government owns and administers some state-owned industrial enterprises directly, the majority of firms under public ownership are, and always have been, vested in lower level local authorities. These authorities range from the provincial level down through municipalities and counties to the township and the village.

As one moves down the hierarchy the scale of enterprises in terms of output and employment drops. So also does the number of enterprises overseen, falling from the hundreds at the provincial level down to what might be two or three for a village. It is this greater ability of the lowest levels to monitor effectively their enterprises that in large measure accounts for their success relative to the state enterprises under higher-level authorities. The monitoring is more effective as it operates directly, with fewer levels of bureaucracy and supervisory bodies to slow and distort the flow of information.

The quality of scrutiny is not the only factor to move in favour of improved enterprise financial performance as one moves downwards in the scale of government. At the lowest level, among the township and village enterprises, there has never been the comprehensive provision of social welfare benefits in housing, health and retirement associated with the state-owned enterprises under the control of central and higher regional authorities. This split between state-owned enterprises and collectives in terms of the provision of such benefits has been estimated by one study to account for 40 per cent of the difference in profitability between the two (Xiao 1991).

Township and village collective enterprises not only did well in comparison with state-owned enterprises. They also outshone local private rivals, at least during the early years of the reforms. This resulted from a number of factors. In the first place, it must be remembered that the ideological suspicion surrounding private business did not disappear overnight. It was to ebb only gradually, returning at times during periods of political rectification. This was not an atmosphere conducive to the protection of private business against the demands of state bodies. Private enterprises stood little chance of success where conflicts arose between them and state enterprises or agencies. A lingering suspicion remained that private entrepreneurs were of dubious morality in their business practices and suspect in their political loyalty. This added to the appeal of putting on a red hat through leasing the title to a collective enterprise or entering into some form of partnership.

Private enterprises were also in a weaker position in comparison with the collectives in terms of access to resources. The shift from planning to the market took time, and took longer in relation to the factors of production than to the commodities they produced. In the meantime, connections with regard to administratively distributed resources remained a key to success. In the case of land, administrative allocation has continued to play a role down to the present day. Land remains in public ownership, despite long-term leasing arrangements and some ability to transfer rights to its use. Planning restrictions and compulsory repossession still give local government officials a forceful say over the use and disposal of land.

Private firms also fared worse than collectives in gaining loans from banks and rural credit cooperatives. Local authorities were able to offer themselves as guarantors of loans to their collective. Private entrepreneurs, in contrast, have generally held much less in the way of collateral and could not provide local authority guarantors. The collectives also benefited from the influence of the local authority with local bank branches and credit cooperatives. Another source of finance, widely resorted to, is through the compulsory purchase of shares by residents. One way in which this can be enforced, where necessary, is by withholding of payments due from the compulsory sale of grain to the state. In raising funds for new enterprises, or to assist established enterprises, the local authority was also able to call upon transfers from other collectives under its jurisdiction. The township or villages operated, in effect, like one corporation, shifting resources from one 'division' to another. This was not always completely straightforward, as at times it met with resentment and resistance on the part of the more successful firms who were having their resources drained in this manner. Negotiation might be called for, and the transfer arranged in terms of an interest-bearing loan from one enterprise to the other (Oi 1998).

The financial position of collectives was also bolstered by the active cooperation of the local authorities in various tax avoidance ploys. Funds, for example, could be shifted into non-budgetary areas controlled by the township alone. These included profits remitted from local collectives and fees charged to them. While a percentage of the taxes raised locally above a certain level was returned to the local government, revealing a high revenue capacity incurred the danger of having the threshold for tax remittance ratcheted up in future years, further increasing the appeal of tax avoidance.

An interesting feature of tax evasion by collective enterprises is the openness with which it is admitted to in conversation with those involved. In the eyes of the local officials and managers, such tactics are only to be expected in the struggle over the distribution of resources between the centre and the locality. It is a view summed up in the saying: 'The higher levels make policies and the lower levels find ways to get around them' (*shang you zhengce, xia you duice*). This is not to say that upper levels ignore such practices. Far from it. Circulars prohibiting the

Box 6.1 Tax evasion and collective enterprises

Among the 25 collective enterprises in the townships of Wuxi and Shanghai that were interviewed by Whiting, managers and accountants of 19 enterprises described practices involving tax evasion. They did not hesitate to discuss these practices because they perceived tax evasion in collective enterprises as legitimate. One manager described how his enterprise inflated costs to reduce taxable profits. He defended the practice stoutly: 'This is not tax evasion, because the state didn't invest in this enterprise and because it is for the collective.' Another manager stated that tax evasion 'is no problem because it's not an individual evading taxes for himself' (Whiting 2001: 198).

Township officials have an incentive to collude with the enterprise managers in tax evasion so that they can shift revenues from budgetary channels shared between the township and the state to non-budgetary ones controlled by the township alone. Collusion takes many forms, often taking advantage of the preferential policies granted to collective enterprises. A common practice reported by the managers was to rename the factory or one of the factory's workshops, and register it with the township industrial and commercial bureau as a new enterprise, which is then eligible for a multi-year tax exemption or reduction. Meanwhile the township officials still governed divided enterprises as one unit with one set of performance targets, one manager, a single set of internal account books and a single bank account. Such divisions and mergers occurred in cycles, with one enterprise dividing, merging and dividing again as tax exemptions expired. Although, under the state regulation, tax-exempt funds are only to be used within the enterprise, township officials often tapped into them to finance other activities.

Another form of preferential treatment often abused is tax exemption for new products. One manager described how his enterprise had been awarded tax exemption on one new product. This subsidy was stretched to embrace other and older products by the simple expedient of issuing receipts for them written in the name of new tax-exempt product. According to the manager, the township officials were aware of this practice, but his enterprise had contributed significantly to the township, including a donation of 80 000 yuan for the construction of new township government buildings.

Tax-exemption for welfare and school-run enterprises offered another route through which to evade tax. Local officials created welfare factories simply by listing a number of handicapped individuals on enterprise payrolls. Schools that supposedly sponsored enterprises often did not actually exist. In Wuxi there were so many 'school-run' enterprises that the local government had to put a ceiling on the level of exemption.

Higher level bureaucracies also joined in tax evasion, often bribed by county and township officials or enterprise managers. In the case of granting tax exemptions for new products, provincial or national level state agencies were involved in certifying the new products. According to one manager, his county government officials influenced the Shanghai municipal tax bureau to grant more approvals through bribing technical experts from the Shanghai science and technology commission.

Source: Whiting (2001: 198–201)

abuse of tax breaks abound, as do attempts to plug similar loopholes. However, in the face of the persistence of evasion, pragmatism points to a role for flexibility and negotiation in place of any hope of being able rigidly to enforce a code of uniform rules.

Technology has been another area in which collectives were better placed than their private counterparts to benefit through officials using connections with state-run enterprises to establish various forms of cooperation or subcontracting. This particularly benefited rural areas near large cities rich in state-owned industrial enterprises and research units. Yet, even for more remote areas, study tours by local cadres and their visits to successful models, often far away, can enable them to serve as a valuable conduit of information concerning new products and techniques.

Personnel recruitment and development were also easier for township and village collectives. Part-time work by personnel from state-owned enterprises was more acceptable when seen as assisting with the public sector than with the private. Residence permits for staff and their families were also in the gift of the local authority when it came to recruiting from outside the area. Managerial and technical staff were also attracted to the collectives by better tems and conditions of service than those on offer from private entrepreneurs.

Enter the manager

The organisational edge that township and village enterprises enjoyed over the state-owned firms and private enterprises put these local enterprises in an excellent position to benefit from the reforms. Able to take advantage of the gaps left in production by the large state enterprises and the unleashing of pent-up consumer demand, township and village collectives began to grow in size and number. The increase in the number and scale of their operation meant, however, that local officials no longer had sufficient time free from their other duties to devote to the detailed control of the collectives. The result was the emergence of a group of professional enterprise managers. Whereas, initially, managers of the collectives were often regarded as little more than technicians or foremen transmitting the instructions of the local cadres, they began to assume increasing power and autonomy.

Just who were these managers? Chen's (2000: 77–79) survey of township and village enterprises provides us with a broad sketch. Her sample found managers to be drawn almost entirely from the locality (85 per cent). They were, however, better educated than others in the locality and 75 per cent were members of the Communist Party. Doubtless this last factor carried some weight in appointments, but it is clearly not sufficient nor in every case necessary. Indeed, the reverse pattern of cause and effect is known, with successful managers being invited to join the Party to integrate them into the local power structure. More importance attaches to proven financial acumen, as is attested in some areas by the use of open bidding to fill posts. Prior to their appointment, 19 per cent of the sample were Party cadres, 36 per cent managers of other township or village enterprises, 33 per cent former employees (frequently technicians or in the field of procurement or marketing), 7 per cent were employees of state-owned enterprises, and 5 per cent were private owners. All were men, reflecting in part the greater strength in rural areas of traditional prejudice in their favour.

Contracts and collectives

Broadly speaking, there are three types of contract that have developed to govern the relationship between these enterprise managers and the local authority. They form a continuum stretching from fixed wage through profit sharing to fixed payment made by the manager to lease or purchase the firm. As one moves away from the fixed wage end of the continuum, greater responsibility is assumed for the running of the firm. Along with this goes an increase in profit share and exposure to risk. The three types contain within themselves variants on this general theme. Thus, fixed wages can be supplemented by bonuses related to performance, and profit sharing can be divided between non-mortgage and mortgage varieties. In the latter case, the manager has to pledge a certain sum that may be forfeited to defray any losses that arise. Fixed payment includes both leasing for a specific period and outright purchase through auctions or other means. With fixed payment, the reward of profit and the risk of loss is transferred to the manager–entrepreneur.

The pattern of such contracts has tended to change with time, shifting away from the fixed wage end of the continuum. At the same time, despite this trend, all three types can still be encountered, often coexisting in the same community. There are also regional differences in the types favoured. Why has this trend taken place? What accounts for variations within one area? And what accounts for variations between areas?

Part of the answer to these questions lies in the changing nature of the transactions involved in managing these enterprises. As such, it can be illuminated by insights drawn from transaction economics, with its emphasis on the costs that shift reliance for completing transactions back and forth between markets and hierarchies (Williamson 1975; Chen 2000).

Together with the shift in patterns of reward has gone a change in the distribution of managerial duties. First, *internal* management activities concerned with organising daily production are delegated to managers. These include assigning and coordinating tasks, and monitoring performance and quality control. As the number and size of enterprises under a local authority grew, the local cadres had no option but to delegate such tasks to enterprise managers. This introduced a principal–agent problem. How were they to ensure that managers would not shirk their responsibilities? Close monitoring was out of the question, as it would have drawn cadres in to the very commitments from which they were trying to extricate themselves. The alternative was to align the manager's interests with those of the local government through offering to share the profits from the enterprise.

At the same time as managers were taking over internal management, the continued involvement of the local cadres was needed in matters of *external* management, the area covering tasks such as the procurement of inputs of raw materials, energy, investment funds and equipment, the marketing of output and the recruitment of personnel. This was in large measure due to the undeveloped nature of the markets in such areas, which placed a high premium on the privileged access accorded to cadres, both through official channels and through unofficial connections. This function was vital to the success of the enterprise. This division of labour between managers and local officials also introduced a further twist to the principal–agent relationship. Managers needed to see that officials did not shirk the responsibility they had assumed for external management. Profit sharing served this purpose too, giving the cadres an incentive to fulfil their part of the understanding. For this reason, managers also preferred profit sharing as the form of contract best suited to the prevailing business environment. For them to move towards a fixed payment leasing arrangement would have been a less optimal solution. Indeed, this partly accounts for private entrepreneurs at this stage not simply donning a red hat in name only but actively entering into various forms of closer collaboration with local authorities in establishing and running enterprises.

Yet having local cadres on board to cope with the problems posed by market irregularities was not without cost. The goals of local officials are not confined to maximising the profits of the enterprise and so this single goal may at times be sacrificed as a result. With the gradual improvement in the operation of markets, the balance of costs and benefits of cadre involvement in business was to shift yet again. By the early 1990s, this process of improvement had speeded up dramatically. Between 1990 and 1993, for example, the proportion of retail goods subject to market pricing rose from 53 per cent to 93 per cent and the proportion of production factors from 36 per cent to 81 per cent (Chen 2000: 144). As a result, the external management functions of the local government shrank.

With less involvement in the running of the enterprise, as external management moved to join internal management in the hands of managers, it became increasingly difficult for local authorities to obtain precise information on the actual performance of the firm. Were profits being hidden? With less involvement in the firm's affairs, monitoring became ever more expensive as an option. With more and more transactions mediated by the market, in the absence of reliable accounts the number of supervisory staff needed to make monitoring effective was simply uneconomical. A fixed fee system offered a solution that proved less demanding not only for local cadres, but also for enterprise managers, who no longer had to rack their brains over how to conceal profits. Moreover, divested of the multiple aims of the local cadres, the firm was in a more competitive position with its focus on profitability before all else.

Such a focus became more important as township and village enterprises fell victim to their own success. As more and more townships and villages entered the market on the heels of their neighbours, often choosing what to produce solely on the basis of imitating what appeared to have achieved success elsewhere, overproduction started to bite into profits everywhere. For those who had turned to foreign markets, the profit squeeze intensified as higher quality demands increased the price of inputs. For the local township or village, firms that earlier had been assets began to be liabilities.

The inability of local authorities to sustain loss-making enterprises was further increased by tax reforms undertaken in 1994 and 1996. These replaced reliance on local authorities to collect taxes and divided taxes into three categories: local taxes, national taxes, and those shared between both. National and shared taxes were placed under the responsibility of a new central taxation authority. Restrictions were also enforced that discouraged the transfer of funds into realms that could escape taxation. While the effectiveness of these measures was reduced by difficulties in implementation they nevertheless began to subject local authorities to tight budget constraints.

Credit started to get tighter and more expensive. Banks were becoming increasingly commercial in their outlook. While the large state-owned enterprises continued to be allocated loans, the collective sector had never been favoured to the same extent. Unlike the large state enterprises, the size of single collectives left them outside the category of companies too large to fail because of the unemployment implications. With increasing failures among the township and village enterprises, banks found themselves facing increasing levels of bad debts. Townships and villages no longer had the resources to back up their guarantees. Bankruptcy offered little compensation – the banks were placed last in line for whatever was left. With the tighter market of the 1990s forcing more closures, townships and villages were less able than before to make up for the shortfall in bank loans by shifting resources from one collective to aid another.

These changes led local politicians, in areas that had previously frowned upon or ignored private enterprise, to turn a more kindly eye in its direction. This left them more ready to contemplate disposing of enterprises to cut losses and raise funds, a move that quickened in pace as the 1990s progressed. This result in many areas reproduced a local version of the national policy of 'keeping hold of the big and letting go of the small', leaving many townships or villages with a variety of different types of enterprises within their borders.

Which enterprise is held on to and which shifted to the private sector has partly been shaped by differences in technical structure. Where marketing and other external management tasks are relatively unimportant in comparison with quality control and internal monitoring, the balance of forces favours fixed payment leasing and sale. In contrast, for those firms with high capital investment that is specific and cannot readily be transferred to other uses, the balance shifts back towards the local authority retaining ownership, even to the extent of using a variation of the fixed wage system. Differences in the extent and intensity of the public ownership of township and village enterprises also remain between areas. In the poorer areas, where collective enterprises are fewer,

Box 6.2 The rise and decline of the village as a corporation

Some townships and villages have long attracted attention because they operate much like corporations. Qiaolou, a village in Sichuan, is typical. As Ruf (1999) illustrates in his study of the village, its history has revolved around the attempts of local officials to manage all the village enterprises as if they were subdivisions of a single firm. The village was to operate as one business, with the village leader at the helm.

When the contract-responsibility system for farming was introduced in Sichuan, Qiaolou was among the last villages to abandon collectivisation. Instead of implementing the state-mandated reforms, which would diminish their control over the economic life of the village, the leaders were endeavouring to strengthen their power by establishing a new non-agricultural collective sector. The finance for the new sector was provided from a capital accumulation fund established previously by the village when it was a brigade under the commune system.

The first major investments were made in 1976. The village cadres purchased 3 000 tangerine saplings and transplanted them into two orchards. In the same year, the village cadres opened the first collectively owned factory to produce bricks. The collective nature of this factory, set against the background of the agricultural reforms, drew support from higher authorities. The county government arranged deferred interest loans of approximately 300 000 yuan from the Agricultural Bank and granted the village a one-year tax exemption for its efforts in promoting collectively owned and operated rural enterprises.

Established at the beginning of a house-construction boom in Sichuan, the brick factory flourished. The village repaid the bank loan within three years. The rest of the income was mainly employed in establishing more enterprises. These included a transport team with five trucks in 1983, a second brick factory in 1984 and a sorghum distillery in 1985, all of them owned collectively by the village.

Each family in the village also financed the brick factories through the compulsory purchase of shares. Families without cash to buy them had their income from compulsory state grain sales withheld by the village leaders. Despite this contribution, the villagers had little influence over any decisions regarding the enterprises, which were managed by committees of the village council. In turn, the Party secretary, nominated by the county Party committee, controlled the village council.

The Party secretary exercised his power over most important issues regarding the enterprises. He nominated managers and staff, set production targets, budgetary allocations, and revenue projections. Revenue from profitable enterprises was repeatedly appropriated to subsidise those less productive.

During the 1980s, collective enterprises in Qiaolou were very successful. The brick factories were benefiting from the booming construction market, the distillery was producing an award-winning spirit popular at banquets and the orchards exported oranges to Russia and Japan. Production was up and so were profits. Families in the village enjoyed advantages unavailable to those in neighbouring villages. The enterprises provided them with waged employment. The village leaders used the revenues from the enterprises to support family tax subsidies. Basic health care was free of charge through a 'barefoot doctor'. A primary school was built. Roads were laid. The village was repeatedly awarded titles such as 'advanced civilised village' by the state. Visiting delegations from all over the nation toured village enterprises for inspiration. Village leaders would proudly recite to the visitors a growing list of consumer goods owned by the villagers: bicycles, washing machines, refrigerators, colour televisions and VCRs.

However, in the early 1990s, markets for products from the enterprises began to tighten. The housing construction boom started to slow down, while new kilns set up by neighbouring townships using better quality clay began to pose serious competition. A large number of distilleries had been set up throughout the province and began to depress the market. Orange cultivation had become a universal family enterprise in the province, bringing prices down. Many townships and villages started to lease out their collective enterprises.

In Qiaolou, however, the Party secretary was determined to maintain the village and its enterprises as one unit.

In pursuit of this objective, he set up a joint venture with a private group of technicians from a state-owned institute in Chengdu to convert one of the brick factories into a zinc refinery. The technicians provided the joint venture with knowledge and skill, while the village paid for the equipment. The technicians managed operations, with authority over decisions regarding supply, production and marketing. However, one year later the joint venture fell apart when the Party secretary wanted to use the refinery revenues to subsidise other enterprises in the village.

In 1995, using their political capital with county authorities, the village leaders obtained another low-interest loan with which they purchased a production line imported from Italy for manufacturing automobile tyres. However, with the loan not enough to provide operation funds, the facilities lay idle.

Faced with mounting debts, costly production lines and discontented families, the Party secretary decided to take a dramatic departure from his earlier stance. He started to seek a foreign partner to invest in a joint venture in order to get production rolling at the tyre factory. He had also to agree to contract out the loss-making distillery to its production supervisor. Paying a one-time fee, the manager was given a long-term lease with authority to run the distillery as he wished. With funds raised from a family fruit enterprise and borrowed from friends and relatives, the manager now entered into a partnership with a technical expert from the county to improve on the quality of the products. In a short while, it was returning a profit.

Further inroads into the village corporation were made when the Party secretary was made an offer for the lease of several street-front rooms in the village office building from a young villager. He paid a one-time fee for a long-term lease and then refurbished the rooms into a small restaurant and karaoke bar. The young man was once in prison and his success in persuading the Party secretary to abandon long-held socialist convictions was rumoured to be due to a threat to blow up the village office building in the event of refusal.

Meanwhile, a new generation of young village leaders and managers is coming of age. Although many of these are heirs of old village cadres, most of them lack the ideological commitment to collectivism and the memories of hardship and scarcity that fuel the anxieties and concerns of the older generation. Neither do they regard collective enterprises as a means to pursue their own interests. The nephew of the Party secretary, for example, is now managing one of the brick factories as well as deputising for the Party secretary. He is has acquired the reputation for being more concerned with economic development than with politics. Unlike his uncle, it is his belief that collective village enterprises must ultimately be contracted out to individual entrepreneurs if managerial efficacy, high productivity and profitable returns are to be achieved.

Source: Ruf (1999)

and with each more central to the economic well being of the local community, their position allows – and demands – more attention from local leaders.

Rural industrial growth did not everywhere follow the same general trend outlined above. Along the coastal fringe of south-eastern China, rural officials never played such a leading role in running township and village enterprises as elsewhere. Such village enterprises that did exist in such areas were sold off or leased at an early stage in the reforms and officials confined themselves more to a supporting role in fostering the growth of private enterprise. The roots of this difference can partly be traced back to the Maoist era. As mentioned earlier, townships and villages had their origin in the communes and brigades of that time. In many areas, these operated rural industries, providing cadres with capital and business expertise from which to launch or expand enterprises. With the abolition of collective farming, cadres turned to these to bolster their declining power.

The coastal regions, however, had never been well endowed with communes and brigades that had accumulated resources, such as those necessary for large-scale farm mechanisation and irrigation control. Nor had they developed rural industry to any great extent. Where they did have access to resources, however, was in the form of private capital. Provinces such as Fujian have a long history of emigration that provides family connections to the overseas Chinese business community. Further funds come from remittances home from migrant workers in more prosperous parts of the country. The coastal regions have had a long history of commercial involvement, stretching back to the days before collectivisation. One final ingredient in producing a climate more favourable to private enterprise was the remoteness of these enterprises, offering greater independence from the centre. In a situation where 'the sky is high and the emperor far away', local authorities had a freer hand in exploring the new possibilities opened up by the reforms.

Differences also exist between enterprises operating under townships and those under villages (Kung 1999). A township can consist of several thousand households and, consequently, relationships between officials, managers and employees tend to be rather more impersonal. Those responsible for failing township enterprises may find themselves moved to less desirable posts, but the very movement brings some escape from the scene of their disgrace. For village officials who are not full-time members of the bureaucracy there is no such escape. If they lose their place, they are likely to continue residing and working in the village and to be subject to the censure of their neighbours for the unemployment resulting from their mismanagement.

Village residents are also likely to take a more proprietorial interest in village collectives. This is partly the result of the village being designated a self-governing organisation rather than a tier of the government bureaucracy, as is the case with the township. This can make labour discipline more of a problem for managers of collectives where the employees view themselves as privileged by their joint ownership. This is especially so where funds have been raised from the workers or other villagers in the form of shares or bonds. Their purchase is often regarded as including within it the right to a job.

There is also resistance to increasing the rewards of managers relative to workers, from norms of social equality that make themselves more strongly felt than in the townships. Nevertheless, the need to restrain the growth in earnings differentials between workers and managers is felt up to national level, with Ministry of Agriculture officials warning against allowing these to increase too far on the grounds they may de-motivate workers. Ironically, back at the local level, such sentiments and norms can lead to their own undoing. Driven by the need to find a means of motivating and empowering managers on the one hand and subject to critical scrutiny by villagers on the other, some village Party secretaries find the prospect of distancing themselves from a troublesome enterprise by lease or sale beginning to have unexpected appeal.

Despite the small size of villages, it would be a mistake to view village enterprises as invariably small in character. Some have grown from

modest beginnings to enormous dimensions, as in the case of
Daqiuzhang, a village on the outskirts of Tianjin in northern China.
On the verge of starvation in 1966, by 1988 it was producing an output
valued at 403 million yuan with assets valued at 90 million yuan. All this
was achieved for a local population that stood at 3886 in 1989, enabling
it to enjoy in 1990 a per capita income ten times the national average
(Lin and Chen 1999: 151).

As with almost any area of Chinese life, one cannot pass over the topic of
township and village enterprises without mention of family influence and
Daqiuzhang was no exception. The driving force behind the success of
the village was its Party secretary, Yu Zuomin. By the time the village
enterprises had expanded to the level outlined above, his grip over them
was reinforced through the placement of his relations at key points of
what was by then known as the Daqiuzhang Agricultural-Industrial-
Commercial United Corporation. Yu combined the roles of Chairman of
the corporation, secretary-general of the local Party, and village head.
One of his sons served as general manager, while a cousin, a son-in-law,
and a niece's husband headed three of the five groups into which the
organisation was divided. The Board of Trustees contained two of Yu's
cousins and the office of administration was presided over by his
mistress, Shi Jiamin. One of Shi's brothers handled development zone
enterprise, another was in charge of the electricity office and a third led
the electronics company. Her sister ran the Tianjin office (Lin and Chen
1999: 153).

Yu Zuomin suffered a spectacular fall from grace in 1993 when he was
jailed following an incident when he had encouraged local resistance to a
police investigation into the beating to death of an employee by company
security personnel. Had he not been caught up in the toils of hubris there
is every reason to believe his family power would have continued
unabated. In many ways, Daqiuzhang merely writ large the drive to
interlace family networks with political power and economic enterprise
that has been common to many villages and townships.

Satisfying this drive does not come without cost, however. The need
to employ on grounds of talent becomes more pressing as competition
sharpens, and this has been reflected in the recruitment policies of many
of the more dynamic township and village enterprises. Thus, while they
tend to recruit line-workers from within the township or village to satisfy
local expectations, larger firms are increasingly turning to wider markets
in their search for technical and managerial staff (Ding et al. 2001).

Box 6.3 Raising our heads above the fields

At the beginning of the 1980s, a local township enterprise built a 24-floor hotel in Pudong, then a rural area to the east of the city of Shanghai. The hotel was the tallest building in Pudong at that time, although now the surrounding skyscrapers completely dwarf it. The hotel became a household name in Shanghai almost immediately. The fame was brought about by its name: *Youyou*.

Tian – field   You – to free

As can be seen, the character for the Chinese word *you* is very similar to the character *tian*, meaning 'field'. *Tian* itself resembles the Chinese paddy fields. Allowing the vertical line dividing the square to escape through the top, the ideograph turns into *you* – roughly speaking, to free. It was just this that the hotel promised the farmers, the choice of a better life, one free from days spent toiling in the sun. For them, the character 'shows us raising our heads above the fields', as one employee remarked.

Youyou grew out of what was the commune of Yanqiao. In the beginning of the 1980s, the commune started to build a factory subcontracting work for a state-owned garment factory. The factory was a success and provided funds for setting up other enterprises.

Although the enterprises were successful, there were problems related to their ownership. The head of the town was the general manager of every enterprise. He and other township leaders freely moved money from successful enterprises to subsidise loss-making enterprises or to provide funds for other township bodies. As a result, successful enterprises could not accumulate enough to expand and managers lost motivation. It was partly in an effort to tackle the problems that, in 1992, the enterprises were turned into shareholding cooperatives. The change, however, proved difficult. The main difficulty was how to divide the assets among the enterprises and the township government, and over how many shares should be sold and at what price. Since there was no clear government policy on these issues, the township and the enterprises fought hard for their interests. Both parties approached government bodies above the township level, but the government officials felt equally at a loss in the absence of any state guidance. Eventually it was agreed that the township People's Congress should decide the issue. The congress met and voted on the share percentage issue. The congress decided that the collective should hold 60 per cent of the shares, with the rest sold to the managers, workers and residents of the town.

In the event, the shareholding cooperatives failed to provide sufficient incentive to the managers and employees. In the late 1990s, it was decided to abandon the cooperatives in favour of the, by then, fashionable joint stock company form. Shares of the companies were sold to individuals and private businesses outside the township, and managers had to buy additional shares if they wanted to retain their positions.

At the same time, Pudong began to develop into a financial centre. As a result, most the township and village enterprises in Yanqiao lost their land. The township also disappeared, with most of its residents moved to allow redevelopment. The government relocated the enterprises to one area and merged them into the Youyou Group. The group now has 18 subsidiaries involved in property development, hotels, tourism, manufacturing car parts, car sales and maintenance, storage and transportation, textiles and clothing, and food processing.

The governing body of Youyou Group is the shareholders meeting. The board has seven members. One member is from the former township collective asset management committee, another is a representative of the employee shareholders. Three more are representatives from external shareholders. The final two are independent board directors. One is a lawyer, the other a professor from the management school of a local university. According to the vice-chairman of the group, nobody on the board is from a government body. However, the nominations of the board members have to be approved by the local government and the Party committee. In the words of the vice-chairman: 'they had to have a look at the members to make sure everybody is all right.' There is also a supervisory committee, which is supposed to exercise supervision over the board, but in practice it appears, like the great majority of such bodies, to have little real influence. The vice-chairman remarked of it: 'we put the retired leaders in that committee, it is a most suitable place for them.'

Economically, Youyou does not have a direct relationship with any government body apart from paying taxes. The Pudong government asserts its influence on the company mainly through industrial policy. Politically, the Group is under the leadership of the Industrial Committee of the Pudong government. The Industrial Committee has two subcommittees in charge of Party affairs and trade unions. In these two areas, the Group is under the leadership of these subcommittees. At the Group level, the Party is still very important. The Party secretary is also chairman of the board. At the subsidiary level, some of the Party secretaries are also general managers. The vice-chairman remarks that he does not think there is any conflict between the management and the Party; in many cases, they are the same people. The Party mainly propagates state policies and assists managerial work. In 2001, a dozen managers and staff from the group joined the Party. The vice-chairman said: 'We realise that we have to rely on ourselves. If we do well economically, most of the things will be all right. But of course we need the Party to create a favourable macro-environment.'

The group does not borrow money from state banks. The vice-chairman says: 'we believe that we should rely on ourselves. We save money so that we can expand. But I do not think the banks would refuse us if we went to borrow money, because they know we have been so successful. It is very important to do well by yourself, then everybody respects you, even though you are a township enterprise.'

Having already accumulated assets worth 40 million yuan, Youyou tried to obtain government permission to issue its shares in the Shanghai Stock Exchange. It failed, however, because most of the businesses of Youyou are not among those the government wishes to assist.

Youyou has been actively seeking strategic alliances with companies from other sectors. Many of its joint ventures are with overseas Chinese with roots in the former township. However, it has also formed a joint venture with a German partner to produce car parts, and a joint venture with a state-owned company in property development.

In its daily operations, Youyou has not been troubled by many unreasonable levies or charges. Nevertheless, as the vice-president puts it: 'When government bodies have some trouble and need help, the Group should help if it can.'

More serious are the many bad debts from state-owned companies. For example, the government-owned land developer has not paid much of the compensation due for taking away the land. The group has been asking for this for two years. Yet, it is still felt important to maintain a good relationship. As the vice chairman explained, 'we have a subsidiary that produces office furniture. When the land developer moved to a new office building, we furnished all its offices for free.'

Youyou has a policy that top managers from the subsidiaries have to buy a certain percentage of shares in the companies they manage. The group signs performance contracts with them on a yearly basis. In addition, the Group nominates directly all the chief accountants of the subsidiaries. Every week the chief accountants return to the Group to report on the financial situation of the subsidiaries.

Most of the managers of the subsidiaries were managers of the former enterprises, but some were openly recruited from outside. It is difficult, however, to attract experienced managers and skilled technicians to the company, as most prefer to work for foreign-owned companies. The Group signs a two-year contract with these externally recruited managers, and a one-year contract with externally recruited workers. However, managers and workers from the former collective enterprises have lifetime contracts as a compensation for the loss for their agricultural land. The Group and its subsidiaries find it difficult to discipline these employees.

The employees enjoy social welfare similar to state enterprises in terms of the provision of medical insurance and pensions. The municipality, the group and the employees themselves share the costs. Youyou is very active in carrying out state policies and conducting campaigns as instructed by the Party. It has a family planning office. It also fulfils the government's blood donation quota better than other companies. And every year it fills its official quota of titles to be awarded to model workers and model managers.

Fieldwork notes, 2001

A helping hand

As we have seen, local officials started to take a more sympathetic view of private involvement in establishing or taking over township and village enterprises in the 1990s. At the county level, it was increasingly appreciated that the private sector could not only provide increasing tax revenues to the local authority, it could also relieve the authority of both the risk and the burden of running the enterprises. The response of the local authorities to this recognition was not, however, to retire from the fray and to watch from the sidelines. There was recognition that, while entrepreneurs could bring an invaluable source of fresh ideas and initiative to rural development, they would only succeed in favourable circumstances. Only then would they be able to marshal the resources and show a willingness to take on the risks necessary to develop on a large scale. Just as the local authorities had earlier assisted the growth of the collective sector, they now started to take private rural enterprise under their wing, providing these enterprises with similar assistance in their external management. Officials in the more business-friendly counties now lobby for loans for key private enterprises and direct local credit associations to expand their lending to the sector. Technical assistance and market information, often crucial at the early stage of enterprise development, is now made available to the private sector through the same bureaucratic channels as assisted the collectives in their take-off. Approvals and licences are granted with greater ease.

The hand held out by local authority is not always there simply to help, however. In addition to receiving help, rural enterprises find themselves receiving a variety of unreasonable and arbitrary charges levied by local officials. This has worsened as cadres struggle to make up for having to cut back on levies on farmers due to the increasing resistance to such charges. With limits on what the cadres can extract from the farmers comes increasing needs as the rural bureaucracy has grown in size, partly in response to increased expectations regarding the provision of local services. Desperate for funds, the cadres have resorted to the only target to hand, the local enterprises.

From a beginning when they were ignored by the state, township and village enterprises have become the subject of planning up through the provincial to the national level. One result is that they are now being encouraged to look beyond their immediate community with the hope that they will grow into industrial groups, based around successful enterprises, capable of establishing recognised brands. With this in mind, there is a move to encourage rural enterprises to relocate to newly created industrial parks, often catering to one particular line of business. Often these will be created at, or near, county or town seats. The aim is partly to secure improvements in purchasing, marketing and technological development, partly to provide a better environment to attract outside technicians and also to stem the flow of rural labour to the large cities.

The plan aims to promote selected industries at the same time as discouraging others, such as brick-building, from diverting land away from agriculture, and discouraging coal mining because of the associated pollution problems. Those making the plans hope that they may be able to alleviate excess capacity in certain areas, but in this as with state-owned enterprises, the tradition of regions duplicating lists of industries to be encouraged leaves little likelihood of success. Enterprises may have grown out of the plan, but the planners certainly have not.

Box 6.4 Into leather

The shift towards a greater reliance on private enterprise within the townships and villages has not resulted in the government retiring from active participation in business to the role of a mere regulator. As Blecher and Shue (2001) illustrate in their account of the development of the Xinji leather industry, the guiding hand of the state has lost none of its firm paternal grip.

The city of Xinji in Hebei province had a long tradition of leather production and trade, a tradition that gave way in the Maoist era to the production of chemicals and machinery under the state plan. Beginning from the 1980s, however, under the initiative of private businesses and rural township and village enterprises, the tradition revived. In the 1990s, with the state-owned sectors faltering, the leather industry once again became the major industry in Xinji, with total output value exceeding 200 million yuan per year.

Starting from 1991, the local government of Xinji decided to take the development of this up-and-coming yet largely private industry in hand. It had a vision of turning the industry into a major player in the domestic and international market. To achieve this goal, the mayor conducted a survey of the industry and decided that most of the enterprises were too small and geographically dispersed to be competitive. So it was decided that a large central marketplace was needed to house all the enterprises under one roof. The mayor argued that the big marketplace would attract more investment and businesses from home and abroad. Moreover, with the gathering of the industry into one marketplace, business information and technology could be dispersed more effectively.

The inspiration of the mayor fitted well with the state policy for rural development. The government was looking for ways to revitalise the faltering township and village enterprises. One of its solutions was to merge the small enterprises into groups and to move them into industrial parks in county seats. This, according to the government, would enable the township and village enterprises to achieve economies of scale and would also help them to upgrade their technology. Therefore, Xinji's proposed marketplace became a project included in the state plan. In 1992, it was designated one of the country's ten primary projects in that year. The total project would cost over 800 million yuan.

However, it proved difficult to persuade private businesses to invest in the project. The mayor and his colleagues in the local government had to employ financial and administrative resources under their control to persuade private entrepreneurs to build stores in the marketplace. Many incentives were given to investors. The municipality, for example, granted the investors full rights over the use, rental and sale of buildings they constructed. Under the influence of the municipality, local state banks provided investors with loans to cover 70 per cent of the building cost. The banks also promised to provide future loans and preferential treatment to investors. The local tax bureau offered tax exemptions on investment in new property and on business income. The public security bureau offered city residence to investors and their families and the education committee agreed to accept children of the investors into their school – both important considerations. The state-owned telecommunications company offered price cuts on its services.

At the same time as the marketplace was launched, the officials turned their attention to the tanneries. The officials had a vision of a garden-like industrial park, with state-of-the-art facilities and machinery producing top-quality leather products for export. In 1995, three special zones were built, all of them equipped with modern tannery machinery, pollution control laboratories and water purification facilities. Although part of this multi-million yuan investment was funded by the state, private businesses were ordered to pool their money together to buy into these facilities so that they could produce products up to the standard the government desired.

With the completion of the marketplace and the tannery zones, government officials also established ways to administer the industry. A supervising commission was established to lead and shape the development of the private businesses. The commission employed about 60 full-time staff and 100 part-time staff from various local government bureaux. Its presence was felt everywhere. It worked with the tax bureau to collect tax, with the police to keep order and the Party to carry out ideological campaigns. The quality office of the commission rigorously checked on the quality of the goods traded to ensure there were no fake or sub-quality goods in the market. The office also encouraged and helped businesses to establish their own trademarks. The labour office checked all the labour contracts to ensure that they met the requirements of the labour law.

However, more importantly, the supervision commission managed many aspects of production and trading for the private businesses. As one official put it, 'we changed the past practice of letting enterprises develop of their own accord. Instead of letting the water run here and there on its own, we have relied on providing guidance and services, and top-to-bottom planning of enterprise development, so that the trade centre grows along the path to excellence . . . we have supported the strongest and the most superior firms, so that the trade centre will develop in the direction of more large- and medium-sized backbone firms' (Blecher and Shue 2001: 386).

Among many of its efforts to promote the enterprises, the commission spent 11.5 million yuan to carry out a national television advertisement campaign. It organised enterprises to establish direct sales outlets in major cities. It facilitated the establishment of joint ventures between foreign companies and private enterprises.

In 1997, the commission organised a chamber of commerce. The chamber has recruited 57 of the biggest enterprises from the marketplace as members. The chamber helped work on controlling wage competition, the retention of skilled workers and coordinating in the purchase of raw material.

One private owner from the market commented that the Xinji government 'runs the business associations, organised the market, convenes market research conferences, provides information, convenes an annual market fair, and generally works hard at trade promotion by helping us make connections and attract business. So basically we don't have to find customers; the government does it for us' (Blecher and Shue 2001: 387).

Source: Blecher and Shue (2001)

7 Where the twain meet

- Establishing the venture
- Interpreting the law
- The return of the comprador
- Learning and adjustment in the joint venture
- Conflict and control in Chinese organisations
- Us and them
- Formalisation and responsibility
- Human resources
- The homecoming

> I help him communicate, which for a Western businessman is very difficult.
>
> Wendi Deng, Chinese wife of Rupert Murdoch,
> on her role of helping him expand his business in China
> (*Far Eastern Economic Review*, 15 June 2000: 86)

Negotiating a path through the complex world of contemporary Chinese business is enough to tax the ingenuity and talent of Chinese managers familiar with the system. Foreign managers introduced into this world find themselves even more baffled by the system, but more at ease with the challenges thrown up by market forces. International joint ventures should operate at an advantage through blending such complementary strengths. Nevertheless, this is not always easy to achieve.

Part of the problem lies in the conflicting aims and interests of the different parties. Such conflicts are common in any strategic alliance, which nevertheless may go ahead on the basis that the gains outweigh whatever sacrifices are necessary to reach an accommodation. For the Chinese state, the chief aim in encouraging foreign investment is to gain access to foreign capital, advanced technology and managerial skills. At a lower level, for the Chinese firm seeking a joint venture, further considerations such as greater managerial autonomy, higher salaries and tax concessions may also feature in the equation. Local authorities and other Chinese stakeholders in joint ventures may also be more interested in realising short-term profits than in ploughing revenue back into the enterprise for long-term growth.

For the foreign side, the attractions of locating in China frequently include the hope of accessing a large domestic market and the opportunity to benefit from resources not available on such favourable terms elsewhere. Given these different aims, the ideal combination might be conceived as one in which the Chinese side provides labour and materials at low cost, but of sufficient quality, with some access to the Chinese market, while the foreign side provides new technology and foreign exchange earnings. Striking such a balance requires careful negotiation.

Establishing the venture

The first problem faced by the prospective investor is that of securing trustworthy information. Statistics at local and national level are unreliable. This stems from a wide variety of sources. They may be stretched by those seeking to claim credit for expanding output or shrunk by those wishing to avoid tax. Company accounts, as mentioned earlier, share a similarly dubious reputation. Such sources of information have improved over the course of the reforms, but they still fall far short of international standards. Similarly, investment guidelines outlining those areas in which foreign investment is encouraged or forbidden are now published where once they were secret. They remain, however, guidelines, subject to interpretation, narrow or broad as that may be. Reporting remains varied in quality, and Hong Kong based journalists have, on occasion, been arrested for reporting figures about state enterprises which elsewhere would be regarded as open to legitimate public interest.

In these circumstances, one needs inside knowledge. Where formal information is withheld or unreliable, or where rules are so general as to leave much leeway for interpretation, those without access to informal channels of information are at a severe disadvantage. There is a need to know who is in a position to take decisions and to foster good relations with him or her. Knowledge about that person's particular web of official and private interests can also save time from the pursuit of ends that are diametrically opposed. There is a need, in short, to cultivate connections.

For an outsider, these connections do not spring up overnight. One solution is to start with a representative office and to build up one's presence gradually, accumulating knowledge and cultivating connections along the way. Another is to employ the services of Chinese who can span the divide, perhaps as the result of studying or working overseas. Reliance on joint venture partners alone or the officials backing them is insufficient, as it may well lead to being misled when this is in the interests of the partner. Nationalities appear to differ in their response to the information problem. The Japanese, for example, have been characterised as adopting a 'shotgun' approach, setting up several ventures and then seeing which make money. The poor performers will then be starved of resources. European and American firms, on the other hand, are more hesitant to leave the area of their core competence and to take a leap into the dark (Rosen 1999: 33).

Where the objectives of the two sides differ, some compromise will need to be established, an agreement negotiated. The preference of the Chinese authorities is quite likely to lie in favour of investments that are large, export oriented, introduce high technology, provide the Chinese side with a majority share in a joint venture enterprise, and put all the capital up-front in one large initial injection. For a variety of reasons, foreign investors may hold diametrically opposed preferences on any or all of these points. Small investments may be preferred to test the water. Access to the large domestic market may well be the long-term aim. Technology transfers may be approached cautiously because of fear of copying and spawning competitors. Wholly foreign owned ventures may be preferred to joint ventures for the greater control they allow. Gradually phased paid-in capital offers a degree of protection in the event of the enterprise proving a disaster and encourages continuing cooperation from the other side.

Where such tensions exist, they are likely to be resolved through the parties being prepared to make trade-offs among their preferences, such as offering to increase the amount invested or to improve the type of technology transferred in exchange for greater control over the enterprise. Where the balance is struck will depend on what the two sides have to offer and how eager the other is to acquire it. This will shift with time; with the Chinese authorities, for example, frequently easing restrictions on foreign direct investment at times when overall levels show signs of weakening.

The first question that must be decided is on the ownership form the enterprise is going to take: will it be wholly foreign owned or some form of joint venture with a Chinese partner? The number of wholly foreign-owned enterprises grew throughout the 1990s as authorities relaxed their former insistence on joint ventures. Nevertheless, by 1999, joint ventures still held the lead in terms of utilised direct investment (see Table 7.1). In some areas, the authorities still insist on joint venture forms for foreign investment, and this will continue under WTO membership with some areas opening up to foreign investment requiring joint venture participation. In telecommunications, for example, foreign involvement will not be allowed to exceed 50 per cent, and in fund management, 49 per cent.

Where the joint venture option is pursued, a question arises over the distribution of control. Fifty-one per cent can be relied upon to secure 51 per cent of the dividends. However, the logic that equates 51 per cent Western ownership with absolute control is unlikely to be shared by Chinese partners, who see instead a modest 2 per cent difference separating the two sides (Hubler and Meschi 1999: 169). Conversely, a high technology input may secure foreign managerial control even where foreign ownership is relatively small. Similarly, phasing in investment over an extended period can provide incentives for the Chinese partner to continue to go along with the management strategy of its foreign partner.

Which Chinese companies form joint ventures with foreign partners? In his sample of state enterprises in Shanghai, Guthrie (1999) found that profitability on the one hand and losses on the other were both associated with forming such ventures. The greater the success, the greater the attractiveness for foreign partners and, for Shanghai at least, it is unusual for a successful Chinese firm not to have at least one joint venture.

Table 7.1 *Utilised foreign direct investment from 1997 to 1999*

Foreign direct investment	1997 (billions of dollars)	1998 (billions of dollars)	1999 (billions of dollars)
Equity joint ventures	19.50	18.35	15.83
Cooperative joint ventures	8.93	9.72	8.23
Wholly foreign-owned enterprises	16.19	16.47	15.55
Joint explorations	0.35	0.18	0.38
Compensation trade	0.09	0.07	0.01
Others	7.33	2.78	2.45
Total	52.39	47.57	42.45

Source: *Zhongguo Jingji Nianjian 2000* (Almanac of China's Economy, 2000: 945)

On the other hand, government departments have tended to guide prospective partners towards state enterprises viewed as in need of support, using their power over the establishment procedure to get foreign firms to accept as a partner state enterprises they would be unlikely to choose given a freer hand and fuller information. In this, the authorities continue a policy adopted with stronger domestic state enterprises that have their arm twisted to take over poorly performing state firms in the hope that they can turn them around. For the enterprise shouldering such a burden, there is the expectation that favours will be reciprocated, rewarding them for their public-spiritedness.

Many foreign investors come to have cause to regret ill-informed decisions taken at the time of negotiating entry. Some have found themselves conceding distribution rights to partners who prove unable to deliver. Others have entered into agreements concerning the amount of domestic content that they then find difficult to fulfil, given quality and price considerations. Fortunately, not all such undertakings are impossible to escape. Here, as elsewhere in Chinese business, the contract is seldom the final word, but part of a continuing process of negotiation and reinterpretation. Some undertakings appear to be enforced less stringently than others. Undertakings regarding the amount of output to be exported, for example, are tighter for wholly foreign-owned enterprises than joint ventures. In both cases, however, when it comes to enforcement, many local authorities implement such export performance standards with a light hand. This partly depends on location. The closer to Beijing, the tighter the control (Rosen 1999: 69). Export targets may not be a problem, however, as they may well fit with the intentions of investors. Many contractual joint ventures close to the Hong Kong border, for example, have been located there to secure access to cheap labour and land for the production of low value-added consumer items intended for the export market. In other cases, some joint ventures have trimmed the proportion of their output aimed at the Chinese market when their hopes have collided with difficulties in securing payment for goods supplied within China.

Undertakings entered into concerning local content are likely to be more rigorously enforced. Local authorities have a greater interest in this as it provides additional local employment and revenue. In many cases, this may well coincide with the ambitions of the foreign investor. In others, as with the initial stages of the Beijing Jeep project, the foreign investor may be more interested in using the joint venture principally as a point of assembly for imported kits than in hastening the growth of domestic

Holland and Hiebert (2000) describe how China's Unicom devised a scheme in 1995 to get round a government ban on foreign investment in the telecommunications industry with Siemens, France Telecom and others. Early in 1999, however, the central government intervened; issuing a ruling that brought the collaboration to an abrupt halt. The foreign partners were offered 6 per cent return on an investment where they might usually have expected something more in the region of 30 per cent and told to accept or risk being shut out of the market. Unicom, on the other hand, came out of the affair rather better, having gained management skills and capital at little cost.

Source: Holland and Hiebert (2000)

production (Aiello 1991). The Chinese authorities, for their part, have at times found their support for the use of domestic parts in conflict with the need to make enterprises competitive domestically and internationally by allowing sourcing from wherever provides the best quality and price. The poor quality and costliness of domestically produced parts has, for example, prompted the relaxation of domestic sourcing requirements formerly imposed on the Shanghai Volkswagen joint venture.

Interpreting the law

One difference to which Western managers sometimes find it difficult to adapt is that between the notion of the law they are used to and the law as it operates in China. This has deep roots, with the tradition of law in China very different from that in the West. The written law of pre-modern China was overwhelmingly penal in character. This meant that:

> matters of a civil nature were either ignored by it entirely (for example, contracts), or were given only limited treatment within its penal format (for example, property rights, inheritance, marriage). The law was only secondarily interested in defending the rights – especially the economic rights – of one individual or group against another individual or group and not at all in defending such rights against the state . . . If a dispute involved two individuals, individual A did not bring a suit directly against individual B. Rather he lodged his complaint with the authorities who decided whether or not to prosecute individual B.
>
> (Bodde and Morris 1967: 4)

Involvement in this formal system of justice was widely regarded as a road to disaster and therefore to be avoided at all costs. In Confucian thought, law has often been viewed as little more than a necessary evil and it was not unknown for officials themselves to pen articles strongly advising against any resort to the courts (Hsiao 1979: 5). Advocacy was discouraged. Under the Qing code, anyone assisting others to bring a case, whether for a fee or not, was regarded as a troublemaker for inciting litigation and was guilty of a criminal offence (Bodde and Morris 1967: 413–17).

A reluctance to resort to official court proceedings as a way of settling disputes remains and favours reliance on a range of alternative methods of dispute resolution. Prominent among these is mediation. Current Chinese law continues the tradition of discouraging formal litigation in most cases except as a last resort. A great number of Chinese laws and regulations provide negotiation as a preliminary method for settling disputes followed, in order, by mediation, arbitration and litigation (Mo, 1997: 368–69). Most of the leaders involved in founding the People's Republic were from the countryside and were accustomed to the traditional idea of resolving disputes through compromise, and so carried this forward when shaping the system of dispute resolution (Wang, 1993: 525).

Rooted in such a past, the legal system poses a number of challenges for the Western manager. There is, to begin with, often difficulty in establishing quite what the law is. Commercial law on any scale is a relative novelty to China and while many laws have been drafted during the course of the reforms, gaps and inconsistencies remain. Laws are also often framed in vague and general terms. This has often been necessary to allow their passage in the first place, given opposition from conservative political factions suspicious that too much was being conceded to foreign interests; so from the foreign investor's point of view it might be that a vague right is better than none. Vagueness also allows for further experimentation, with details fleshed out in specific regulations later. Unfortunately, these may not be finalised until several years after the initial law. In the meantime, vague laws preserve the pivotal role of officials as sources to be turned to in the hope of securing a favourable interpretation. Even here, however, certainty is elusive. Opinions may be contradictory and the chance of any official committing an opinion to paper remote. Often, the best one can achieve is to submit an outline of one's intentions and to have it stamped with an official seal to indicate that it has been read, a practice reminiscent of commercial practices in imperial times (Rowe 1984). As ever, however, the danger with being given the nod by one sympathetic official is that officials change.

Should the matter come to seeking redress in court, one has to contend with a judiciary that suffers from a lack of well-trained members, with many judges coming from army or police backgrounds rather than from the legal profession. Seeking redress in cases involving disputes between joint venture partners or between the foreign investor and government authorities tends to be avoided due to the lack of independence of the judiciary from the Party and government. Bias against outsiders covers not merely foreigners, but may extend to firms from outside the immediate locality. Judges are not required to give legal reasons for a decision, making arbitrary judgement easier and appeals more difficult.

In these circumstances, many foreign partners in joint ventures seek to have arbitration clauses inserted into the contracts governing the venture. Given the known disposition of the Chinese courts, these clauses are not sought by Chinese partners, but may be conceded. Arbitration may be situated inside China or in a third country, such as Singapore. Within China, it will go before the China International Economic and Trade Arbitration Commission (CIETAC), which is composed of both Chinese and foreign experts. Decisions are binding and are supposedly final. However, while under the Civil Procedure Law a Chinese People's Court is bound to enforce a CIETAC award except in very limited circumstances, they have sometimes shown reluctance to do so against Chinese parties. As Moser (1995: 247) remarks, 'this is mainly because enforcement decisions are rendered by local courts at the place where the assets of the defendant are located. Such courts are especially vulnerable to political and economic pressures from local authorities and interested parties.'

CIETAC also places a high value on attempting to mediate the dispute placed before it rather than proceeding directly to adjudication:

> In practice, this means that once the issues have been defined in the hearing, the arbitrators will often encourage the parties to attempt to resolve their dispute by compromise and mutual accommodation . . . This distinctive Chinese approach to arbitration is reasonable in theory, but it can at times entail problems if a party insists upon its 'legal rights'. Such a party may be viewed by the arbitrators as uncompromising and unreasonable, with the result that the award which it has insisted upon may turn out to be less favourable than it envisaged.
>
> Moser (1995: 246)

Guthrie's study of joint ventures in Shanghai reveals an equal split between those that included an arbitration clause in their agreement and those that did not. Chinese partners more strategically located in the bureaucratic hierarchy are better able to resist foreign partners' calls for the introduction of arbitration clauses. This they are able to do by bringing to the table more to offer in terms of their connections with the bureaucracy and thus their power to speed the establishment of the joint venture and to ease its future dealings with officialdom. From the side of the foreign partner, country of origin plays a part in determining the support for an arbitration clause. Those from Western countries tend to press for this; those from Taiwan and Hong Kong do not (Guthrie 1999: 172–73).

One frequently encountered difficulty concerns the ineffectiveness of the law when it comes to protecting intellectual property rights. This not only entails competition from fake products, but also the poor quality of these can damage the reputation of the legitimate producer. Procter & Gamble estimates that 15 to 20 per cent of products on Chinese shelves bearing their label are fakes, resulting in a loss of 150 million dollars in sales (*Far Eastern Economic Review*, 5 October 2000: 57–59). Going to law is a last resort, as the process can be lengthy and penalties awarded trifling. Gillette, for example, fought a two-year battle against counterfeiters who, in the end, were fined only 20 000 yuan, equivalent to 2400 dollars (*Far Eastern Economic Review*, 23 March 2000: 46–47). Intellectual property infringements stretch far beyond trademark infringement to include patent infringement and the wholesale copying of proprietary technology, through state enterprises and research institutes taking apart machinery in a process of 'reverse engineering' to master how the machinery may be reproduced.

Given the state of the legal environment, success often goes to those who have managed to establish special exemptions and entitlements through cultivating the right connections. This leaves a number of the long-established incumbent foreign enterprises in an ambivalent position with regard to the rule of law. At one moment they may rail against the inequities of favouritism, and in the next be boasting of the special relationships and privileges they have established. Incumbents may in consequence seek to restrain the introduction or implementation at a local level of reforms that may level the playing field for new arrivals.

The return of the comprador

Foreign investors face the same presence of bribery and corruption encountered by domestic firms, intensified by the attention their prosperity attracts on the principle of 'whipping the fat ox'. Most foreign investors face the dilemma that falling in with such practices not only often offends Chinese law, but also runs contrary to ethical and legal requirements in their home countries. In the case of American companies, the Foreign Corrupt Practices Act extends the reach of such obligations to their dealings within China. Generally, however, this act is useful not so much for fear of the threat it poses, as the risk of being charged is usually being regarded as slight. It nevertheless does serve as a useful excuse for companies seeking to resist pay-offs.

Corrupt practices range, as Rosen (1999: 218) remarks, from 'the clearly corrupt (bribes to get customs duties lowered) to the likely corrupt ('rep' fees to facilitate large government procurement contracts) to the murky (gift giving and extravagant entertainment for official customers or children of high-level officials).' He goes on to recite a litany of complaints gathered from managers of foreign invested enterprises. Most concern bribery related to securing approvals and sales. Often, extortion hides behind the offer of various 'consultancies' recommended by supervisory agencies to deal with applications or infractions of rules. Officials may also guide enterprises towards firms related to their departments, either as subsidiaries or through connections that are more indirect.

Given the ubiquity of such practices, few foreign firms manage to remain completely aloof from participation if they are to operate smoothly. Most, however, strive to put a spin on such payments that will give them some vestige of legitimacy. Thus, payments to encourage purchasers are dressed up as post-purchase 'rebates', rather than pre-purchase payments more easily seen as bribes. Various other means may be found to distance the foreign investor from involvement in the more dubious side of the business. Such work may be delegated to the Chinese partner or agents charged with seeking to cultivate good relations with customers and the authorities. The particular methods adopted by this new breed of comprador are not closely enquired into by the foreign side, who do not care to know the details of how they oil the wheels of commerce. Enterprises may run their own loosely defined public relations departments with the responsibility to smooth relations with officials and business associates, but the size and prominence of these tend to shrink and expand in step with the waxing and waning of anti-corruption campaigns.

Nevertheless, many foreign managers accuse fellow members of their fraternity as frequently being the active instigators of corrupt practices rather than their passive victims (Rosen 1999: 220). Many come from societies where similar practices are not unknown. Even among the cleanest societies, campaign contributions to gain access and to secure preferential treatment are common. Corruption has been a problem throughout the history of communist China. It has also been fought throughout the same period. Transgressors have been, and continue to be, sent to jail, sometimes even executed, for such practices, at times in large numbers. This has not stamped out the practice, but it has held it in greater check than in many other transitional and developing societies. Further reduction will take time, as it has in the history of other countries.

Similarly, a reluctance to turn to the law to settle disputes between business associates is not unknown in the West. Even in that most litigious of societies, the United States, other considerations have been known to come into play. In his study of the degree to which litigation was used to settle disputes between American firms, Macaulay notes that disputes were 'frequently settled without reference to the contract or potential or actual legal sanctions . . . as one businessman put it, "You can settle any dispute if you keep the lawyers and accountants out of it. They just do not understand the give-and-take needed in business." . . . Law suits for breach of contract appear to be rare' (Macaulay 1963: 61). And speaking in terms which would not sound out of place applied to China, he goes on to note:

> Even where agreement can be reached at the negotiation stage, carefully planned arrangements may create undesirable exchange relationships between business units. Some businessmen object that in such a carefully worked out relationship one gets performance only to the letter of the contract. Such planning indicates a lack of trust and blunts the demands of friendship, turning a cooperative venture into an antagonistic horse trade.
>
> (Macaulay 1963: 63)

Learning and adjustment in the joint venture

Learning and adjustment is necessary in any cooperative venture. When joint ventures take place across national borders, especially when they take place between societies with differing cultures, political systems and levels of economic development, the degree of mutual learning and adjustment needed will be all the greater. Just how the adjustment is made will depend on a variety of factors. Child (1994: 277–79) suggests that two in particular deserve attention. The first is the power of the partners relative to one another. The second is the attractiveness of the other's management style and of the benefits it can bring to the joint venture. The interaction of the two is illustrated in Figure 7.1. In considering their impact, it should be kept in mind that relative power and attractiveness are not static and that therefore modes of adaptation are likely to change over time and according to the issue at stake.

The forced mode of adaptation results when one party is able to impose its will on the other despite hostility towards its proposals. Its ability to do so may be based on greater resources, such as technical expertise. Alternatively, it may be faced with demands from other sources viewed as more powerful and pressing than the joint venture partner. Thus, the Chinese side in a joint venture may insist on following a particular timetable for the completion of a project, even though this conflicts with the other partner's preferences, when politicians have set a deadline that they insist must be met. Such forcing of a position or a practice on to the other side may, needless to say, give rise to resentment and hostility.

	Low attraction	High attraction
Unequal power	Forced	Dependent
Balanced power	Segmental	Mutual

Figure 7.1 *Modes of joint venture adjustment (adapted from: Child 1994: 271–79)*

Nevertheless, the side imposing its stand may at times feel compelled to do so by the demands made upon it.

More satisfactory from the point of view of the smooth functioning of the enterprise is when the path dictated by the dominant partner enjoys a degree of legitimacy in the eyes of the partner being required to change its ways. This can occur when a foreign partner introduces products and technology that are well respected by the Chinese partner. The mixture of unequal power with attraction gives rise to a dependent mode of adjustment. The amount absorbed can vary from passively going through the motions to full understanding and acceptance of the changes. Frequently, the reception is mixed and selective, with some elements embraced fully and others adopted in a more superficial fashion.

Where the power of the two partners is more evenly balanced and the managerial practices of the other side are not attractive, a segmented form of adjustment is likely. In this form of adaptation, responsibilities are divided between the two partners. Typically, the Chinese side will take care of personnel and administration, the foreign side taking responsibility for other matters. This frequently inhibits information sharing between partners and the development of managerial competence. It also makes it difficult to resolve differences in such areas as remuneration and staffing levels.

The final mode of adjustment is mutual in the sense that managers from both sides attempt to make full use of each other's knowledge and skills to run the enterprise as a coordinated whole. This rests upon a balance of power and agreement on the desirability of a certain way of running the enterprise. It is, unfortunately, one achieved more often in the world of company publicity statements than in reality. It is more likely to be approached, however, with joint ventures entered into by the high-technology spin-offs discussed in Chapter 5 than with more long-established and traditional state enterprises.

What is learned and what is retained and put into practice depends much on the situation in which people are placed. Those Chinese managers who have trained abroad and then return to work in state-owned enterprises often show little sign of change despite their training. Conversely, Western managers can show some tendency to 'go native', picking up Chinese ways of operating at both a personal and an organisational level. For Chinese returning from training overseas, the most dramatic changes occur in those who have worked for several years in a foreign business environment and then returned to China to work for

Box 7.2 On being too Chinese

A Chinese secretary at a Sino-American joint venture voiced the following complaint about her American general manager who had majored in Chinese:

> The trouble is he has turned himself into a fool by reading all those books about us. He often thinks there is a hidden meaning behind whatever we say. Actually, not many people here have the time to think about hiding their true meaning. We simply do not have the time. But he often asks people what they mean by saying this and that. This really annoys people because often we mean what we say and even if we mean something else, we are not going to tell him anyway. He has also learned to eavesdrop. Once he wanted me to eavesdrop on the conversation between the Chairman of the board and the deputy manager two doors away. I told him I wouldn't and that it was no good him trying as they were speaking in the local dialect so even if he could hear anything, he would not be able to understand.

Interview, 2001

a foreign enterprise. Simply working for a foreign enterprise within China often results in a more superficial understanding and level of change. Lacking direct experience of how certain ways of managing are demanded by the workings of the business system as a whole, they do not fully appreciate the worth or rationale of these methods.

Conflict and control in Chinese organisations

Organisations vary according to the way in which conflict is approached and what sorts of remedies are considered appropriate. Based on cross-cultural comparisons of how managers diagnose the causes of inter-departmental conflict, Hofstede (1994: 139ff.) argues that different nations have different ideas about what constitutes the ideal organisation. Borrowing dimensions identified in the Aston studies, he distinguishes organisations according to the degree of concentration of authority and the extent to which activities are structured. Given a dispute between two departmental heads, different nationalities are likely to approach the problem in different ways. The French, for example, are likely to identify the source of the conflict as negligence on the part of the manager to whom the two departmental heads report. The solution is for them to submit the matter to their common boss. The form of organisation advocated has a highly structured hierarchy, a classic bureaucracy. The

Germans, on the other hand, are likely to identify the problem as resulting from a lack of structure. The solution then lies in the elaboration of rules. The British are unlikely to identify the source of the problem as due to insufficient concentration of authority or lack of rules. For them, it is more likely to be seen as a human relations problem and therefore the two departmental heads should receive some training as to how to get along better.

The fourth preferred form of organisation is one in which conflicts are resolved by referral to the boss who rules over an organisation in which duties are not clearly defined by rules. The organisation is seen as an extended family ruled in a paternalistic manner. This is typical, Hofstede argues, of the Chinese.

Box 7.3 Using a cannon to shoot the mosquito

The commencement of the construction of a green field joint venture project was seriously delayed because the joint venture owner and the project contractor could not agree upon the price for construction. Since the contractor, a consortium of a local state-owned Chinese company and a Hong Kong company, was forced upon the joint venture by the local government, the joint venture was not in the position to find a replacement for the contractor. The deadlock had lasted for more than six months and eventually the district governor called a meeting with the intention of solving the dispute.

The meeting took place in a grand room in the district government building. Top managers from companies involved in the project were all summoned. Tea was served, but nobody dared to take a sip. Everybody seated themselves in places appropriate to their rank. Nobody talked loudly, as they would before other meetings.

Ten minutes later, the governor arrived and announced that the meeting would last an hour. He first asked the Chinese deputy general manager from the joint venture to report on the current situation. The Chinese deputy general manager spent most of the time emphasising all the efforts the joint venture had taken to make the situation better. This pleased the governor greatly. After his speech, however, the representative from the German parent company of the joint venture indicated that he would like to mention some problems. The initiative of this German manager surprised the governor and everybody else at the meeting. Nevertheless, the governor granted him five minutes. The representative mentioned various problems with the contractor, the Chinese–Hong Kong consortium, which had been delaying the commencement of the construction for several months. At this point, the governor became very angry and shouted at the chief executive of the Hong Kong company: 'We have helped you to get the project. It was not easy, the Germans put up with a lot of resistance. So if you mess it up, your company will never get another project in my jurisdiction.'

The governor then turned to the German general manager of the joint venture: 'the joint venture managers should learn how to manage, too.You should take up your responsibilities. Don't phone your German parent company over small issues.' The Chinese design institute was not spared criticism either. The district governor told them: 'I know your company is very famous, but not all the buildings you designed are functioning well. So, send a designer onto the site and stay there until the project is over. I don't want to hear whether this service is stated in the contract or not, just do it.'

Without giving anybody an opportunity to express further views, the district governor concluded the meeting by stating that from now on the management of the project would be taken over by the district government. He would send two of his officials to inspect and hold coordination meetings twice a week on the site. He or his deputy would come to the site every Saturday morning to hold meetings. In addition, managers from all the parties should have a meeting every afternoon on the site. Minutes of these meetings should be taken and faxed to him the next day. Before he left the meeting, the district governor set a deadline for the project and threatened all present with the possibility of being stripped of their positions if they did not meet it.

Most of the managers were shattered, but they argued with each other fiercely as soon as the district governor was out of the sight. The chief executive office of the Hong Kong company told off the German representative for reporting the problems: 'In situations like this, we should help each other. We are in the same boat.'

The district governor made his decisions about the project without consulting the contract or the joint venture. Many of his orders therefore were not in accordance with the contract. For example, the deadline set by the district governor was one month earlier than the date stated in the contract. Given that the original schedule was tight and the commencement of the project had been delayed, it appeared impossible. However, not daring to contradict the orders from the district government, the managers now found themselves ending up with new problems. One manager from the Chinese construction company commented:

> The involvement of the government in the project is like trying to shoot a mosquito with a cannon. The cannon ball misses the mosquito, but kills a lot of people. But what else can we do to push things along? People don't know other ways to solve problems. It does not work if anybody else says anything or to ask everybody to do whatever is stated in the contract. You see how frightened people were at the meeting. They could have solved these problems among themselves, but they don't want to. They only listen to the emperor.

Fieldwork notes, 2001

That Chinese firms are high in the concentration of power and lack the structure provided by clearly established rules is true of most overseas Chinese enterprises. The same is true of the mainland, where state organisations have typically combined a concentration of power with the absence of clearly defined responsibilities. The result has been rather unkindly characterised as one in which 'the critical art is to avoid responsibility, diffuse decisions, and blunt all commands that might later leave one vulnerable to criticisms' (Pye 1982: 16). While this situation is changing as a result of the reforms, it often remains the case that solving problems can be a slow affair as matters are passed upwards for decision. The multitude of bureaux that impinge on the way a firm operates can complicate matters further and add to delays. The reputation of large Chinese organisations as unusually slow in reaching decisions may be compounded by the Chinese preference for waiting on the achievement of consensus within peer groups rather than pushing ahead on the basis of a simple majority (Yates and Lee 1996: 346). In such circumstances, it is perhaps not surprising that when a group of Chinese managers was given hypothetical situations in which they had to solve problems though negotiation with Chinese and Canadian firms, they, like the Canadians, considered that negotiations with the latter would be more satisfying and easier to control (Tse *et al.* 1994).

When Chinese and foreigners work together within the same enterprise, expectations often clash concerning the appropriate structure and operation of the organisation. One problem encountered by a number of joint ventures, for example, is a lack of clarity between the partners over which leaders hold authority to resolve certain problems. Conflicts often centre on human resource management, such as attempts by American firms to introduce systems of selection, appraisal, dismissal, or promotion that local employees view as inappropriate (Smith and Wang 1996: 333–34).

In his comparison of Chinese and American co-workers in a privately owned restaurant in China, Yu (1995) found considerable differences in cultural assumptions about work roles. The owner took an active role in overseeing the business, but also employed two managers, one Chinese, the other American. The waiters were Chinese and American. The Chinese staff viewed the managers as having little autonomy, their role being to convey the directions of the owner. Perceived as having little authority, the managers would often find the Chinese workers going over their heads, approaching the owner directly should any problem arise. The Chinese manager seemed to concur with this assessment of his position, and in general played a passive role.

The American manager, in contrast, saw the post as entailing a responsibility to take a much more active role. This included devising ways to improve the running of the business and putting these methods in to operation. In adopting this role, he met with no resistance from the American staff, who considered it his duty. The Chinese staff, on the other hand, resented being told what to do when they suspected the instructions did not originate from the owner himself, often checking with the owner to make sure. The owner was himself a little taken aback by the zeal of his American manager, commenting that he did too much. The Americans, on the other hand, were critical of the Chinese staff for not listening to the manager, and of the owner for not giving the manager enough responsibility and support.

The possibility of a clash of cultures when members of different nationalities work together is not limited to opposing views on authority. Differing expectations in many areas can sow misunderstanding and discord. Quality standards vary, with what may strike some foreign partners as just acceptable, striking the Chinese side as over demanding to an absurd or wasteful degree. Misunderstandings may also spring from differences in the role played by certain occupations. On one joint venture building project in China with which the authors are familiar, the Chinese contractors at first found it difficult working with the Western architect. It soon became apparent that he was not acting like a 'proper' (i.e. Chinese) architect should, refusing, for example, to adjust his plans to allow for their problems. Such adjustment would be expected of a Chinese architect, who generally enjoys a lower status and degree of professional independence than his or her counterpart in the West. The

Box 7.4 Meeting expectations

It seemed that the Chinese team of design engineers had finally learned what the German architects wanted the meeting to be like. There was no longer the usual mobile phone conversation, shouting at each other across the table, running in and out of the meeting room, leaving the table to admire the view out of the window or simply dozing off. Instead, everybody was attentive and kept reminding each other to keep quiet and to ask important questions only. They also appointed one member to speak on everybody's behalf and another to take minutes. The architects were obviously very pleased with this and made many important concessions that would enable the Chinese construction company to save much money and time.

Nevertheless, this did not last. Once the Chinese team had secured the concessions, the meeting rapidly reverted to a more bazaar-like atmosphere.

Fieldwork notes, 2001

first reaction was thus one of indignation. Realisation that the role of the architect in the West was different eventually dawned, but this was itself only one step forward in the learning process, as the contractors were then at a loss as to what to expect of the architect and how to treat him. Eventually, however, they learned. One instance is given in Box 7.4.

Us and them

In coping with potential conflicts, people may behave differently where an outsider is involved. Members of the 'in-group', the group with which an individual feels a sense of similarity and belonging, may well be tackled in a different manner to members of the 'out-group'. Summarising research in this area Weldon and Jehn write: 'Outgroup members are believed to be less attractive, less capable, less trustworthy, less honest, less cooperative, and less deserving than members of the ingroup' (Weldon and Jehn 1996: 98). Behaving differently towards out-group members is particularly characteristic of collectivist societies, of which China is one. In such societies, one can expect greater differences

Box 7.5 Divided loyalties

A Chinese middle manager at an Australian company in Shanghai talks about divided loyalties:

It is much easier for my Australian colleagues and bosses to manage and discipline the Chinese workers. They can simply tear their face down [drop the mask of civility] and tell people that they are not doing their job well. But I can't. I am Chinese myself. I feel that I should be on the Chinese side. I think the workers expect me to be on their side. So it is very difficult for me especially in situations when both the Australian managers and the Chinese workers are present. I have to be very careful as to what to say and do. I have to show the Australian bosses that I am working hard for the company, but at the same time, I have to show the Chinese workers that I have their interests at heart. I know other people in my position simply tell themselves and others that they are loyal to whoever pays them. But I think that is not really right. One should identify with one's own countrymen. So a lot of the times I tell my Australian bosses about what is going on in the workshop and get them to criticise the workers.

Interview, 2001

in behaviour towards people based on their group affiliation (Triandis 1994: 132). National identities thus come to overlay and exacerbate other differences of interest within the joint venture. Language barriers obviously reinforce awareness of these divisions, but language proficiency alone will not necessarily eliminate them.

Hiding information plays just as much a key role in business as does sharing it. Given that strategic partners are likely to have conflicting as well as shared interests, it is not surprising to find them concealing information from one another. Each may harbour hopes of going it alone after mastering the partner's secrets. Each may hinder the other acquiring knowledge precisely for this reason. Barriers to information flow are thrown up as a result; making use of whatever material lies ready to hand, including language. Such barriers effectively stand in the way of establishing solid control over the enterprise, for power depends on the effectiveness of channels of communication. This is why power is so intimately bound up with administration, which is essentially the processing of information. For an organisation to function effectively it needs the coordination made possible by managers taking responsibility. They also need to exercise initiative in a manner that takes into account a broad corporate perspective, rather than limiting their attention to their own narrow field. Unfortunately, the form of Chinese organisations tends to discourage this through division into many hierarchical levels and functional divisions. Instead, it reproduces a tendency to look upwards for top-down initiatives and approval.

Control depends on communicating instructions and monitoring performance, which may be evaded by attempts to misinterpret orders or to hide or distort unfavourable feedback. It is partly in order to overcome this that some foreign partners press for the introduction of formal and recorded procedures.

Formalisation and responsibility

Formalisation, the introduction of a more systematic approach to the transmission of information and to defining the framework of managerial authority and responsibility, is, as we saw in Chapter 3, fostered by experience with joint ventures. Nonetheless, the extent of formalisation that joint ventures adopt varies. It is naturally stronger in larger ventures than smaller, although there also tend to be differences according to the national background of the foreign partner. American firms are generally

Box 7.6 The failings of formality

A senior Chinese manager from a Sino-German joint venture commented on the style of his foreign colleagues:

> They bury their heads behind their computers and spend most of their time writing and writing. This won't work here. You have to spend most of your time mixing with the clients and customers, chatting, smoking, drinking and eating together with them. You make friends with them, so that they feel obliged to help you out. It makes no sense to try bossing contractors about, they need to be treated as partners rather than employees . . . Most problems are solved to the click of chopsticks and the clink of wine cups, instead of by sending dozens of letters to complain or to threaten the contractors with breaching clauses in the contract. Threatening them with penalties or court action can only antagonise them. Besides, when you send the first letter, the contractor may be frightened, but after several such letters, they simply ignore them.

Fieldwork, 2001

regarded as pressing for the full implementation of formal systems adopted by their organisations elsewhere, whereas such an insistence is somewhat less prevalent among European partners. Formalisation is at a far lower level in joint ventures where the partner is from Hong Kong or Japan (Child 1994: 266–69).

The aim of formalisation is partly to encourage delegation and to overcome an unwillingness to assume responsibility. In this, joint ventures have met with varying success. Attempts to introduce reporting systems may run up against reports that are not filed. Attempts to run meetings along formal lines more familiar to the Western boardroom have run up against constant interruptions as participants are called away, as well as a general lack of preparation and follow-up. Practices such as starting on time, using agendas, minutes, reviews of actions undertaken, preparation of documents and speaking to the chair are novelties to many Chinese managers and may conflict with their preferred mode of operation.

The Japanese, in contrast, try to rely more on encouraging greater responsibility through promoting a strong sense of corporate culture among the Chinese employees of the joint venture. Usually results fall disappointingly short of their expectations. Attempts to introduce problem solving sessions along the lines familiar to Japanese enterprises have often met with an unwillingness on the part of Chinese participants to offer suggestions in the presence of Japanese managers (Chen 1995: 285).

Human resources

Under Chinese law, foreign enterprises enjoy the legal freedom to hire staff for their enterprises as they see fit, choosing staff on the open market or selecting those available from their Chinese partner. In the case where they have just established representative offices, however, they must hire staff through a government service company, a requirement that some nevertheless manage to circumvent.

In the case of established joint ventures, control over labour matters is seldom, in practice, left entirely in the hands of the foreign partner. Usually, during the process of establishment, pressure is brought to bear to structure the enterprise in such a way that the Chinese partner has a leading role in matters concerning pay and conditions. A whole range of concerns may lead the Chinese side to favour such an arrangement. It can be used to safeguard employment within the locality and the firm. It can also serve as a means of dispensing patronage for the Chinese side. This may be exercised in favour of friends and relatives – a cherished power where exchanging favours and cultivating networks of support can be of such importance. Joint venture employment is better rewarded than are jobs in ordinary state enterprises and, as such, is a sought after gift to have at one's command.

Conflict between Western and Chinese partners has also arisen from the traditional tendency of Chinese firms to pride themselves on size in terms of headcount, even where this has meant lower output per worker. While this is still present, it is clearly on the wane. Rosen, for example, cites one of the Western managers he interviewed in 1997 about negotiations with a Shanghai petrochemical company. The state enterprise was taken aback and thrown into some confusion by the suggestion of the Western side that it should shed some of its ancillary services such as the crematorium. Who, after all, would wish to cut back the size of their business? (Rosen 1999: 91). When we visited the same company in 2001, however, the management appeared perfectly at ease with such a notion and was well on the way into putting it into effect.

There is often also a lingering caution on the Chinese side about allowing wage differentials among the Chinese workforce to widen too far. This stems from a mixture of enduring attachment to egalitarian norms,

Box 7.7 Putting supporters in place

At a 50:50 Sino-Canadian joint venture in Beijing, most of the department heads had been personally connected with the Chinese deputy general manager before they were recruited into the company. The head of the personnel department is the daughter of a friend. The head of marketing is the son of the former boss. The head of the logistics department is a former subordinate. The head of the secretarial staff is the daughter of a former subordinate. In the accounting department, the head was openly recruited from the job market. However, he had to leave shortly afterwards because he found his orders were not obeyed by a key staff member who was connected to the deputy general manager.

By recruiting personal connections to key positions in the company, the deputy general manager enjoyed much more than the 50 per cent share of control and power in company affairs. The Canadian general manager, although a fluent speaker of Chinese, was often kept in the dark. According to the joint venture contract, every important managerial issue needed to be jointly decided by the general manager and the deputy general manager. However, the general manager's personal assistant, who is connected to the deputy general manager, sometimes deliberately kept papers until the general manager was out of town. This enabled the deputy general manager to make decisions on his own with the excuse that the matter needed to be dealt with urgently.

Fieldwork notes, 2001

anxiety about stirring up resentment among the less favoured parts of the workforce, and concern that word of large payments will spread to stoke demands elsewhere in the state sector.

For many successful joint ventures, a more pressing problem than over-staffing is the need to find and retain talented and qualified staff in an environment where the supply falls far short of the burgeoning demand. This has led to many ventures facing increasing wage pressure as they try to retain those staff with sought after skills. Here, the labour contract has become a means not of freeing the enterprise of unwanted workers, but of attempting to attach workers more closely to the firm. A number of enterprises, both foreign invested and domestic, have been experimenting with providing low cost mortgages for ten-year periods in the hope that the prospect of foreclosure will deter leaving.

Many foreign invested enterprises are known for the quality of their training, but this can add to the problem of high labour turnover among managerial staff as competitors seek to poach trained staff. For those providing training, most prefer the malleability offered by staff recruited straight from school and university on the basis that no experience is better than bad experience. For the most ambitious foreign firms ready to invest substantially in management training, the results aimed at can be profound, as summed up by the Chairman of Johnson and Johnson Investment in China, Jerry Norskog, speaking of the training programme developed at their Xian joint venture:

> When I interview a new recruit, I ask him what advice his father and mother gave him about being successful in life. The answer is usually: 'Keep your head down, keep your mouth shut, ensure you have a good relationship with your boss, be obedient and work hard.' Now I am going to ask him to stand up, to speak out heretical ideas, to fight intellectually, to challenge his boss. I am going to tell him that risk is rewarded, not punished.
>
> (Quoted in Stuttard 2000: 60)

While the training programme aims to displace one Chinese habit and to encourage a positive approach to flexibility and change, it nevertheless takes care to incorporate material from Chinese history when discussing

Box 7.8 Building alliances

The following case study illustrates a number of the problems faced by joint ventures touched on in this chapter.

Britco, a British steel building fabricator and contractor, signed a contract to provide a 7000 square metre factory in north China for an American client. Unable to obtain a construction licence under the Chinese regulations, Britco recommended a state-owned Shanghai construction company with which it was allied, MC, to undertake the installation work. Britco assured the client that it would supervise the Chinese company and make sure that the installation work was up to international standards. With a view to undertaking more projects in China for the same client, Britco persuaded MC to cut its price from the market standard of 8 dollars per square metre to 5 dollars.

Problems started, however, soon after the project began. The construction team that MC sent to the site did not belong to the company. A village team, it consisted of part-time farmers from the countryside outside of Shanghai. MC, like many other Chinese construction companies, often subcontracts projects to such village teams. The village team, however, did not have a construction licence. The solution to this problem was that MC allowed the village team leader to print a name card claiming he was a middle manager of MC and was undertaking the work as part of MC.

The village team was, however, much smaller in number than stated on the contract, while the installation equipment the team brought with it was hardly adequate in quality and quantity to install the building. Some of the equipment, such as scaffolding material and workers' safety goggles, did not meet the safety standards insisted upon by the American client. In addition, the construction team constantly demanded that Britco pay for equipment, such as power generators and lighting for night shifts, clearly stated in the contract as the responsibility of MC.

These conflicts escalated when winter came. The site, being in north China, was cold and windy, which further delayed the pace of installation. Britco was under great pressure from the American client to finish installation on time while the village team was working slower and demanding that Britco pay for more equipment.

One of the authors was brought in to advise on resolving the dispute. Talks with MC managers, requesting them to provide more manpower and resources, secured only verbal assurances. A chance conversation with one of the workers, however, revealed the core of the trouble. MC was upset about the lower price of the contract and felt hurt by the unreasonableness of Britco, with whom they had worked on a number of previous occasions. Nevertheless, they signed the contract believing once the contract was secured, they could demand concessions and turn the deal into a favourable one.

Signing a contract in China is seldom the end of bargaining. The contract is not the final word, not a binding document of fundamental importance. It is, rather, the symbol of willingness to do business with each other, the beginning of a relationship that entails trading favours and concessions. Indeed, before the economic reforms, a state-owned company only signed contracts with the ministry that supervised it. Failure to abide by such contracts was not viewed as so dramatic as refusing to agree on them in the first place, as this would have been an open challenge to the higher authorities.

The failure in pleading for more manpower from MC also revealed different expectations regarding the power of managers. MC, being owned by the state, does not have the same control of its own business as its Western counterparts enjoy. MC, like many Chinese construction teams, was overstretching its capacity during the construction boom. Similar problems are familiar from elsewhere in the world. However, the situation was made worse when MC was handed two politically sensitive projects: the installation of the 80 000 seat municipal stadium and two broad-span hangars for Shanghai airport. The mayor of Shanghai, in order to boost the notion of 'Shanghai speed', ordered MC to finish the two projects ahead of schedule. An MC manager remarked on this that MC managers were constantly 'severely scolded by the mayor' and 'threatened with being stripped of their positions' for not being able to quicken the pace of installation. 'Foreigners threatening us with breach of contract is not as frightening as the mayor's anger,' concluded the manager.

Another constant source of conflict was quality control. Britco, with around 200 employees, survives on its high quality in fierce competition with giants such as BHP and Butler. MC, in contrast, aimed at contracting as many projects as possible rather than quality. During site visits, Chinese workers and managers complaining about the wastefulness of Britco's installation supervisors when they refused to allow the use of sub-standard material often approached the author. The Western supervisors 'throw away steel sheets as if they were millionaires and then charge us enormous prices for new sheets to be air freighted from England to China.' Fights broke out when Chinese workers tried to use slightly dented sheets and Britco's British supervisors jumped on the sheets to cause more damage so that the sheets could not be used.

Efforts to explain the importance of quality to MC workers had little impact. Only when the author visited the workers' dormitory did the difficulty become easier to understand. The workers rented an unfinished and unfurnished farmhouse with cement floors, broken windows and rusty iron bunk beds. There was no heating, no hot water and no indoor toilet facilities. The steel building they were installing was palatial compared with their own accommodation. Having grown up in a scarcity economy, the workers and managers have little understanding of the importance of quality. Indeed, as Britco supervisors remarked, workers often took faulty sheets away from the site to sell to neighbouring construction sites for a good price.

Another cause of disagreement was safety. The American project management team was anxious about any industrial accidents. Anybody entering the site had to have safety boots, goggles, helmets, safety belts and name badges. The village team resented the whole arrangement and nicknamed the site 'the prison'. Safety managers found themselves playing hide-and-seek in order to catch the workers who took off their belts and goggles as soon as safety guards were out of sight. When a safety guard caught one worker violating safety regulations and tried to photograph him, a fight broke out and escalated into hostility between the Chinese workers, Western managers and the overseas Chinese managers. Nationalistic feeling ran high and non-cooperation by the Chinese workers led to the site closing for two days.

At first sight, it seemed that the Chinese workers were very different from their Western colleagues in attitudes to danger. However, later when lunching with Britco's British workers, conversation turned to boasting of how they walked on beams without safety belts back in Britain. The excitement is part of the fun of the job, they remarked. However, safety regulations had become so tight in Britain that violations could lead to losing one's job. Clearly the cultural difference here was not in the workers' attitudes. Young men wishing to be daring seem as common in Britain as in China, but the former have had to get into the habit of giving way before inflexible regulations that are effectively policed.

Deteriorating relationships between Britco's supervisors and village workers were another cause for concern. Village workers started to refuse orders from Britco's supervisors, calling them 'Western imperialists'. This surprised both the Chinese and British management because the supervisors were known to be on 'brotherly' terms with the workers. Initial talks with Chinese workers did not give any clue except the usual eulogy on the friendliness of the supervisors. Not until the author spent a whole day on site did the cause of the problem become clear. Britco supervisors were installation workers themselves back in Britain. At the beginning of Britco's operation in China, the supervisors worked shoulder to shoulder with Chinese workers 'drinking warm beer at lunch time and eating rice out of the same pot', as one of the Chinese workers remarked. However, after two years in China and with more projects to supervise, the supervisors started to spend large parts of their time on paperwork in the office from nine to five rather than working in the rain or snow from seven to seven. Britco's success in China also meant the supervisors were given more fringe benefits, such as a car and chauffeur to share, and extra allowances on food so that they could eat in restaurants rather than on site. In addition, being in China for two years, most of them started to have Chinese girlfriends and preferred to spend their spare time with them rather than with the workers. The result was the workers felt a growing sense of distance between themselves and their erstwhile British comrades, a growing sense of 'us and them'.

A long-standing issue between Britco and MC was the prospect of forming a joint venture. It was one entangled with conflicting interests. Britco, like most Western companies investing in China, was aiming at China's domestic market. It wanted to obtain a licence enabling it to contract projects that were restricted to Chinese companies. By a joint venture with MC, Britco hoped to share MC's licence and to construct buildings with steel sheets produced back in Britain. MC, on the other hand, was interested in a special product of Britco's that was unavailable on the Chinese market. MC wanted to be able to produce such a product itself. A joint venture with Britco would be the most economical way to get the machinery and technological knowledge. However, for Britco, this special product was, and is, its life's blood. Introducing the product to China, a country with problematic intellectual property protection, would be a dangerous move to make.

Both Britco and MC were aware of this difference in interests, but both hoped to be able to influence each other to fall in with their own wishes. Numerous talks had taken place but with nothing of consequence resulting. The Chinese would praise Britco for its high quality goods and Britco flatter MC on its relations with the government. The vagueness ended when Britco finally found itself with sufficient funds to invest and pressed MC for a definite answer. To Britco's dismay, it found out that four years of expensive visits, dinners and talks had failed to bridge the gulf. Yet it was, perhaps, just as well that the joint venture did not proceed. The underlying differences in aims would undoubtedly have continued, blighting the venture as similar conflicts have other ventures.

Fieldwork notes, 1997

matters such as leadership, building on Chinese pride with the explicit aim of creating not an American company but a global company with Chinese characteristics (Studdard 2000: 65–66).

The homecoming

Although we have been focusing largely on management issues related to Western investment in China, throughout the reform period the bulk of foreign direct investment into China has come from ethnic Chinese in the region, principally from Hong Kong and Taiwan. Between 1979 and 1993, for example, overseas Chinese invested more than five times as much as the USA, Japan and the European Union combined, contributing over 80 per cent of the number of foreign funded projects and the amount invested (Yeung 2000: 91–92). Although the level of new Chinese investment plummeted during the depths of the Asian crisis, it remains the dominant share of foreign direct investment.

The main attractions have undoubtedly been economic, principally access to a cheap and plentiful supply of labour. Yet, at the same time, the owners of many of the small and medium sized businesses involved were also attracted by the expectation that sharing a common language and culture would smooth operations in China. Many, however, found certain of these expectations disappointed. In the case of Taiwan, for example, the differing paths followed by Taiwan and the mainland since the split between the two in 1949 has resulted in numerous differences in outlook and the conduct of business.

The Taiwanese entrepreneurs interviewed by Schak (1999) in the Pearl River delta region of Guangdong found the most striking differences between operating in Taiwan and in China to lie in the levels of corruption and the skill, work habits and attitudes of workers. Corruption is not unknown to Taiwan, but it has declined sharply in recent years to a level far below that to which Taiwanese establishing their businesses on the mainland find themselves forced to adjust. While challenges to some impositions, such as unjustified customs charges, may eventually succeed, the amount of time this would require made most feel it necessary to pay. This is particularly so in those factories producing orders for export. These rely on their reputation for meeting delivery dates. Any disruption to production could endanger this, a vulnerability that corrupt local officials are well aware of when pressing their demands. New charges tend to multiply when the head of a local township changes, so that the new incumbent does not have to wait upon the arrival of the next billing period. The Taiwanese resent not only the costs incurred, but also the unpredictability of the fines and fees foisted upon them. China, they complain, is ruled by individuals (*renzhi*), not by law (*fazhi*). Their resentment is compounded by a sense of superiority over their mainland compatriots, whom they view as backward and incompetent in comparison with themselves (Schak 1999: 242–44).

Even more unexpected and troubling for many Taiwanese entrepreneurs than the level of corruption is the difference between the labour force in Taiwan and on the mainland. Mainland workers are criticised for being slow and lazy, in need of constant surveillance if they are to be stopped from malingering or producing poor quality goods. Another complaint concerns the casual attitude workers display towards moving from one job to another. Migrant workers come to the coastal area to work for a few years to accumulate enough to return home and settle down. They are young and footloose, having a very casual attitude towards work, with no interest in taking on responsibilities or buckling down to learn a trade. Many are quick to leave one job for another for just a little extra or to work in the same factory as others from their home province.

This casual attitude means that many migrant workers are content to master just enough to enable them to complete one small task and lack an overall view of the process of production. Taiwanese managers complain in consequence that, while in Taiwan one manages people (*guan ren*), in China one must manage the work (*guan shi*), splitting it down into simple component parts. Unless they are allocated just one simple step it is felt the workers will not have the application to keep track of what they are about. Taiwanese workers, on the other hand, simply need a general instruction as they understand the process of production as a whole and have greater commitment to completing the task on time and in good order. Managers also complain of what they see as the mainland tendency to hoard knowledge to safeguard one's job. This makes training more difficult, with longer established workers not volunteering to teach the new ones.

Hometown loyalties (*laoxiang guannian*) can lead to problems. Workers from a similar locality will tend to side with their compatriots in disputes between workers or between workers and management. Solidarity is expected of foremen from one's own locality. This extends to expectations of receiving favourable treatment from supervisors from one's own locality and fights have been known to break out when such expectations, felt to be perfectly reasonable, have not been met (Schak 1999: 250).

Fights are not uncommon, despite being invariably met with dismissal. The same applies to theft among the workforce. This is not only more common than in Taiwan, but is also more indiscriminate, with managers expressing astonishment that almost anything that is not nailed down will disappear. The problem is exacerbated by the mobile nature of the workforce and the immense size of China, leaving culprits free to escape with ease should the necessity arise.

Much of the blame for the shortcomings of the workforce is placed by the Taiwanese on the lack of any moral education teaching the virtues of honesty and hard work. Some responded by holding classes for management and workers in an attempt to change their outlook toward work and life in general. Another educative approach is to bedeck the factory with slogans urging greater dedication to work, a tradition as popular with the Kuomintang as with the Communist Party.

Faith is not placed in exhortation alone. In keeping with the traditional Chinese family-business management style, many overseas Chinese firms adopt an authoritarian approach. Many have detailed factory handbooks listing rules and the associated penalties for non-compliance. The rules can be numerous and cover matters in fine detail. Huang lists several: not wearing an identity tag, fine five yuan; punching cards for others, fine three days' wages; not lining up to punch cards, fine two yuan; spitting or littering, penalty, cleaning lavatories for a week; smoking in dormitories, fine ten yuan; disobeying a supervisor, warning followed on the third occasion by dismissal (Huang 1999: 224). In some cases, workers are required to memorise the rulebook. For those coming from the countryside and used to a less regulated lifestyle, such a precisely defined and structured environment is alien and alienating, making it quite plain to them that they are not trusted.

Another point on which the outlook of the migrant workers diverges from their employers is in what might seem, for the Chinese, to be an uncharacteristic individualism. Young and footloose, cut off from surveillance by family and neighbourhood, they do not readily respond to traditional collectivist arrangements and appeals. As one interviewed by Huang (1999: 227) remarked: 'I don't have a sense of being part of the factory, because I am always being myself at work and after work. Many others feel the same as I do.'

8 Conclusions

- **The World Trade Organisation**
- **Continuity and change: a case study**

At the end of the previous chapter we saw the expectations of Taiwanese entrepreneurs seeking to establish businesses on the mainland disappointed as they came up against a culture that, in some ways, differed markedly from their own. They might have been less surprised if they had thought to look back into Taiwan's own past. In the 1950s and 1960s, Taiwan's workforce had low levels of skill and little appreciation of the importance of quality standards and meeting delivery dates; a situation comparable to that now complained of in China. Westerners also have a history that offers many parallels to what is being experienced in China today as industrialisation shifts workers from the countryside to the towns. In the West, factory owners in the early phases of industrialisation also sought to tame a workforce unused to discipline and routine through their own harsh equivalents of the Taiwanese rulebooks. These similarities suggest that certain problems faced by managers in China are transitional, a conclusion at once encouraging and discouraging. It is encouraging because it provides every reason to think that development will run its course on the Chinese mainland as it has elsewhere, eliminating or reducing some of the problems it now confronts. It is discouraging because experience suggests that such change does not occur overnight. Accumulating resources and experience, building institutions, take time.

This is not to say that China will finish up adopting practices that make it indistinguishable from the West. Taiwanese managers, for all their irritation at mainland attitudes and work practices, are more at home in a business system that relies heavily on cultivating connections through gifts, favours and banquets (Yang 1994). They tend to share with mainlanders a lack of faith in law and in contracts in the conduct of business (Guthrie 1999: 172). Similarly, Hong Kong managers in joint ventures find less to complain of than their Western or, for that matter,

Japanese counterparts (Child 1994). The experience of Taiwan and Hong Kong suggests that modernisation can take place while retaining Chinese characteristics. Indeed, some traditional Chinese values, such as diligence, frugality and a respect for learning, may well give Chinese communities a certain competitive edge.

Nevertheless, the experience of modernising Chinese societies beyond the mainland cannot serve as a ready guide to China's future, as these societies differ among themselves in terms of values and institutions because of their different historical paths. Business and the business system in Hong Kong, for example, differ markedly from those in Taiwan given the different courses their development has followed. As Redding writes in relation to family businesses in Hong Kong, any full understanding of their mode of operation requires knowledge of Hong Kong's recent history. This includes a government policy that mainly eschews intervention, the role of traditional Western trading companies and banks, the weakness of the labour movement, the provision of subsidised housing for half the population, and the form of the education system. The background in Taiwan differs in a number of important respects. There is the background of 50 years of Japanese colonial rule, several decades of close ties with the United States and advanced technical training in that country, the involvement of the state in important sectors of the economy and the state's active steering of the economy (Redding 2000: 46).

If diversity exists in the Chinese business world beyond its borders, so it does within. Indeed, the reform process is, in many ways, best seen not so much as the wholesale abandoning of one set of practices in favour of another, of communism for capitalism, but of increasing diversity. Development abounds, but it is development that entails a broadening of the repertoire of organisational forms embracing state enterprises, local collectives, private enterprise, joint enterprises and wholly foreign owned ventures. The balance between these has shifted with the progress of the reform, but a mixed economy, firmly anchored in the gradualist approach of the authorities towards reform and in the continuing faith in the state taking an active role in economic activities, will be the reality into the foreseeable future.

Predicting the future in China is as fraught with difficulty as elsewhere, perhaps more so. Few, for example, would have predicted in the early 1990s the withdrawal of the Chinese army from active involvement in the economy. This involvement began to grow in the late 1980s to reach a total of several thousand enterprises, including the country's largest pharmaceutical company, 999. Concern at this increasing involvement distracting the army from its proper function led to the order that it was to divest itself of all its enterprises by December 1998. Another concern was suspicion that some of the enterprises were benefiting by their association to evade taxes and customs duties. The People's Liberation Army complied, transferring 2937 enterprises and closing another 3928. In 1999, the year after the divestiture order, customs duties leapt by 80 per cent (Lawrence 2000). The change was sudden and dramatic, indicating the power of the central authorities to bend matters to their will when they have a mind to do so. The same applies in their relations with local authorities, as the special economic zone and port of Xiamen has discovered in recent years through a spate of prosecutions of local officials on corruption charges spearheaded by the central government. Once again, customs duties and smuggling have played a part in this conflict. In any tussle between the centre and the periphery the centre is likely to get its way. Its principal problem is that it cannot direct its attention everywhere at once. Those caught in the beam of its searchlight have little hope, but those beyond can carry on safely providing they do not attract unwanted attention by flagrantly flouting directives. The sky is high, and the emperor far away.

The World Trade Organisation

China became the 143rd member of the World Trade Organisation on 11 December 2001. The motive behind China's push for entry cannot be understood independently of the struggle over the reform of the state-owned enterprises. The will to pursue both energetically had to await the replacement of Li Peng by Zhu Rongji as premier, given the identification of the former with entrenched bureaucratic interests. Doubts nevertheless remain, within government circles and more broadly, as to the balance between the costs and benefits of entry, and these advantages and disadvantages will shape the enthusiasm with which the agreement is implemented.

Nevertheless, state-owned enterprises are increasingly tackling their long-standing problem of over-staffing by laying-off workers, some modestly, others dramatically. The figures, as noted earlier, are too unreliable to be worth quoting, but the reality is everywhere apparent on the streets of China's cities, where one constantly encounters laid-off state workers trying to make a living through street trading. However, underemployment is not the only problem plaguing many state ventures. Another is the level of investment needed to upgrade their facilities where foreign investment interest in such a project is proving minimal. This, combined with overcapacity and the associated move over the period of the reforms from a sellers' market to a buyers' market, threatens the viability of many state enterprises. For those exposed to still greater competition under the terms of the WTO provisions, the pressure will increase.

If one takes the automobile industry for example, tariffs on imported cars are set, under the terms agreed, to drop from 80 to 100 per cent down to 25 per cent. If the latter figure had been in operation in the middle of 2000, the price of an imported Buick would have been 330 000 yuan, whereas the price of a Buick produced at General Motors in Shanghai at that time was around 390 000. The company feels confident that it can cut its costs by the necessary 11 per cent within the five-year period allowed for the phasing in of the changes. Shanghai Volkswagen would similarly be at a disadvantage in terms of price if other comparable models produced by the company outside China were to be introduced at once. Like General Motors, however, the company expresses confidence in being able to cut prices over the next five years, aiming to reduce them by 25 to 30 per cent (Harwit 2001: 666).

Whether the reductions can be made and quality raised to world standards remains to be seen. A fall in car sales, as purchases were delayed by hopes of being able to obtain an imported car, signalled a lack of confidence in how up-to-date and reliable the domestically produced alternatives are (Harwit 2001: 669). Against this must be set the government's plans for 90 per cent of the market to be supplied by domestic production. This might be obtained by improving the quality and price of domestic producers. Equally likely is that is will be buttressed by erecting barriers to trade beyond the reach of WTO rules. Chinese officials note with approval the various devices that protected the automobile industries in Japan and Korea. Adapting rules on environmental and safety grounds to favour local products is one manoeuvre.

Such non-tariff barriers at the national level will doubtless be reinforced by the continuation and elaboration of similar strategies already in use by local authorities to favour local producers. A glance at the traffic flowing though the centre of Shanghai, an almost endless stream of Shanghai Volkswagens, is ample evidence of the power of a determined local authority to shape local purchases. The city of Wuhan likewise favoured purchases of the locally produced Citroen-Fukang cars through tax relief and the imposition of additional charges on those purchasing other makes. The accession to the WTO is likely to lead to the elaboration of more subtle measures rather than any abandonment of restrictions in favour of enthusiastically embracing a policy of free competition.

The same is true elsewhere in the economy. The impact of WTO membership on the management of state enterprises began to be felt well before accession. The reorganisation that took place was not aimed at preparing a level playing field for competition to thrive, but at strengthening domestic enterprises so that they are better able to fend off foreign inroads into their markets. This can be seen, for example, in the flurry to buy up petrol stations to dominate distribution on the part of the two state petrochemical companies.

Penetration of the market by foreign firms will also be limited in certain industries by such involvement being limited to joint ventures in which the government will retain a controlling interest. This will be the case for telecommunications. To conform with WTO requirements, the regulating authority in the industry was split from direct involvement in network operations through the establishment of the Ministry of Information Industry (MII), replacing the former Ministry of Posts and Telecommunications (MPT). This transformation had important consequences for domestic competition, for the MII set out to strengthen and favour Unicom, a fledgling competitor to China Telecom. It would seem that having the regulatory authority separate from operations did indeed encourage it to be more even handed in encouraging completion. Such impartiality is unlikely to be extended to conflicts of interest between foreign partners and state firms, however. Both the telecommunications industry and the MII remain firmly the creatures of the government (Zhang 2001).

Similar restrictions on foreign investment apply in parts of the financial sector. Asset management companies will limit participation by foreign firms to a minority stake. The same applies to securities companies, while life assurance will be limited to 50 per cent and non-life insurance to 51 per cent. Joint ventures will thus continue to play a pivotal role in foreign investment in certain sectors of the economy. Foreign banks will be allowed to operate freely after a five-year interim period. During this period, they will be allowed to expand their presence throughout the country, but only in a very gradual manner (Langlois 2001).

Many laws have been, or are being, redrafted to enable China to comply more fully with the terms of membership. This process is far from complete and, indeed, is unlikely to be fully completed if interpretations that view China as obligated to remove certain references to the Communist Party and socialism from the constitution are accepted (Potter 2001). As we have seen earlier, the laws and rules on the statute books are of less importance than how they are interpreted and implemented. Even if China wanted to abide strictly by all the rules, it does not presently have the institutional framework to enable it to do so. In such circumstances, it will more fruitful for China's trading partners to expect a generous measure of 'acceptable non-compliance' rather than insisting on a strict implementation of the agreements.

Continuity and change: a case study

We conclude with a brief case study of a diesel engine manufacturer that we visited in the spring of 2001. No one could fail to be impressed by the intelligence and dedication evident among the managers as they struggled to adapt their company for survival in an increasingly difficult environment. It cannot claim to be representative of other state enterprises in every respect, but it does contain within itself many of the elements of continuity and change present in contemporary Chinese management.

The company traces its history well back into the era before reform, so has had far to travel in transforming itself from an all-inclusive *danwei* of the planned economy into a modern company operating under increasingly competitive conditions. A major step on this journey was taken in 1992 when it incorporated before listing on the local stock market in the following year. The state remains, however, the majority shareholder through a holding company that exercises control over major investments and appoints senior management. In 1999, it enjoyed a net profit of just under 70 million yuan on sales of 1150 million yuan with a workforce of 9000.

As it is not designated a pillar industry, the firm has greater freedom in determining its own restructuring. This freedom is matched, however, by the absence of preferential treatment from the state and increasingly hard budgetary constraints. This has clearly concentrated the minds of management, who have employed the services of a leading Western management consultancy to assist with a wide-ranging reform of the company. This has covered the responsibility system, strategy formation, procurement, marketing and client relationships, quality management, and the structure of the company and its subsidiaries.

Reforming the company is viewed as a continuing process, building on numerous small steps, combined with two episodes in which the restructuring took place on a major scale. The two major reforms were very similar. The first, however, ran up against numerous obstacles, so the second was needed to push the plan through to completion. The main thrust revolved around significant downsizing of the workforce. By the time of the second major reform, resistance was less as people had become, however reluctantly, used to the notion of cutting staff and workers and were prepared to accept that the company was facing a crisis. The management of the company has initiated all the reforms, rather than simply implementing instructions from above, as would have been the case formerly.

In terms of its appearance, the organisational chart remained much the same after the reform as before. The same divisions remain: Human Resources; Technology; Product Development; Procurement; Marketing and Sales; Planning; Information; Strategy; Subsidiaries; and Manufacturing, which presides directly over the factories. What has changed is their mode of operation. Following the recently instituted internal reforms, the factory heads, for example, are given far greater autonomy in areas such as production planning and remuneration. This is part of a broader pattern of delegation, with the general manager signing a yearly achievement contract with all the division heads. The division heads will, in their turn, sign an achievement contract with the factory heads and the factory heads will sign with department heads and the department heads will sign with the workers. The achievement contracts include three areas: financial, covering matters such as cash flow, preservation of assets and profits; operational, covering production, marketing and sales; and organisational, covering satisfaction of the workers and staff, and the satisfaction of other departments.

Top-level managers (around 30 of them) are nominated by the parent company. Middle level managers are recruited through advertising on the job market. The general manager will decide the heads of the divisions and the heads of the factories. The division head can nominate the deputy division head and the factory manager can decide the deputy factory manager. Promotion of middle and high-level managers has to be approved and finalised by the Party Committee. In theory, the personnel department of the Party Committee should check these candidates. However, the Human Resources Department undertakes the actual checking. The Human Resources Department can also finalise promotion of lower managers.

Salaries for technicians and managers are no longer closely related to the state cadre salary system, with salaries now depending more on the importance of the post. In the past, no matter how important the post, the salary would be decided by qualifications and length of service. The basic salary as a proportion of earnings has fallen in parallel with the increase in bonuses. The total salary amount of the company, the divisions, the factories and the workshops is negotiated with the high-level managers. Salary differentials remained small until three or four years ago, but have since widened. Fringe benefits are fewer than in the past, when there were allowances for all manner of things, such as a hair cut allowance and a newspaper subscription allowance. Now these have all gone. However, there is clinic and a vocational school. There are still also the occasional treats, such as when Coca-Cola comes to the company on a promotion drive and the factory or company will buy drinks and distribute them to everybody.

The Party Committee secretary is also the chairman of the board; while the general manager is also the Deputy Party Secretary; and the head of the trade union also doubles as the head of the Cadres' Disciplinary Committee. All agree on the need to run the firm in a commercial fashion. The size of the Party apparatus has been shrinking and its officials have been assigned additional duties, such as running the militia. Heads of the Party apparatus at divisional, factory and workshop levels all have managerial positions. Only in some departments, such as those with more highly educated or young people, is there a Party secretary specialising in ideological work, as these people are thought to be more in need of it.

The old system of state enterprise titles being awarded to individuals and teams remains. The firm is given a quota to fill for a broad variety of titles, such as National Model Worker; National Trustworthy Quality Team; National Model Union; the Red Flag Ladies Team; the Labour Day Model Worker; the Pioneer Woman Worker; the Civilised Work Team; the Red Flag Civilised Post; and the Union Official Good in Ten Ways. This is all taken as part of the Party's remit to attend to spiritual matters in addition to material matters. In the event, however, the many competitions and activities organised by the Party Committee, the Youth

League and the union tend to be harnessed in assisting improvements in production. In addition, there is now much talk, under the influence of the Western consultancy company, of the need to develop a company culture. This is mainly taken care of by the Party Committee. Managers remark, however, that nobody really knows what the company culture is or ought to be, with different meetings and different bosses saying different things. Despite these efforts, it remains difficult to make people feel that they belong to the company and that they should try hard to contribute more.

This is understandable in relation to the job cuts that have accompanied the two major reform drives. These have cut back the workforce by over 30 per cent. Some of the redundant workers have been transferred to subsidiaries established in the service sector. Others have been laid off with a subsistence allowance and the right to enter employment centres in the hope of finding other work, usually in services, such as hotel maintenance workers. Redundant managers were offered the choice of early retirement or demotion.

Other reforms were more easily achieved. In marketing and sales, the company formerly had no system or policy. Customers were managed according to their area, or the type of the diesel they bought. Now there is one system, with customers divided between key customers and non-key customers. There is a problem with securing payment from some customers, a problem handled by the company's debt collection office. The company also has a lawyer, formerly employed by the trade union to assist the workers. Now he is in charge of every legal issue. To assist with this he is expected to devote himself to cultivating a good relationship with the court.

The company has many subsidiaries, some of them related to the core business, others in services such as hotels and restaurants. At present, the company is going through a process of allowing these subsidiaries greater autonomy subject to profit targets, in place of the close direction that ruled formerly.

As far as procurement is concerned, in the past, the company had many suppliers. Relationships were not stable and were subject to constant haggling. Quality suffered as a result. Now the company has decided to concentrate on fewer suppliers, to forge a lasting relationship with them, and to provide them with more technical input. Through placing larger orders, they are also hoping that suppliers will be able to advance their own research and development.

This is perhaps a trifle optimistic given the company's own weakness in providing resources for R&D. The main hope the company has of improving this and in advancing its competitive position in general is through seeking a joint venture partner. The advantages of this strategy are brought constantly to mind by the fierce competition the company faces from its main rival, a joint venture with Cummings.

Some areas of reform have proved more difficult and slower than others. The search for a potential joint venture partner has yet to succeed. It is also very difficult to reform the R&D department. The R&D department was very important under the planned economy, when sales and marketing were of little relevance. As a result, the members of the R&D department continue to think it is the most important department and it is very difficult to get them to adapt. Another area difficult to reform is quality management. The quality inspection department only inspects the products. It has little idea of what is good quality and how to introduce a total quality management system.

As we were leaving, talk turned to the position of state-owned enterprises in general. Our host remarked how many new companies in new industries were running quite well recently. However, old companies, and especially those companies that were very successful under the planned economy, were finding it very difficult to change. Their organisation, technology, products and approach were very difficult to adapt to the new environment. 'Our company,' our host concluded, waving us off with a wistful smile, 'was very successful under the planned economy.'

Notes

1 Of different minds

1 Although the authorities currently encourage anonymous denunciation, wiser heads prevailed in the past. An imperial edict of 1818 gives the practice short shrift as 'extremely harmful to morality and custom, its prime motivation being private hatred and the desire for revenge. Investigation of accusations of this sort serves not only to smear the accused, but through its repercussions also ruthlessly implicates innocent outsiders. With a few anonymous words, the schemer induces officials to poison the lives of ordinary people, while he himself looks on with folded hands, thereby satisfying a private grudge. The resulting evil is worse than that caused by demons' (Bodde and Morris 1967: 400).

2 A vivid illustration was provided by the saffron-robed monks to be seen cycling across Tiananmen Square in May 1989. They were carrying food for the protesters and streaming banners proclaiming 'Buddhist monks support the students'. They clearly felt at ease mixing traditional beliefs with supporting calls for greater democracy, leaving an enduring image of old China in tandem with the new.

4 Taking the capitalist road

1 There is a general belief that the choice of this apparently arbitrary figure was hit upon because Marx in *Capital* had used an imaginary example of a capitalist employing eight workers to illustrate how surplus value accrued to the capitalist through the efforts of these workers (Marx 1930: 291–92). Whatever number was to be permissible, eight stood revealed as morally dubious.

Bibliography

Aiello, P. (1991) 'Building a joint venture in China: the case of Chrysler and the Beijing Jeep Corporation', *Journal of General Management*, 17: 47–64.

Black, J. S. (1993) 'Resolving conflicts in Japan', *Sloane Management Review*, Spring, 49–59.

Blecher, M. and Shue, V. (2001) 'Into leather: state-led development and the private sector in Xinji', *The China Quarterly*, 166 (June): 368–93.

Bodde, D. and Morris, C. (1967) *Law in Imperial China*, Cambridge, MA: Harvard University Press.

Boisot, M. and Xing, G. L. (1992) 'The nature of managerial work in the Chinese managerial reforms', *Organization Studies*, 13(2): 161–84.

Bond, M. H. (1991) *Beyond the Chinese Face: Insights from Psychology*, Hong Kong: Oxford University Press.

Bond, M. H. and Hwang, K. K. (1986) 'The social psychology of the Chinese people', in: M. H. Bond (ed) *The Psychology of the Chinese People*, Oxford: Oxford University Press.

Bond, M. H. and King, A. Y. C. (1985) 'Coping with the threat of westernisation in Hong Kong', *International Journal of Intercultural Relations*, 5: 137–52.

Bond, M. H. and Lee, P. W. H. (1981) 'Face-saving in Chinese culture', in: A. Y. C. King and R. P. L. Lee (eds) *Social Life and Development in Hong Kong*, Hong Kong: Chinese University Press.

Brahm, L. J. and Lu, S. X. M. (1999) *Re-engineering China*, Hong Kong: Naga.

Bruun, L. Y. (1995) 'Political hierarchy and private entrepreneurship in a Chinese neighbourhood', in: A. G. Walder (ed) *The Waning of the Communist State*, Berkeley: University of California Press.

Chen, H. (2000) *The Institutional Transition of China's Township and Village Enterprises: Market Liberalization, Contractual Form Innovation and Privatisation*, Aldershot: Ashgate.

Chen, M. (1995) *Asian Management Systems: Chinese, Japanese and Korean Styles of Business*, London: Routledge.

Child, J. (1994) *Management in China During the Age of Reform*, Cambridge: Cambridge University Press.

Child, J. and Lu, Y. (1993) 'Negotiation in organizational hierarchies: a comparison of British and Chinese investment decisions', Research Paper in Management Studies, 28, University of Cambridge.

Child, J. and Markóczy, L. (1993) 'Host-country managerial behaviour and learning in Chinese and Hungarian joint ventures', *Journal of Management Studies*, 30: 611–31.

Colson, E. (1975) *Tradition and Contract: the Problem of Order*, London: Heinemann.

Dardes, J. (1991) 'Childhood in pre-modern China', in: J. M. Hawes and N. R. Hiner (eds) *Childhood in Historical and Comparative Perspective*, New York: Greenwood.

Ding, D. Z., Lan, G. and Warner, M. (2001) 'A new form of Chinese human resource management? Personnel and labour-management relations in Chinese township and village enterprises', *Industrial Relations Journal*, 32(4): 328–43.

Ding, X. L. (2000) 'The illicit asset stripping of Chinese state firms', *China Journal*, 43, January: 1–28.

Duckett, J. (1998) *The Entrepreneurial State in China: Real Estate and Commerce Departments in Reform Era Tianjin*, London: Routledge.

Easterby-Smith, M. and Gao, J. (1996) 'Vision, mechanism and logic: understanding the strategic investment decision making process', in: D. H. Brown and R. Porter (eds), *Management Issues in China, Volume 1: Domestic Enterprises*, London: Routledge.

Francis, C.-B. (1999) 'Bargained property rights: the case of China's high technology sector', in: J. C. Oi and A. G. Warder (eds) *Property Rights and Economic Reform in China*, Stanford, CA: Stanford University Press.

Frye, T. and Shleifer, A. (1997) 'The invisible hand and the grabbing hand', *American Economic Review; AEA Papers and Proceedings 87* (May): 354–58.

Gabrenya, W. K. and Hwang, K.-K. (1996) 'Chinese social interaction: harmony and hierarchy on the Good Earth', in: M. H. Bond (ed.) *The Handbook of Chinese Psychology*, Hong Kong: Oxford University Press.

Gao, G., Ting-Toomey, S. and Gudykunst, W. B. (1996) 'Chinese communication processes', in: M. H. Bond (ed) *The Handbook of Chinese Psychology*, Hong Kong: Oxford University Press.

Gilley, B. (2000a) 'Moment of truth', *Far Eastern Economic Review*, 15 June: 58–60.

Gilley, B. (2000b) 'A mine full of possibilities', *Far Eastern Economic Review*, 13 July, 61–63.

Gilley, B. (2000c) 'Huawei's fixed line to Beijing', *Far Eastern Economic Review*, 28 December: 94–98.

Gore, L. L. P. (1998) *Market Communism: the Institutional Foundation of China's Post-Mao Hyper-growth*, Hong Kong: Oxford University Press.

Gu Shulin (1999) *China's Industrial Technology: Market Reform and Organizational Change*, London: Routledge.

Guthrie, D. (1999) *Dragon in a Three-Piece Suit: the Emergence of Capitalism in China*, Princeton: Princeton University Press.

Hall, E. T. (1976) *Beyond Culture*, Garden City, NY: Doubleday Anchor.

Harwit, E. (2001) 'The impact of WTO membership on the automobile industry in China', *The China Quarterly*, September, 167: 655–70.

Hertz, E. (1998) *The Trading Crowd: an Ethnography of the Shanghai Stock Market*, Cambridge: Cambridge University Press.

Hildebrandt, H. W. (1988) 'A Chinese managerial view of business communication', *Management Communication Quarterly*, 2: 217–34.

Ho, D. Y. F. (1986) 'Chinese patterns of socialization: a critical review', in: M. H. Bond (ed) *The Psychology of the Chinese People*, Oxford: Oxford University Press.

Ho, D. Y. F. (1996) 'Filial piety and its psychological consequences', in: M. H. Bond (ed) *The Handbook of Chinese Psychology*, Hong Kong: Oxford University Press.

Hofstede, G. (1980) *Culture's Consequences*, Beverley Hills, CA: Sage.

Hofstede, G. (1994) *Cultures and Organizations*, London: Harper Collins.

Hofstede, G. and Bond, M. (1988) 'The Confucian connection: from cultural roots to economic growth', *Organizational Dynamics*, 16(4): 4–21.

Holland, L. and Hiebert, M. (2000) 'Sure bet?', *Far Eastern Economic Review*, 22 June: 21.

Hsiao, K. C. (1979) *Compromise in China* (Seattle: University of Washington Press).

Huang, C. (1999) 'The *qiaoxiang* irony: migrant labour in overseas Chinese enterprises', in the Pearl River delta', in: L. Douw, C. Huang and M. R. Godley, *Qiaoxiang Ties: Interdisciplinary Approaches to 'Cultural Capitalism' in South China*, London: Kegan Paul.

Hubler, J. and Meschi, P.-X. (1999) 'European direct investment in China and Sino-French joint ventures', *Asia Pacific Business Review*, 7(3): 157–80.

International Finance Corporation (2000) *China's Emerging Private Enterprises: Prospects for the New Century*, Washington, DC: International Finance Corporation.

Keister, L. A. (2000) *Chinese Business Groups: the Structure and Impact of Interfirm Relations During Economic Development*, Oxford: Oxford University Press.

Kornai, J. (1992) *The Socialist System: the Political Economy of Communism*, Princeton: Princeton University Press.

Krone, K., Garret, M. and Chen, L. (1992) 'Managerial communication practices in Chinese factories', *The Journal of Business Communication*, 29: 229–52.

Kung, J. K.-S. (1999) 'The evolution of property rights in village enterprises: the case of Wuxi county', in: J. C. Oi and A. G. Walder (eds) *Property Rights and Economic Reform in China*, Stanford: Stanford University Press.

Langlois, J. D. (2001) 'The WTO and China's financial system', *The China Quarterly*, September, 167: 610–29.

Lardy, N. R. (1998) *China's Unfinished Economic Revolution*, Washington, DC: Brookings Institution.

Lawrence, S. (2000) 'A model people's army', *Far Eastern Economic Review*, 13 July: 14–16.

Leung, K. (1987) 'Some determinants of reactions to procedural models for conflict resolution: a cross-national study', *Journal of Personality and Social Psychology*, 53: 898–908.

Lin Y. (1939) *My Country and My People*, London: Heinemann.

Lin, N. and Chen, C.-J. J. (1999) 'Local elites as officials and owners: shareholding and property rights in Daqiuzhuang', in: J. C. Oi and A. G. Walder (eds) *Property Rights and Economic Reform in China*, Stanford: Stanford University Press.

Lu, Q. (2000) *China's Leap into the Information Age: Innovation and Organization in the Computer Industry*, Oxford: Oxford University Press.

Ma, R. G. (1992) 'The role of unofficial intermediaries in interpersonal conflicts in Chinese culture', *Communication Quarterly*, 40(3): 269–78.

Macaulay, S. (1963) 'Non-contractual relations in business', *American Sociological Review*, 28(1): 55–67.

Marx, K. (1930) *Capital*, London: Dent.

Mead, R. (1990) *Cross-Cultural Management Communication*, Chichester: Wiley.

Mintzberg, H. (1973) *The Nature of Managerial Work*, New York: Harper and Row.

Mo, J. S. (1997) 'Alternative dispute resolution', in: C. G. Wang and X. C. Zhang, *Introduction to Chinese Law*, Hong Kong: Sweet and Maxwell.

Montagu-Pollock, M. (1991) 'All the right connections', *Asian Business*, January: 20–24.

Moser, M. J. (1995) 'Dispute settlement', in: D. Lewis (ed), *Life and Death of a Joint Venture*, London: Asia Law and Practice.

Naughton, B. (1995) *Growing out of the Plan: Chinese Economic Reform, 1978–1993*, Cambridge: Cambridge University Press.

Ng, S. H. and Warner, M. (1998) *China's Trade Unions and Management*, London: Macmillan.

Nolan, P. (2001) *China and the Global Business Revolution*, Basingstoke: Palgrave.

Oi, J. C. (1998) 'The evolution of local state corporatism', in: A. G. Walder (ed), *Zouping in Transition: the Process of Reform in Rural North China*, Cambridge, MA: Harvard University Press.

Pearson, M. M. (1997) *China's New Business Elite*, Berkeley: University of California Press.

Pollock, S. M. (1986) 'Strive to conquer the Black Stink: decision analysis in the People's Republic of China', *Interface*, 16(2): 31–37.

Potter, P. B. (2001) 'The legal implications of China's accession to the WTO', *The China Quarterly*, September, 167: 592–609.

Pye, L. (1982) *Chinese Commercial Negotiating Style*, Cambridge, MA: Oelgeschlager, Gunn and Hain.

Ralston, D. A., Gustafson, D. J., Cheung, F. M. and Terpstra, R. H. (1993) 'Differences in managerial values: a study of U.S., Hong Kong and PRC managers', *Journal of International Business Studies*, 2: 249–75.

Ralston, D. A., Yu, K. C., Wang, X., Terpstra, R. H. and Ho, W. (1996) 'The cosmopolitan Chinese manager: findings of a study on managerial values across the six regions of China', *Journal of International Management*, 2: 79–109.

Ralston, D. A., Egri, C. P., Stewart, S., Terpstra, R. H. and Yu, K. (1999) 'Doing business in the 21st century with the new generation of Chinese managers: a study of generational shifts in work values in China', *Journal of International Business Studies*, 30(2): 415–28.

Redding, S. G. (1993) *The Spirit of Chinese Capitalism*, Berlin: de Gruyter.

Redding, S. G. (2000) 'What is Chinese about Chinese family business? And how much is family and how much is business?', in: H. W-C. Yeung and K. Olds, *Globalization of Chinese Business Firms*, Basingstoke: Macmillan.

Redding, S. G. and Ng, M. (1983) 'The role of "face" in the organizational perceptions of Chinese managers', *International Studies of Management and Organization,* XIII, 3: 92–123.

Rosen, D. H. (1999) *Behind the Open Door: Foreign Enterprises in the Chinese Marketplace*, Washington, DC: Institute for International Economics.

Rowe, W. T. (1984) *Hankow: Commerce and Society in a Chinese city, 1796–1889*, Stanford, CA: Stanford University Press.

Ruf, G. A. (1999) 'Collective enterprise and property rights in a Sichuan village: the rise and decline of managerial corporatism', in: J. C. Oi and A. G. Walder (eds) *Property Rights and Economic Reform in China*, Stanford: Stanford University Press.

Schak, D. C. (1999) 'Culture as a management issue: the case of Taiwan entrepreneurs', in the Pearl River delta', in: L. Douw, C. Huang and M. R. Godley, *Qiaoxiang Ties: Interdisciplinary Approaches to 'Cultural Capitalism' in South China*, London: Kegan Paul.

Schwartz, S. H. (1992) 'Universals in the content and structure of values: theoretical advances and empirical tests in 20 countries', in: M. P. Zanna (ed) *Advances in Experimental Social Psychology*, San Diego: Academic Press.

Shenkar, O. and Ronen, S. (1987) 'The cultural context of negotiations: the implications of Chinese interpersonal norms', *The Journal of Applied Behavioural Science*, 23(2): 263–75.

Smith, P. B. and Wang, Z.-M. (1996) 'Chinese leadership and organizational structures', in: M. H. Bond (ed) *The Handbook of Chinese Psychology*, Hong Kong: Oxford University Press.

Solinger, D. J. (2001) 'Why we cannot count the "unemployed"', *The China Quarterly*, September, 167: 671–88.

State Development Research Centre (2000) *Almanac of China's Economy*

[*Zhongguo Jingji Nianjian*], Beijing: Almanac of China's Economy Publishing House.

Steinfeld, E. S. (1998) *Forging Reform in China: the Fate of State-owned Industries*, Cambridge: Cambridge University Press.

Steinfeld, E. S. (2000) 'Free lunch or last supper? China's debt-equity swaps in context', *The China Business Review*, July–August: 22–27.

Stern, E. (2001) 'China's response to the global downturn.' Speech, Developmental Research Centre of the State Council, Beijing, 13 June.

Stuttard, J. B. (2000) *The New Silk Road: Secrets of Business Success in China Today*, New York: Wiley.

Tam, O. M. (1999) *The Development of Corporate Governance in China*, Cheltenham: Edward Elgar.

Tang, Q., Chow, C. W. and Lau, A. (1999) 'Auditing of state-owned companies in China: practices, problems and future developments', *The International Journal of Accounting*, 34(2): 173–87.

Tang, S. F. and Kirkbride, P. S. (1986) 'Developing conflict management skills in Hong Kong: an analysis of some cross-cultural implications', *Management Education and Development*, 17(3): 287–301.

Thomas, K. (1976) 'Conflict and conflict management', in: M. Dunnette (ed) *Handbook of Industrial and Organizational Psychology*, Chicago: Rand McNally.

Triandis, H. C. (1994) 'Cross-cultural and organizational psychology,' in: H. C. Triandis, M. C. Dunnette, and L. M. Hough (eds), *Handbook of Industrial and Organizational Psychology*, 2nd edn, Vol 4, California: Consulting Psychologists Press.

Tse, D. K., Francis, J. and Walls, J. (1994) 'Cultural differences in conducting intra- and inter-cultural negotiations: a Sino-Canadian comparison', *Journal of International Business Studies*, 25: 537–55.

Walder, A. G. (1995) 'Local governments as industrial firms: an organizational analysis of China's transitional economy', *American Journal of Sociology*, 101(2): 263–301.

Walder, A. G. and Oi, J. C. (1999) 'Property rights in the Chinese economy: contours of the process of change', in: J. C. Oi and A. G. Walder (eds) *Property Rights and Economic Reform in China*, Stanford: Stanford University Press.

Wang, G. G. (1993) *Business Law in China*, Hong Kong: Butterworth.

Wank, D. L. (1995) 'Bureaucratic patronage and private business', in: A. G. Walder (ed) *The Waning of the Communist State*, Berkeley: University of California Press.

Wank, D. L. (1999) *Commodifying Communism: Business, Trust and Politics in a Chinese City*, Cambridge: Cambridge University Press.

Warner, M., Goodall, K. and Ding, D. Z. (1999) 'The "myth" of human resource management in Chinese enterprises', in: M. Warner (ed) *China's Managerial Revolution*, London: Frank Cass.

Weber, M. (1951) *The Religion of China*, Glencoe, Ill: The Free Press.

Weber, M. (1978) *Economy and Society*, Berkeley: University of California Press.

Weldon, E. and Jehn, K. A. (1996) 'Conflict management in US-Chinese joint ventures: an analytical framework' in: J. Child and Y. Lu (eds), *Management Issues in China, Volume 2: International Enterprises*, London: Routledge.

White, G. (1996) 'Chinese trade unions in the transition from socialism', *British Journal of Industrial Relations*, 34(3): 443–57.

Whiting, S. M. (2001) *Power and Wealth in Rural China: the Political Economy of Institutional Change*, Cambridge: Cambridge University Press.

Williamson, O. (1975) *Markets and Hierarchies*, New York: Free Press.

World Bank (1997) *China's Management of Enterprise Assets: the State as Shareholder*, Washington, World Bank.

World Bank (2001a) 'China update', Beijing, March. Mimeo.

World Bank (2001b) 'China update', Beijing, September. Mimeo.

Worm, V. (1997) *Vikings and Mandarins: Sino-Scandinavian Business Cooperation in Cross-cultural Settings*, Copenhagen: Handelshojskolens Forlag.

Wu, D. Y. H. (1996) 'Chinese childhood socialization', in: M. H. Bond (ed) *The Handbook of Chinese Psychology*, Hong Kong: Oxford University Press.

Xiao, G. (1991) 'Managerial autonomy, fringe benefits, and ownership structure: a comparative study of Chinese state and collective enterprises.' Research Paper Series 20, Socialist Economics Reform Unit, World Bank, Washington, DC.

Yang, K. S. (1986) 'Chinese personality and its change', in: M. H. Bond (ed) *The Psychology of the Chinese People*, Oxford: Oxford University Press.

Yang, K. S. (1996) 'Psychological transformation of the Chinese people as a result of societal modernization', in: M. H. Bond (ed) *The Handbook of Chinese Psychology*, Hong Kong: Oxford University Press.

Yang, L., Tang, Q., Kilmore, A. and Hong, J. Y. (2001) 'Auditor-government associations and auditor independence in China', *British Accounting Review*, 33: 175–89.

Yang, M. M.-H. (1994) *Gifts, Favors, and Banquets: the Art of Social Relationships in China*, Ithaca, NY: Cornell University Press.

Yates, J. F. and Lee, J. W. (1996) 'Chinese decision-making' in: M. H. Bond (ed) *The Handbook of Chinese Psychology*, Hong Kong: Oxford University Press.

Yeung, H. W.-C. (2000) 'The dynamics of the globalization of Chinese business firms', in: H. W.-C. Yeung and K. Olds, *Globalization of Chinese Business Firms*, Basingstoke: Macmillan.

You Ji (1998) *China's Enterprise Reform*, London: Routledge.

Young, L. W. L. (1982) 'Inscrutability revisited' in: J. J. Gumperz, (ed) *Language and Social Identity*, Cambridge: Cambridge University Press.

Yu, X. (1995) 'Conflict in a multi-cultural organization: an ethnographic attempt to discover work-related cultural assumptions between Chinese and American co-workers', *International Journal of Conflict Management*, 6: 211–32.

Zhang, B. (2001) 'Assessing the WTO agreements on China's telecommunications regulatory reform and industrial liberalization', *Telecommunications Policy*, 25: 461–83.

Author index

Subject index